Riding in Style

RIDING IN STYLE

The First 25 Years

Alan McGowan

Library and Archives Canada Cataloguing in Publication
McGowan, Alan, 1930–, author
    Riding in style : the first 25 years / Alan McGowan.
ISBN 978-0-9947512-0-1 (paperback)
    1. McGowan, Alan, 1930–. 2. McGowan, Alan, 1930–
Childhood and youth. 3. British Columbia—Biography. I. Title.
FC3826.1.M36A3 2015   971.1'03092   C2015-904539-8

Editor: Audrey McClellan
Cover and book design: Frances Hunter

alanmcgowan@gmail.com

This book is dedicated to my family and

extended family, especially to my late mother

who never lost her sense of humour or her

dignity throughout all her hardships.

Contents

A PRELIMINARY NOTE

Some overly observant relatives, friends or enemies may spot something that could be an error. They might even consider phoning or writing me to point out my misconceptions. But they should not waste their time or mine, or get agitated, because there are deliberate and accidental memory mistakes . . .

PART ONE

Early Family Life

Before Birth

Deciding to write my memoirs in chronological order has brought me smack up against the most sensitive, and controversial, story of my life. I originally thought I would start off with events that happened when I was young and build up to the major events. But strange as it might seem, one of the major events of my life happened before I was born, and remembering it has plagued and sustained me all my life. In my long life, I've only shared this incident with close family.

I was born in the little, isolated, company town of Port Alice on the northwest coast of Vancouver Island. I became aware of life in a void. I couldn't see, couldn't hear, couldn't talk, couldn't feel, but I could think, with no past up to this moment, in something like time. It was comfortable. I could sense other friendly spirits around me, and some were vaguely familiar, as if I knew them or had known them. They could communicate to me. I didn't feel that I was communicating to them, although in some way they were allaying my worried thoughts: *Where am I? What's happening? Am I going somewhere?*

A strong clear thought came to me: *You are going back to be born.*

Somehow I knew what that meant. Time or something happened. Then a second clear thought came to me: *It is not going to happen now.*

Another time of comfort passed from other spirits that I could sense were all around me. Then another strong clear thought: *You are now going back to be born.*

Maybe I can blame all this on my mother having a very difficult labour for three days before I was born. Maybe the umbilical cord cut off the blood supply to my brain. The sense of feeling cold, and strangulation, are other memories from this time, and I am stuck with them. I carried them with me throughout my early childhood and thought they were perfectly normal, but never mentioned them to others.

When I became older, nobody ever discussed this before-birth phenomenon, but in Sunday school, and later in church, some biblical stories came close to describing the same sensation and made me feel I wasn't the only one to experience something like this.

Mentioning these events resulted in quizzical looks, so I kept my mouth shut and lived my life believing it and not questioning it.

Well, we have now got through that, so let's get on with my and my family's life.

Coping with the Great Depression

Over the years I've talked to various people who lived in isolated company towns through the many years of the Great Depression and was flabbergasted to find out that many of them were not aware there was a depression going on. One of these unaware people must have been my dad, because in 1931 he quit his steady job at the pulp mill in Port Alice and moved Mum, my three-year-old brother, Hughie, and me, one-year-old Alan, to Vancouver, smack dab in the middle of the Great Depression. He didn't get another job until 1938.

Joe McGowan, my father, was what was called a "Boomer," always moving from one boomtown to the next. He had been born in 1900 in Glasgow, Scotland. At the age of ten he was apprenticed as an electrician in the Glasgow shipyards. Around the same time, his dad died of tuberculosis. In 1917, Joe joined the Army and saw active duty as a machine gunner, then served for nine years in occupied Germany. He chose to be demobbed in Canada and slowly worked his way across the country, taking on odd jobs and helping farmers with their harvesting. He got a job as an electrician in Princeton, British Columbia, where he met Mum, and they were married in 1927.

Mum and Dad first moved to Bonnington, where Dad had a job at

Top: Joe McGowan, getting ready for the Army, 1917; Joe McGowan 1919.
Below: Margaret Hunter 1926; Mum and Dad, 1927.

Top: Parents' marriage, 1927; Below: Joe McGowan, electrician 1928;
Mum and Hugh, 1929.

Hugh (left) and Alan (second from right),
Port Alice, 1931.

the hydroelectric dam just outside of Castlegar. They then moved to Powell River, where Hugh Hunter, my brother, was born on August 10, 1928. A year later they moved to Port Alice, and on March 4, 1930, I was born, Alan William. A year after that, they moved to Vancouver, right in the middle of the Great Depression, and Patricia Ann, my sister, was born on April 25, 1932, in Mum's hometown of Princeton, B.C.

Dad's way of life, casually moving from job to job, had an enormous impact on him and his way of thinking, which, in turn, affected his marriage and his three children. Each of us kids was influenced differently by our father, and sometimes it was hard to believe we were all from the same family.

As it turned out, the worst place to be during a depression was a big city—people in the country could at least grow food—and we ended up on what was called Government Relief, which amounted to the meagre sum of forty dollars per month for rent, food, light, heat and clothes.

My early memories are of the endless arguments between Mum and Dad driven by their opposite views of a situation. My dad came from a poor, socialist upbringing in Glasgow. My mother was the only daughter of the government agent in the small town of Princeton, and her well-to-do parents were one of the leading families. Dad did not believe in owning a home; he thought it was a waste of good money to pay a mortgage when you could rent more cheaply. For Mum, home ownership meant stability and position. Dad did not believe in banks, and he didn't trust them. Mum had $2,000 in the bank when she married Dad, and he insisted that she withdraw it.

Dad was a strong believer in, and adherent of, his union, the IBEW (Industrial Brotherhood of Electrical Workers), which was run by Communists at that time. When he couldn't find work, some of his union brothers told him, "Join the Communist Party, and we will find union work for you." He played around with the idea, but I don't think he went all the way.

Some of Dad's supposedly strong Communist union brothers found non-union work on the side, such as wiring a house. They would come over and tell Dad about the radios, cars and clothing they had bought with the money earned, and then they would ask Dad to work with them. He flatly refused unless it was a union job. Mum would argue endlessly with him as we desperately needed the money, but he would never bend. Mum's attitude was "If it pays money, there's no disgrace in honest work." She resorted to making slippers and selling them on the street to earn some much-needed cash. Dad did what he could by raising rabbits for food and growing a large vegetable garden, even though he didn't know anything about gardening.

One of the most exciting things for us kids during these tough years was receiving the many parcels from Dad's mother in Glasgow, Scotland. She would send chocolates, scarves, gloves, sweaters and socks of the highest quality. One of those scarves I wore for fifteen years. She also sent Scottish comics that we read and reread. I picked up a lot of the Scots slang from those comics, which came in handy later on in life. I still remember Andy Capp, the Wee Bairn and Silas the Truant Officer.

Free Fish for Everybody

One day when I was six, Mr. McMillan, our next-door neighbour and landlord, came over to see Dad. He was a natural scrounger, and he was always making money moving something or delivering something with his old truck. He told us that the Fisherman's Union had gone on strike and, as a protest, had dumped over fifty tons of fresh herring on the Pier C dock for people to help themselves. He offered to take us there to load up on fish for the whole neighbourhood.

Dad refused, because as a strong union member he would not cross a picket line. Mum asserted herself and asked us two boys to go. Hughie refused, always siding with Dad. I jumped at the chance to ride in the truck, eat fresh fish and help the neighbours, as well as enjoy the excitement and fun of it all. We went up and down our block of Walden Street, explaining what we were doing and asking for buckets and sacks. The reactions we received from each house were remarkably diverse, from a cold "No, not interested," or suspicion to enthusiasm and thanks.

We got to the dock and drove through the picket line, and there was the fresh herring spread out all over the dock. Surprisingly, hardly anybody else was there to help themselves. We dug in and loaded the truck real fast, and we all ended up covered in slime, blood and fish scales. Back we went to Walden Street, delivering an equal portion to each household that wanted some herring.

That night, Mum fried up about five pounds of herring roe. I had never tasted herring roe and it was delicious. To this day, I can still taste those eggs.

Dog Bones for Soup

Living on a restricted budget of forty dollars per month, Mum developed into an excellent cook. She could cook any meat and it would be a masterpiece. Tripe, heart, liver, kidneys—all came out of her kitchen fit for a king.

One day she asked me to take my scooter to the butcher shop and dig in the free dog-bone box for the biggest bones with lots of meat on them. I went off, confused, because Mum wouldn't explain why we were getting dog bones when we didn't have a dog.

When I asked the butcher for the bones, he said, "Oh, you got a dog now have you?" with a small grin.

I replied, "No."

He said, "Oh well, help yourself anyway."

I thanked the man and brought home two giant beef hip bones, some kidneys and tripe. Mum was pleased, and we had great soup the next week.

Where we lived on Walden was near Main Street, the dividing line between those people on the west side of Vancouver who had jobs, and those on the east who were on relief. As the butcher explained one time to my mother, "With the price of meat so low, those that are working can easily afford the best cuts and those that are not working can't afford the poor cuts, so I am stuck with them." I guess that's why we got really excellent dog bones, with lots of meat on them.

The scooter I rode on has its own story. We couldn't afford to buy bikes, scooters or wagons, so various ingenious fathers came up with substitutes that made us kids happy. My scooter was a handmade soapbox type: scrounge one roller skate, nail the front two steering wheels to a three-foot-long piece of two-by-four lumber and nail the other two wheels to the back end. Nail a wooden soapbox to the front end, and then nail two feet of an old broom handle to the top of the box. Voila! You have a scooter. Strangely, some of the richer kids in the neighbourhood, who could easily afford "boughten" scooters, talked their dads into making them soapbox scooters just like ours.

Block Parties on the Street

The government relief workers realized "relief families" didn't have money to go anywhere, but they could have a break from routine by holding an outside street party with dancing and food. So they would supply us with Japanese paper lanterns, wiring, a sound system, tables and chairs, and maybe a band. We were expected to supply food and beverages. The street was blocked off and the party was on. As kids, we had a great time until we were forced to go to bed. For the adults, it was good to get together to talk over common problems.

One spinoff of the block parties was that everybody registered their trades and talents so they could help each other out, gratis. Dad was registered as an electrician, so anybody needing an electrician for a small job asked Dad. Another man, who was a barber, cut everybody's hair. It got people talking to each other about their lack of money, and sharing ingenious ways to help each other, although there were many people too proud to admit they were poor.

The Streetcar Pass Scam

During the summer it was often too hot to play on the street, so we'd all head to the beach on the streetcar. We had worked out a way to get a bunch of us on for the price of one pass. The ideal number for our scam was four. We would wait at the streetcar stop until there were a few other customers to give us some cover. Then the one kid with a pass would get on, show his pass, grab the first seat on the right side of the streetcar and hand his pass out the window to the next kid. The process would be repeated until all four were aboard.

One time we did this when there were no other people waiting to get on. There was such a long break between each boy, it started to look ridiculous, and a blind man could have seen the pass being handed out the window. I looked at the conductor and saw he had a small smirk on his face; he knew exactly what was going on. They had inspectors for such fare dodges, but a lot of compassionate conductors turned a blind eye because of the tough times.

We would usually take the streetcar to English Bay, where all the other boys would tear off their clothes and charge into the water. I was petrified of water, so my job was to watch the clothes. I didn't know why I was scared of the water, but it was so bad that when we kids bathed in a galvanized tub in the kitchen, I would scream bloody murder unless they took out all but six inches of the water. Mum could only wash my hair with a damp cloth.

Government Make-Work Projects

By 1936, my dad had been on relief for over four years. The relief people had found him jobs as an electrician, but Dad would always turn them down because they were not union scale. This caused many arguments in our household. Finally the relief workers gave Dad an ultimatum: "Either take a job digging ditches or we will take you off relief." He agreed and started working a six-day week for twenty-five cents per hour.

After a few weeks, Dad had accumulated enough money to buy a used bicycle, and his whole demeanour changed for the better. He was happier, and the tension in the house lessened. His friends called him "The Flying Scotsman." The job lasted six months, and then we went back on relief.

In 1935, hundreds of unemployed workers had gathered in Vancouver, occupied the city museum and organized protest rallies, strikes and a trek to Ottawa to protest the poor conditions for working people. In response, the government set up work camps in isolated areas where they could send the unemployed, troublemakers and pro testors to get them off the streets of Vancouver. At these camps, the men did "make-work" projects, such as building roads with picks, shovels, wheelbarrows and horse-drawn scrapers. For six months, Dad was forced to work in one of these camps, out beyond the town of Hope, a hundred miles east of Vancouver.

Years later, Hughie and I asked Dad to come up to Princeton, where we were living, to go fishing for a few days. I drove down to Vancouver on the new Hope–Princeton Highway to pick him up. As we were driving back, just a few miles past Hope, Dad pointed out the old work camp he had stayed at. Five miles farther on he suddenly told me to stop. I pulled over to the side of the road and we both got out. I wondered what was going on.

Joe McGowan (left), Hope-Princeton Road Relief Camp 1935.

He pointed up the side of the mountain and said, "Do you see that old road [which was now a trail] about forty feet up the mountainside, ending nowhere?"

"Yes," I said.

"I helped build that with a pick and shovel." Then he added, "Look farther up. Do you see the road above it, running parallel to the lower one, also ending nowhere?"

Looking very hard, I finally saw what he was pointing to.

He said, "I helped build that too. We lived in the camp but we had to walk to work at the end of the road, which got farther away each day. Finally the end was too far from the camp for us to do any more work, so we started back at the camp again, building another useless road, parallel to the original.

"And you wonder why I don't like government officials."

Respect for Food

One Sunday morning we were sitting around the breakfast table when Mum announced that this morning was special because Dad was going to have bacon and eggs. We kids were going to have our usual mush because there was only enough bacon and eggs for Dad, and he had not had them for a very long time.

As a six-year-old boy, I wondered what was so wonderful about bacon and eggs. I had never seen a fried egg before, and it looked slimy, runny and ugly to me.

Dad cut and ate the bacon, meticulously, and with precision. Then he turned his knife and fork to the egg. With a touch of showmanship, or reverence, he cut the yoke, and the runny yellow liquid flowed onto the plate.

Repulsed, I said, "Why would anyone want to eat that gooey mess?"

Quick as a flash, Dad's left arm came around and, wham, I was sprawled on the floor.

Dad said, "Food is precious. You don't criticize the cook, and you eat whatever is put on your plate." This was a brutal lesson and it stuck.

How well it stuck I didn't realize until, in my mid-fifties, I attended an international conference in Charlotte, North Carolina, related to my work. I had made friends with another fellow, Juan, attending from Mexico City. At one of the meals, after we had both finished off large servings of fish, Juan said, "Would you be offended if I asked you a personal question?"

I said, "Certainly not. We're probably just ships passing anyway."

He asked, "Was your family very poor when you were a child?"

Taken aback, I answered, "Yes, but whatever made you ask?"

Juan gestured at our scrupulously clean plates and said, "I too was very poor, as you can see."

We Now Have a Real Flush Toilet

At this time in South Vancouver there were still many houses with outside pit toilets against the back lane, cleaned by the honey wagon. One day, Mr. McMillan, our landlord, came over to talk to Mum and Dad. Apparently in his scrounging he had gotten hold of an old toilet from an ancient hotel that was being torn down. He and Dad announced they were going to convert our pantry into an indoor bathroom with a flush toilet!

It was a small house, and for a couple of weeks Mum had to put up with a real mess as Dad and Mr. McMillan tore up floors and dug a sewer-line ditch under the house to the back lane.

Finally the great day arrived when the bathroom was finished. All the neighbours came over to have a look. The toilet had a reservoir fastened high up on the wall near the ceiling, with a long chain hanging down. You pulled the chain and, *whoosh*, the toilet was cleaned. All the men took turns pulling the chain and making wise comments, and then Mum and we kids had our turn. What a fantastic invention.

Salvation Army Clothes

During the seven years we were on relief, Mum did a great job of getting us good, warm, used clothes from the Salvation Army or Sally Ann, as we called it. There was only one problem—most of the clothes were twenty to forty years out of style.

In late summer 1936, Mum was busy getting our clothes together for the opening of school. I was entering Grade One, and the day before school started she presented me with an old, used pair of pants. I looked at them in horror—they were woven from thick, dark brown wool and had ugly long black laces up the sides. They looked like the pants worn by Little Lord Fauntleroy, which were last in style in 1890.

Not wanting to hurt Mum's feelings, I reluctantly accepted them.

Hughie got the same style of pants, and he was as upset as I was about going to school wearing them. He told me, "The first guy that says anything, you have to hit him, and then nobody else will be brave enough to say anything." So that's what I did, and we both wore those pants for the full year. Getting in and out of them was a real problem, but they were very warm.

Peeing in Class

My first year of school was at Brock Elementary. We had a tall, plain-looking teacher named Miss Lanarchuck. All the little kids were scared of her. Maybe because we were afraid, we had to pee more than normal.

After lunch one day, a little girl in my row put up her hand and asked for permission to go to the toilet. A few minutes later, another little girl was let go.

By then, I had to go, but Miss Lanarchuck said, "There are too many children going to the toilet and it is disturbing my teaching. You can't go."

I can't go? I thought. But I've got to go.

Looking at this stern, homely teacher, who was glaring down at me, I was too scared to protest. After a while, though, I couldn't hold out any longer and let it go onto the floor. One of the kids across from me spotted the large pool of pee and promptly blabbed to the teacher. Now the whole class had to have a look. I was scared and embarrassed.

Miss Lanarchuck grabbed me by the ear and marched me down to the principal's office. Indignantly, she told the principal her version of what had happened. I was not allowed to speak or to tell my side.

The principal pulled out the dreaded strap. He said, "For peeing in class, you get two on each hand, and maybe you won't do that again."

Then I was marched back to class. The strapping didn't hurt as much as the embarrassment and the teacher lying.

I came home and told Dad what had happened. He just looked at me and didn't say anything.

By this time, Hughie had heard about it and said, "What a stupid thing to do, peeing all over the floor, ha, ha, ha." I guess he was embarrassed to have a little brother who would pee his pants.

The next morning as I was going out the door to school, Dad casually said, "Wait a minute, Alan, I think I'll come with you."

He held my hand and we walked the two blocks to the school. Then he casually asked me where the principal's office was, and I took him there.

We walked into the office and Dad asked, "Are you the principal?"

The principal answered, "Yes, what can I do for you?"

Dad let go of my hand, stepped forward and ploughed him, knocking the principal ass-over-teakettle onto the floor. Then Dad calmly and quietly said, "Don't you ever punish my son before letting me know what he has done."

With that, Dad turned to me and said, "Now, Alan, you go to class, and be a good boy."

When I got home from school, there was never a word spoken about the incident. This was a side of my father that I had never experienced before. Looking back, I realize that, having been brought up by a widowed mother beside the dockyards of Glasgow, with only a Grade Four education and nine years in the army, he had to be tough to survive.

Juvenile Sex

One day when I was six, I was running past a vacant wooded lot on my way to play with some friends down the block. Two girls were playing in the lot, and one of them called me over. She was the little girl from next door, Julie, and she was seven, way older than me. She said, "Do you want to play Mummy and Daddy?"

I said I wasn't really interested, but then she offered me a cookie and I agreed to do it if it didn't take too long. I didn't want my friends seeing me playing with the girls.

We sat down and played at drinking tea. I was getting bored when Julie said, "Now we're going to play Mummy and Daddy and go to bed." She led me into the bushes, where they had spread a blanket. Without any preamble, she took off her panties, pulled her dress up to her armpits, lay down and opened up her legs. Now I was interested. This was something new.

Julie said, "Now you have to take your pants off and get in bed with me, but you got to make that thing of yours hard."

I did as I was told and lay down beside her, but she said, "No, you're supposed to lie on top of me and put that thing of yours inside of me—see, that's where it goes. And you go in and out, in and out."

I found this rather enjoyable and very warm and didn't want to stop. But Julie said, "Now that's enough, you can get off me now and put your clothes back on. We're finished playing Mummy and Daddy, and you can go play with the boys."

Throughout this whole experience, the other girl—let's call her Hazel—stood there watching, but it turned out she knew my brother Hughie had a crush on Julie, and she told him what had occurred in the bush. Oh, was he mad! Hughie was always beating me up for no reason other than he wanted to, but he sure had a good reason to beat me up now, and he proceeded to do just that.

Many years later, when I was a single adult, I was shopping in Vancouver's Hudson's Bay store and needed to cash a cheque. I went up to the fifth floor to the service department. The pretty dark-haired girl behind the cashier's counter had a nametag on her jacket. Sure enough, it was Julie. Now what do you say in that situation? "Remember playing Mummy and Daddy on Walden Street in 1936?"

Too Proud to Pick Apples

We had a nice English family across the street from us on Walden, Mr. and Mrs. Watts and their son and daughter. They were renting and were also on relief, like us, but they had something we didn't have—two apple trees. They never looked after these trees, and for some reason they never picked the apples, which were small and scaly because the trees were neglected, but still edible.

Our mother, coming from a farm, could not understand how anybody could ignore fruit trees and, worse yet, not pick the fruit. Many times she looked across the street at their trees and murmured something about wasteful people. We couldn't afford to buy apples from the store, though sometimes we would scrounge fallen, bruised apples from a farmer a block away.

One day Mum invited Mrs. Watts over for tea and delicately

broached the subject of the apples. Mrs. Watts's answer nearly floored Mum, and when the whole of our family was together for supper, she repeated it, mimicking Mrs. Watts's English accent. She stuck her nose up in the air, pursed her lips and said, "My dear, [long pause] where we come from, we are city folks. Picking apples is for poor country folk or gypsies. We buy our apples in the store."

The end result, though, was that she gave Mum permission to pick their apples. Mum even pruned some of the branches to keep the tree healthy.

You can take the farmer away from the farm, but you can't take the farm out of the farmer.

Spike and the Salesman

During the Depression, there were many door-to-door salespeople trying to sell just about anything. Sid Sherman, an electrician friend of my dad's who lived a block away from us, was tired of dealing with these aggressive salesmen and wanted to do something to stop them bothering him. Signs didn't stop them and verbally abusing them didn't work, so Sid thought maybe a big dog would do the job. Off he went to the animal shelter, returning with a large German shepherd that he named Spike.

Spike was a highly intelligent, friendly dog, and he roamed loose, usually playing in the street with us kids. But Sid had taken the time to give him some special training. No matter where he was, Spike would always spot a salesman with a briefcase coming down the street. His ears would stand straight up and his posture would grow tense. When the salesman climbed the stairs to the Sherman house, Spike came up behind him without making a noise. As the salesman reached out to knock on the door, Spike gently grabbed his wrist in his mouth.

If the salesman was stupid enough to attempt to pull away, Spike's grip became firmer, and he snarled. Holding the salesman by the wrist, Spike turned him around and walked him down the stairs, out to the sidewalk and down the street past us cheering kids. At the end of the block, Spike let him go, then came back to where we were playing and lay down, job done. We thought Spike was the greatest.

My family also finally acquired a dog, after much pleading by me. One day I was out for a walk and found a stray dog who followed me home, thanks to a hastily found piece of rope. He was a smaller-sized dog, and I promised he wouldn't eat too much, so he became a member of our family. We named him Blackie for the colour of his short-haired coat.

A Lost Fortune

When I was six, Mum called me into the house one day, handed me a ten-dollar bill and told me to go to the Safeway grocery store four blocks away and get three pounds of butter that was on sale for four cents a pound. She lectured me on how much a ten-dollar bill was worth and told me exactly how much money to get back from that ten dollars.

Off I went on my scooter, got the butter, stuffed the change and the bills in my front pocket and took off for home.

I proudly gave my mum the butter and reached into my pocket, only to find that the bills were not there! I frantically looked through all my pockets, but the money was gone. Mum and I both ran back four blocks down Main Street to the Safeway store, but found no bills.

I felt terrible, as this was twenty-five percent of our total money for the month. Mum and Dad argued for days about how to cope with the loss of this money. During these discussions I wanted to crawl in a hole someplace and pull it over me.

No Christmas This Year

Two days before Christmas, Mum and Dad got all us kids together and announced that there would be no turkey or presents this year because we had no money. Knowing how proud both my parents were, each in their own way, this must have torn the guts out of them. I, on the other hand, felt guilty for losing all that money.

When Christmas Eve came, we had supper, though the house was unusually quiet.

Then there was a knock on the door. A man and woman in uniform were standing on the doorstep with a great pile of wrapped presents and a turkey. They were from the Salvation Army, and they asked Mum and Dad if they would accept these gifts.

Mum's eyes lit up, and with a big smile she immediately said yes. Dad was a lot slower and reluctantly said, "Well . . . Okay."

With that they put the gifts and turkey on the table and left, after wishing us a Merry Christmas.

Mum and Dad both received a pair of slippers. Pat got a beautiful old doll. Hughie and I each unwrapped large, hand-built, two-motor airplanes, with propellers that turned as you pushed them across the floor.

The next evening we enjoyed the turkey. I don't know about my two siblings, but since I reached the age of twenty-one, I have repaid the Salvation Army many times over for saving that one Christmas for us.

Defying Death on a Sleigh

The winter of 1936–37 gave us loads of snow. Hughie and I desperately wanted a sleigh, but we knew that Mum and Dad couldn't afford to buy one. Eventually, Dad built us one that was different than a "boughten" one. It was low to the ground, about three inches high, but with real steel runners. Hughie was ordered to share it with me.

The favourite sledding spot near our house was the steep, S-curved hill on Little Mountain Road off 33rd Street. All the kids would gather at the top, and a little kid would be assigned to stand halfway down, at the curve, and give an "all clear" when there were no cars coming up. Then everybody would jump on their sleighs and go flying down the hill.

Hughie went first to "break in the sleigh," and then I had my turn. Hughie went back up again, for a second run, and I waited at the bottom of the hill. Standing there, I saw a large oil tanker truck with chains turn off Main Street and head past me up the hill. I waved frantically for the little kid standing guard, but he had vanished. Then my brother came flying down around the curve, going to beat hell, heading straight for the truck.

All kinds of questions rushed through my mind: *Will he come out mangled? Will the truck stop? What will I tell Mum and Dad?*

Hughie disappeared from view. Seconds later he came shooting out from under the truck with not a scratch on him! I couldn't believe it. If he'd been on a sleigh of normal height it would've been "goodbye Hughie."

As was typical of him, he never said a word about his close call. He just looked at me and said, "It's your turn."

The Radio Inspector

One day Dad came home with an old wooden mantel radio. He was keen to get it working so he could hear the soccer results from Scotland, so he scrounged a long length of insulated copper wire and spent the day cutting the insulation off to make an aerial. He fastened the wire to the top of a wooden pole and nailed the pole to the peak of the roof, then ran one end of the wire into the house, to the radio on the kitchen table. The other end he needed to have fastened fifty feet up a tall fir tree.

We were all anxious to hear the entertainment this great invention could supply, so we were standing by, eager to help, when Dad said, "I'm too heavy to climb that tree. It might break. Alan, could you fasten the wire onto that tree if I tell you where and how?"

My father was asking little old me to do something for him, rather than asking my favoured older brother. I was overjoyed, even though I knew he knew that I had no fear of heights and could climb better than Hugh.

Dad fastened an insulator to the end of the wire and tied a thin rope to the insulator and onto my belt. Then I climbed up the tree, pulled up

Alan, Hugh and Pat, Walden Street, Vancouver, 1936.

the wire and screwed the insulator into the tree. I was so proud that I had contributed to the installation of the radio.

A few weeks later, Dad was sitting at the kitchen table, reading the newspaper and listening to the radio. My sister, Pat, and I were on the floor by the door, playing with wooden blocks and pretending they were cars. There was a loud authoritative knock on the door. Without waiting for an answer, a man opened the door. From our position nearly underneath him, he looked enormous.

Dad put down the paper, leaned forward and said, "What do you want?" slightly raising his voice in a threatening manner.

The man replied, "I am the government radio inspector, and I see you have an aerial outside. Do you have a radio? If you do, it requires a five dollar per year radio licence."

From my position on the floor, the eighteen-inch-high Chisholm radio was in plain view, sitting on the table for a blind man to see. Dad slowly picked up the newspaper, unfolded it and placed it over the radio, carefully tucking in the corners. He then leaned farther forward, as if to get up, looked the radio inspector in the eye and in a firm voice said one word. "NO."

The man stood over us for a long moment, then said, in a more subdued voice, "Well then, I'll be on my way." He quietly left, closing the door.

Nothing more was heard from the government radio inspector, and Dad spent many a happy hour listening to soccer games and Scottish music. He enjoyed music so much that sometimes he would pull out his mouth organ and play along.

But the incident was a revelation to seven-year-old me. I had never known my father to lie before, and here he had not only lied but done it deliberately. To a government inspector. It left an impression on me, teaching me that adults sometimes lie to maintain their dignity.

The Cat Who Hated Dogs

Shortly after the radio incident, our dog, Blackie, and a neighbour's dog, Duke, chased our little grey tabby kitten, Rags, practically to the top of the fifty-foot aerial tree. Rags clung to the top of the tree, meowing pitifully. Some of the neighbour men came by and stood around below the tree, giving Dad advice on how to get her down.

I got fed up with all the palaver because Rags was still crying, so I started to climb the tree to get her down. Everyone stopped talking and started watching me, up there at the top where the trunk was so narrow it was whipping back and forth. I climbed down the tree with Rags in my shirt, just in time for Mum to come rushing out of the house. I gave her the kitten but had my ears boxed for taking such a risk.

It was great to have a kitten, and at first we kids thought it was cute the way Blackie and Duke played with Rags. But after a couple of weeks the play started to get rougher, and Rags would try to hide when the dogs came around. Blackie always found her, grabbed her by the scruff of her neck and dragged her, crying, to where Duke was anxiously waiting, wagging his tail. Duke would lunge at Rags's head and put it in his mouth, Blackie would grab her tail and they would drag her through the garden, having a grand old time with Rags meowing mournfully. She was always covered in slobber and mud, and we christened her Rags because this made her look like a dishrag.

Naturally, Rags grew up to hate dogs with a passion. After she developed her claws, if Blackie or Duke got in her way, *slasho*! She would sit on the six-foot-high fence in our alley, and when some unsuspecting dog came meandering down the alley, checking out all the garbage pails, Rags would leap on his back, hook her front claws in his neck and tear out fur, skin and blood with her back claws. The poor dog would run hell-bent for leather down the alley, yelping all the way, with Rags riding on his back. At the end of the block, the cat would jump off and, with a bit of a swagger, trot back to her post to await the next poor victim. Whenever we kids saw Rags wake up from her morning snooze and head for the fence, we would climb up on the woodshed roof to watch the fun.

TB and the Pervert

TB, polio, scarlet fever, smallpox and dog rabies were all over Vancouver. You could hardly go down the block in our neighbourhood without seeing a dark red government sign on at least one front door, warning people that the occupants were quarantined. We also had loads of whooping cough and mumps; nobody escaped getting these two. We were routinely tested at school, and, just as school ended for the summer, Hughie tested positive for TB. Although Pat and I tested negative, the government forced all three of us kids into a so-called summer camp to get healthy.

The camp was at Crescent Beach, and there were counsellors there to take us swimming and on nature walks, or to lead us in outdoor games. There must have been 150 to 200 kids in the great big dormitories that were stuck up on pilings with a three-foot crawlspace underneath. The beds for us three kids were together: Hughie on one side, Pat in the middle and me on the other side, with aisles in between and little lockers by the head of each bed for our clothes.

One of the young counsellors took a shine to our pretty little sister and paid her a great deal of attention. Neither Hughie nor I were naïve. Where we lived, we grew up fast, and we didn't like what was going on here. One night Hughie caught this so-called counsellor trying to climb into bed with Pat, and he put the run on him. We didn't know what to do, because adults don't believe kids in situations like this, so that night we decided we would protect Pat by all sleeping together under the dormitory in the crawlspace.

The next morning we were discovered missing, and when they found us under the building, we were dragged before the head counsellor. Eventually, out came the story. The pervert was fired and everything settled down again. Hughie was rechecked in the fall and was cleared, and we were allowed to come home.

How to Treat Broken Bones

When I was eight, we moved from Walden Street into a large tenement building with eight families around 22nd and Main. We lived on the second floor and went in and out via an outside staircase that ran up the back of the house.

One day, Hughie, who was outside at the bottom of the stairs, yelled up, "Wally's here to see you."

I was excited to see Wally because I wanted to show him the silver Eversharp automatic pencil I'd found the day before at the local dump. I had recently developed an interest in wrecking yards and dumps, and Wally was a fellow scrounger. With the pencil in one hand and a sandwich in the other, I decided to slide down the wooden banister to where he was waiting with Hugh below.

Big mistake. With both hands full, I couldn't hang on. I fell over the banister and straight down, twelve feet, onto the concrete sidewalk. I had the wind knocked out of me, and when I tried to stand up, my left leg wouldn't work. The leg bone bulged out at the hip, and it hurt like hell.

Mum and one of the neighbour women came down and packed me back up the stairs. There was much discussion regarding an ambulance, a doctor, x-rays, hospital and the big subject of no money. Then, along with two more knowledgeable women, they gave me an aspirin, took off all my clothes and placed me in a tub of hot water to soak. I was in so much pain that my extreme fear of water was overcome as long as they didn't fill the tub too high. Mum came in every fifteen minutes to pour more hot water into the tub. They left me there for over two hours, until the pain had subsided and localized in my left hip.

I was confined to bed for two weeks as I couldn't walk. Somebody made a small crutch for me, and for the next two weeks I was able to move around the apartment. No doctor, no nothing, but in the fifth week I could limp around without the crutch. Six weeks after the accident I was back at school, nearly as good as new. The only long-term effect was that my left leg would partially pop out of the hip socket when I lifted it up too high to put on socks or shoes. If I put the leg back down before the muscles went into traction, it would pop back in again. Calcium build-up over the years finally solved this problem, and my hip doesn't flip out anymore.

A number of years ago, after another accident, I had x-rays taken of my back and hips. The doctor remarked that it looked like I had broken my hip as a child.

If we had known the hip was actually broken, would it have made any difference? With no money, I doubt it. There was no medicare then, and no way we could have paid for doctors and hospitals.

Dad Finally Gets A Union Job

In 1938, Dad finally got a union job as an electrician in a large sawmill in Youbou, a small company town on Vancouver Island. We had to move from the big city.

We didn't have a car, so our old landlord took us down to the Canadian Pacific pier and we got on the old CPR steamship *Princess Elaine*. There we were, Mum, Dad and us three kids, along with our luggage and our dog, Blackie. We took Blackie down into the hold, where he was locked in with the freight. After we got underway, though, we could hear him making a heck of a fuss below the decks, so we got permission to bring him back up with us.

We were all excited about being on the boat, charging from stem to stern on the upper deck with Blackie. Mum didn't seem too worried about us, and I guess we were out of her hair. It was a heavy sea that day, and the waves would splash right up over the bow, with the spray coming down all over us. We thought it was great.

Mum had prepared a large bag of sandwiches that we ate for our lunch and supper. When we got to Nanaimo, we walked up the pier with our luggage to the old CPR hotel, where we stayed overnight so we could catch the Vancouver Island Stage Lines bus to Youbou the next day. This was the biggest thrill of our lives, to actually stay in a hotel. Mum, Dad and Pat slept in one bed; Hughie and I slept in the other. Blackie was locked in the basement.

In the morning, Mum announced that we were going to have breakfast in the hotel dining room—a real restaurant. Wow! Mum and Dad ordered a boiled egg breakfast, and we kids had toast and jam. I guess that's all we could afford. The toast was a big disappointment; it was thick, cold and rock hard, and you could have used it for the puck in a game of shinny.

After breakfast we got on the old stage, which I hope is now in a museum somewhere. The outer coachwork was varnished wood, and the seats inside were also wood, and hard as a rock on the bum. There was a railing around the roof of the bus so that we could put our

Hugh, Alan, Pat, Youbou, Vancouver Island, 1939.

luggage up there. God help you if it rained. Jack, the driver, didn't want the dog in the bus, so we boosted Blackie up on the roof as well, and tied him down.

Away we went, with a couple of other passengers, on the two-lane paved road. At Ladysmith we unloaded the mail and passengers, then continued on to Duncan. Goodbye, paved road. Hello, gravel and dust.

The road grew narrower and narrower as we approached the little logging town of Cowichan Lake, at the foot of Lake Cowichan. Naturally, the town's nickname was "The Foot." Big old maple, aspen and cottonwood trees formed a beautiful arch over the road.

As we drove, we could hear Blackie yelping. For a while we ignored him, thinking he was just lonely, but Jack finally realized what was happening. Blackie was being beaten to death by the overhanging branches. Jack stopped the bus, and we climbed the ladder at the back to the roof. Sure enough, there was the poor dog cowering, fearing for his life. We brought him down and put him in the bus under the seat, where he was as good as gold.

The distance between "The Foot" and Youbou was less than ten miles. Halfway there, Jack stopped the bus in the middle of nowhere, and Dad announced that we were home. Jack climbed up on the roof of the stage and handed the luggage down to Dad, and the bus left us standing on the gravel road. Below us was a narrow-gauge railway, and below that was Cowichan Lake. In the other direction, up toward the mountain, I could just make out a small, unpainted, weather-beaten cabin half buried in the trees. This was our new home?

Dad explained it was only temporary. He was building us a new house n Youbou, but it would be a few months before we could move in. However, it was summertime, and Mum soon made a great home for us.

We didn't have electricity or running water, so we didn't have a refrigerator, but there was a small stream beside the house where we could get our water. There was also a pipe sticking out of the ground with cold water dripping out of it. Mum placed a waxed butter box under the pipe's outlet, draped a large towel over the box and had a nice cooler where she could keep food and butter cold. We kids roamed endlessly by ourselves—exploring the mountains and endless beaches, picking blueberries and swimming in the lake. Other than having no other kids to play with, it was a kid's heaven.

Drown to Swim

I said that we swam in the lake. In fact, Hughie and Pat could swim like seals and would spend hours out in the lake, but I roamed the shore, playing in six inches of water. Ever since I was a baby, I had been deathly afraid of lakes, oceans and even bathtubs filled more than six inches. Finally, when I was sixteen years old, my mother reluctantly told me why I was so scared of the water. I guess she had a guilty conscience and had been too embarrassed to tell me sooner, but it sure would have saved me a lot of grief if she had explained the circumstances earlier.

Apparently, when I was six months old and we were living on a floathouse in Port Alice, on the west coast of Vancouver Island, she had put me in a wicker basket on the open windowsill in the living room for some fresh air. She was busy cooking supper and I must have been rocking in the basket. However it happened, the basket overturned and I fell into the saltchuck. She never heard the splash.

Luckily Dad came home from work a short time later and asked Mum, "Where's Alan?"

She replied, "On the windowsill."

"No he isn't," said Dad. He looked out, and there I was, lying at the bottom in five feet of water, looking up at him. How long I had been under water is anybody's guess. Dad was a great swimmer, and he dove through the window, got me and gave me mouth-to mouth resuscitation.

But long before I learned the origins of my fear of water, I was having a miserable time in Youbou, with my siblings cavorting in the lake day after day and me sitting on the shore. When waves were high, they liked to swim inside a large log boom, as the logs stopped the waves.

I thought, *Maybe I can get out there and join them.* I dragged a large slab of wood from the beach into the water, sat on it and then slowly moved it out into deeper water, until the soles of my feet were just off the ground.

This was quite a thrill for me, and I was enjoying myself, but Pat and Hughie were still sixty feet away when I got another bright idea. One of the logs in the boom pointed straight toward them, and I figured if I held on to that log while sitting on my makeshift raft, I could slowly work my way out to them. I was doing fine, but when the water was over ten feet deep, the log ended. Now there was fifteen feet of open water between me and Pat and Hughie. I gave a mighty shove and thought I could coast to them, but my raft immediately flipped over. Luckily I went into the water feet first. Sinking to the bottom, I pushed myself up and reached the surface right beside the log, which I desperately grabbed, coughing and throwing up water.

Pat and Hughie came over to investigate. Panicking, I wouldn't let them touch me or help me, and I slowly worked my way back to the shore, sliding along the log.

This was very scary for me, but for some unknown reason I was determined to try again. I waited until I had calmed down; then I cautiously waded into the water and got all the way to my hips before I started to feel fear. I returned to the shore and then lay down in the shallow water and pushed myself along with my hands on the bottom. *Wow*, I thought, *I am nearly swimming*! Pat and Hugh saw what I was doing and came to shore to encourage me.

That night, excited about the progress I had made, I psyched myself up for another attempt and tried not to think about drowning. It worked. The next day I was dog paddling, believe it or not. From then on I couldn't be stopped when it came to swimming, but it took me another four years before I could put my head under water. Maybe a psychiatrist could explain what happened, but my fear of water was much lessened, and I had achieved some control over it.

Always Get In the First Punch

As fall approached, we got ready to attend yet another new school. Hughie and I had already been to two different schools, and in both schools we had had to defend ourselves from bullies.

I said to Hughie, "Well, I guess we're going to get beat up again."

Hughie replied, "I don't get beat up. I beat."

When I asked how he did that, he replied, "Simple. Pick out the first kid that looks like he's going to pick a fight with you, and before he can get ready, sucker-punch him in the gut as hard as you can. The rest will leave you alone."

Sure enough, on the second day of school a kid called me a name and came over. I did what Hughie had told me and it worked like a charm.

We went to five other schools after this one, and the same tactic worked in four out of five. In the fifth school, one kid sucker-punched me first. There's always a kid at the bottom of the pecking order who wants to move up by picking on the new kid.

The Day Dad Blew the Stump, or The Great Explosion

We lived in that old shack in the woods for about five months, but Dad and his friends worked like dogs to build our new home, and the big day finally came when we could move into our house in Youbou.

Youbou, at that time, was a company town. Industrial Timber Mills owned the land and sold building plots to each employee for forty dollars. The company also sold the employees lumber at cost. It must have been quite a change for Dad, with his socialistic rental philosophy, to now be forced to be the owner of a house, like the "toffs" back home in Scotland.

We moved in a long time before the house was completely finished. There were no interior walls or insulation, no electricity or running water. But it was home, and over the next three years Dad got it nearly finished. Our front yard faced the main road, and our large backyard faced the railroad tracks and, beyond them, Cowichan Lake. All the large timber had long since been logged off our land, leaving only some tall, large, ugly stumps.

Dad hired a man with a bulldozer to remove the stumps, and he managed to get all but one of them out. That last stump was enormous, eight feet tall and over seven feet wide, and smack dab in the middle of our backyard. As kids we liked to play on this stump. We nailed pieces of two-by-four lumber up the side, as a ladder, and the top was so big that we could put two double orange crates back to back up there and still have room to spare. We would sit in the orange crates and imagine flying airplanes or racing cars.

Dad didn't like this stump, though, and decided he wanted to get rid of it. The sawmill was coming out of the Depression due to the Second World War, and the managers had put on three shifts. This required more workers and more houses, so there was a housing boom going on around us. Houses were being built and stumps were being blown up all around us, so Dad, having no experience blowing up stumps, asked questions of the so-called experts. This was a different time and place—there were no regulations, no permits required. Just buy dynamite, blasting caps and fuse, and blow up whatever you wanted.

The first advice Dad received was to burn the stump, so he dug around the very large roots and stuffed kindling between them. The centre of the stump was rotten, so he dug it out and stuffed wood and paper down the centre. The hole was nearly big enough for me to climb into, and Dad thought it would act like a chimney. He lit the whole thing on fire, and it looked real good, with the smoke billowing out the centre, but after a day of smouldering it went out. The consensus of the neighbours was that it was still too wet to burn. I think that old stump wanted to live, and the roots were still sucking up water.

After further discussion with the so-called experts, Dad decided that fourteen sticks of stumping powder placed directly under the stump would lift it and its roots clear up in the air, slick as a whistle. Further instructions from the "specialists" were that Dad should seal off the holes he had dug around the roots, and he should also seal the centre hole.

Being a meticulous tradesman, Dad diligently did as instructed. He got clay and worked like a dog to seal over the roots and covered them with fresh branches. He borrowed a wheelbarrow, collected large rocks and handed them up to Hughie, who was on top of the stump. Hugh then dropped them down to seal the hole. Dad carefully placed the dynamite bundle, with a blasting cap and ten feet of fuse, directly under the centre of the stump. With a fuse calculated to burn one foot every thirty seconds, Dad had then exactly five minutes to get away after he lit it. All of the neighbourhood experts came over to inspect the preparations and make wise remarks.

We kids were of two minds about our stump. We had enjoyed play-ing on it, although after Dad tried to burn it there was a much larger hole to stumble into, plus soot covering everything. But we were also looking forward to seeing it "float up in the air" with a great explosion.

Before the big day, Dad went out and informed all the neighbours, five up the street and five down, that he'd be blowing up the stump on Sunday at two o'clock. He also sheeted over the windows on the back of our house so they wouldn't break with the concussion from the blast. Now all was in readiness.

At 1:30 Sunday, everybody vacated their houses and gathered at least two hundred yards away. My mother took us kids down the road to the Hamiltons' house, where, if we got in the right spot near the raised railroad tracks, we could see the stump and my dad lighting the fuse and running away.

We all waited and waited; that was the longest five minutes ever. People were mumbling, "Maybe the fuse went out," "Maybe it got wet," "Maybe he didn't light it right."

Finally the great moment came, and there was an explosion all right, but not as loud as we were prepared for. And we definitely were not prepared for what happened a split second afterward. Rocks came shooting straight up out of the centre of the stump, as if we had mounted an eight-foot cannon, vertical, with a fourteen-inch barrel.

The two- and three-pound rocks went up and up and up. Then they slowly started to spread all over the neighbourhood as they came down. One went through the eaves of the Hamiltons' house. But, miracle of miracles, there was no further damage to the nearby houses or people.

Everybody had to go up and look at the stump. Dad had done a good job; none of the coverings around the roots were disturbed, but the centre of the stump was blown out, clean as a whistle. From that day until we left Youbou, none of our neighbours would let Dad forget "the day Joe blew the stump."

Errol Flynn in Robin Hood

Mr. Pepper, a local family man, had a small sideline business showing movies he brought by boat to places up and down the lake—The Foot, Youbou, Honeymoon Bay and a couple of logging camps. In Youbou, the theatre was an old, broken-down bunkhouse. The interior was unpainted dark clapboard, and it was furnished with various seats and benches collected from who knows where.

The upcoming Saturday matinee was every boy's dream. Errol Flynn, a very famous actor and by far the most handsome actor in Hollywood, was starring in Robin Hood. Better yet, it was in the new thing called Technicolor, not the usual black and white. All us kids had been making bows and arrows for weeks and practising with them. There was only one problem: my buddy Harvey and I had spent all our allowances on the new Superman comics and didn't have the twenty-five-cent entrance fee for the show.

Checking out the old bunkhouse for a way to sneak in, I noticed a small trap door on the roof at the end of the gable that looked promising. Saturday came, the show started, and Harvey and I went up on the roof and snuck through the trap door. There wasn't much light in there, and we had to walk on the two-by-four stringers or we would fall through the ceiling onto the audience below. Everything was going fine. Down on my hands and knees, I had just got my eye to a knothole when Harvey fell through the roof into the theatre. He hung from a ceiling rafter by his two hands, silhouetted in front of Errol Flynn on the screen, swinging his legs to and fro and trying to avoid falling on the audience.

The show stopped and the lights came on. Mr. Pepper came out and told me to come down, so I grabbed Harvey's stringer and swung to the floor—it was only an eight-foot drop from the ceiling. By now, all the kids were booing us and wanting the show back on.

Mr. Pepper escorted us to the door and said, "Don't come back or I'll see your parents." It all ended up as a big stupid joke on us that hurt more than if we had gotten spanked.

Annie Oakley for a Grandmother

My dad had won a lot of money playing poker in the spring of 1940. He bought new furniture for the house and sent us on vacation for the summer to stay with my mother's parents, or, rather, adoptive parents, on their farm. Mum's family history is, to say the least, colourful and complex.

Her real grandmother, Alice Maude Blythe, and grandfather, Charles Eagles, came over from England with five children—three boys and two girls—and settled in New Westminster. Mum's father, an itinerant Canadian miner named John Moffat, was born October 22, 1864, in Perth, Lanark County, Ontario, and had travelled the world hunting for gold. He went up to the Yukon in the late 1880s, long before the Klondike Gold Rush. Along with some other miners, he came back down by boat and landed in Seattle with two suitcases loaded with gold. Newspapers around the world went wild. This was one of the events that triggered the Klondike Gold Rush.

Grandfather, now a very wealthy man, came north to Vancouver and wooed my grandmother, Agnes Eagles, much to the disgust of her parents, who for some reason wanted nothing to do with him. John and Agnes were married in 1897 and took off on a two-year honeymoon cruise around the world. My eldest aunt, Vi, was born in Australia. The three of them came back to Vancouver and bought a house in the new residential area of Kitsilano, but soon gave it up because the one

John Moffat and Agnes Eagles Moffat with Vi and Charles.

and only crossing to Vancouver was a rickety old wooden bridge across False Creek. They then settled on Seymour Street, close to Granddad's business interests—a sawmill and a cannery.

They continued to have children until 1908: six red-headed girls and one boy. Everything went to hell at this point. A depression hit and Granddad lost everything. Grandmother got tuberculosis and died. Granddad headed back to the Yukon to remake his fortune and was never heard of again, until my mother, many years later, started trying to discover what happened to him. She finally found him in the Mountain View Cemetery in Vancouver, where he was buried in 1938 (strangely, his grave was only two blocks from where we were living on Walden Street at the time).

Mother and her siblings were turned over to the Orphan's Society and adopted out all over British Columbia to seven different couples. The strange law of the day decreed they were to be split up and not allowed to have contact with each other, which was brutal, especially for two of the girls who were twins. The separation was also extremely hard on Aunt Vi, the much older elder daughter, who was like a second mother to her siblings.

Mum, who had been born Ivy Moffat, was adopted by Jesse and Hugh Hunter on May 23, 1906, when she was three years old, and re-named Margaret Hunter.

Jesse Olding Hunter, my grandmother, came from Nova Scotia in the 1880s to teach the Native children in the Lower Nicola Valley outside Merritt, B.C. She married Hugh Hunter in the 1890s, and they had their first home in Granite Creek, ten miles from Princeton, where Granddad, a former member of the Northwest Mounted Police, was the gold commissioner during the second-largest gold rush in B.C., the Granite Creek or Tulameen Gold Rush. This is the rush that nobody today has ever heard about, with over two thousand men panning for gold. In 1902, after the gold rush ended, the Hunters moved to their farm in Princeton, and Granddad was appointed government agent for the Similkameen district.

Grandmother was a tall, stately lady who never raised her voice. She

*Top: Hugh Hunter and Jesse Olding Hunter in their cabin at Granite Creek.
Below: Hugh and Jesse Hunter, 1890s.*

never drank or smoked, and she played the organ in church every Sunday. In a corner of her pantry stood a .22 Winchester single-shot target rifle with octagon barrel, three sights and a drop breach. As a little boy, I was fascinated by it. What was my God-fearing, non-smoking, non-drinking, churchgoing grandmother doing with a rifle? Well, one day I found out.

It was a hot summer afternoon, and Grandma had let the white Leghorn pullets out into the field "to get some greens," as she would say. We had picked a huge tub of peas, and Grandma was sitting in the shade on the back porch, shelling them. She had a large apron on and held a bucket between her knees. The shelled peas fell into the bucket, the hulls went into a tub off to the side.

I happened to look toward the chicken house, where all the pullets were eating the fresh green alfalfa and grasshoppers, and saw a giant hawk tearing a pullet apart. I ran and told Grandma.

She looked down toward the chicken house and quietly said to me, "Alan, go into the pantry and bring me my rifle, would you please."

I ran into the kitchen, cautiously grabbed the gun and handed it to her. I'd never seen a gun fired. She calmly took the rifle, dropped the breach, reached into her apron pocket and pulled out a .22 long rifle cartridge. She put it in the breach, then closed the breach, turned around in her chair, rested her elbow on her knee, cocked the hammer, aimed the gun and pulled the trigger. The large hawk fell over with a few flutters—dead.

Grandma lowered the rifle, dropped the breach, took out the spent cartridge and put it in her apron pocket, and handed the gun back to me, saying, "Please put the rifle away and go and bury that hawk and pullet for me, will you, dear." And then she continued shelling peas.

I went over to the dead hawk. She had shot it straight through the head at over a hundred feet. Was I impressed! I buried the bird and came back to the house.

Mum was in the kitchen, and I asked her about Grandma and the gun. According to Mum, the gun was a wedding present from Grandma's parents and the rifle club she had belonged to in Nova Scotia.

Never Play in a Sawmill

The sawmill Dad worked at in Youbou was huge, but there was no security. If I wanted to see my dad, I would just walk in. Underneath the sawmill was a whole labyrinth of moving machinery that totally captivated a ten-year-old boy. The predominant machinery was a series of large chain conveyors in wide wooden troughs that extended for hundreds of feet. The chains moved through the troughs at about one mile an hour, picking up scrap wood and sawdust as they went along under all the saws and planers on the floor above. They eventually dumped their load through a large hole directly into a fire pit below the boilers that generated the steam to turn the turbines that produced the electricity for all the electric motors running the mill.

All this intrigued me, and I talked my friend Harvey into coming with me to ride this machinery around, under the mill. We had the birdbrained idea to get a small board, squat on it and ride the chain right up to the fire-pit hole, where we would jump off and do it again somewhere else. If, by chance, our foot or clothing had got caught under the chain or on a crossbar, away we would have gone, straight into the open fire.

There was also a large pile of sawdust at the entrance to the mill, and we decided to build a tunnel in it. We found a couple of shovels and proceeded to dig. The outside foot or so was rock-hard, but the rest was easy going. We worked like dogs and after two hours had made a tunnel three feet wide, four feet high and fifteen feet long. Just about then, along came a man who started yelling at us and ran us off the property. Looking back, good for him, because once that sawdust was exposed to air and started to dry out, the tunnel would have collapsed, and we would have been smothered.

Around the time that we lost interest in riding the chains to the fire-pit holes, a tragedy occurred at the mill. One of the firemen, who looked after the fires in the pit, was a middle-aged man who had worked in the sawmill for over twenty years. He had been saving all his money to retire back in China with his family, and this was his last day of work. He had his ticket and all his life savings, nearly $20,000, in a billfold in his shirt pocket. Apparently when he leaned over the fire-pit hole to check the fire, his wallet fell out of his shirt pocket into the blazing fire. Without thinking, he screamed and dove in after it. He would have been dead within seconds.

Riding in Style

Mr. Bond, Harvey's dad, was a quiet, independent man who was a wonderful photographer. He made his living taking school class photos as well as selling his wildlife and scenery pictures to magazines and the *Vancouver Sun* newspaper, and he often went out on little trips in search of subject matter.

One sunny day, Harvey and I saw him loading his camera equipment into his old 1928 Essex car, and we talked him into letting us go along. With all the equipment, there was no room for us inside the car, so Mr. Bond got some pieces of plywood, wrapped them with old sacking, and placed them on the bumperettes at the back of the car for us to sit on. The bumperettes were little bumpers, and when we sat on them, our feet dangled about six inches off the gravel road. Away we went, tootling along, doing about twenty miles per hour with only the spare tire to hold on to.

We would go maybe ten miles at a time, wandering up old logging or farming roads. Then Mr. Bond would stop, set up his camera and take pictures of giant trees, waterfalls and flower patches while Harvey and I explored the area. At the end of the day we made the long trip home, hanging off the back of the car again. If we had fallen off, it wouldn't have been a big deal. We might have gotten a few cuts and bruises, but that's about all. There was little danger of being hit by a passing or following car. In those days it was unusual to see another car on the road. Nobody, including either set of parents, thought anything of Harvey and me travelling in this way.

The Great Detective Caper

One of my friends, Frank Sherman, wanted to become a detective when he grew up, and he practised for that big day by spying on everybody.

He came to Hughie and me one day with this tale about a couple he had followed to a little trysting place half a mile down the train tracks, in the woods by the lake. According to Frank, they were having sex down there. Just as he finished telling us this story, he looked up and said, "Hey, there goes that couple now!" Was it great timing or were we being manipulated? With Frank, you never knew.

Anyway, we went after the couple. We were actually going to see grown-ups having sex! We followed well behind them until they stopped and lay down on some planks. Then we crept up behind a log to watch the proceedings.

This was our first chance to watch adults having sex, and it was quite funny. With all the rapid movement of the man's bum, his pants would gradually slide down around his knees; then the woman would reach down and pull them up and giggle. The weather was cool, so I guess his bum was getting a little cold.

After a while we started to get bored, so Hughie stood up and yelled out, "Need some grease there, buddy?"

She was up, with her dress down, and he was up, with his pants up, faster than you could say "Jack Rabbit."

We jumped over the log to tease them. The woman, Sonia, seemed to enjoy the attention, but Danny, the man, was less pleased. After some more teasing, we said goodbye and went home.

Soon after this, summer holidays began, and we kids spent hours searching the beaches for split cedar logs. We would turn them into rough kayaks by cutting the ends off the logs, forming a point at each end, and then nailing the points together with boards, stuffing rags into the gaps to prevent leaks. When the kayak was more or less water-proof, we would sit in the middle, with our legs in the water for balance, and use a double-bladed paddle to propel ourselves a mile across the lake or along the beaches, trailing a fishing line for trout. We could also put our feet up on the deck to go fast, but that was tricky, as it was easy to tip over.

One day, after a fruitless search for kayak logs, Darryl Brown, one of the younger boys, invited all of us kids up to his place near the beach for snacks. His mother sat with us while we ate, and as we were leaving she asked Frank's older brother, Lloyd Sherman, to stay behind. She said she had something she wanted him to do for her. Lloyd was fourteen and big for his age, the biggest boy in our group. I happened to look back as the rest of us walked away and saw that Mrs. Brown had put her hand on Lloyd's shoulder. When she saw me looking, she suddenly pulled it back.

At the time, I didn't think anything of it, but a few days later our amateur detective, Frank, who was eleven (I was ten), asked me if I wanted to make some money—twenty-five cents an hour! He explained that Mrs. Brown's husband had approached Frank and told him he suspected Mrs. Brown was playing around. He wanted to hire Frank to keep an eye on her when he was on afternoon shift at the mill. Frank said he couldn't do it alone and wanted me to help him. According to Frank, Mr. Brown was not getting along too well with his wife. He had been checking his supply of mail-order condoms, and it was slowly dwindling, so he suspected that when he was on shift, somebody was creeping into bed with her. He wanted to have evidence in case of a divorce.

I was a little suspicious and asked Frank, "With all the kids in town, why did he ask *you* to do this?"

Frank said he didn't know. Something seemed not quite right about this, but I couldn't figure out what it was. So I agreed to talk to Mr. Brown, and that evening we rode our bikes up to the mill to see him. He was a small, quiet man and I immediately felt sorry for him if he really was being canoodled.

We decided to start surveillance that night. I slipped out at ten o'clock, when it was dark and everybody was asleep, and met up with Frank down at the railway tracks. The Browns' house was only a few hundred yards from our house, on the other side of the tracks. Both Frank and I carried flashlights, and we crept up the path behind the house until we could see the back window. Then we hid behind some bushes. Mr. Brown had said he thought the night crawler was coming in through that back bedroom window.

We stayed there until nearly midnight, when Mr. Brown came home, but saw nothing the entire time. The next night we followed the same procedure. Just as we settled in our hiding spot, we saw movement by the bedroom window. A man came out the window and down the path, then stopped right in front of us.

My heart was in my mouth. I could have reached out and touched him, he was that close. The man looked up and we saw his face.

Holy mackerel! It was Lloyd, Frank's brother. He was screwing a grown woman!

I realized that Frank must have known weeks earlier what was going on, and he had gone to Mr. Brown with some cock-and-bull story to try and make some money. I knew Frank and Lloyd were not the best of brothers. Lloyd was a bully, but to turn him in and make money off it was pretty rotten in my books. And to set me up as the impartial witness was nasty. I should have followed my first instinct and have nothing to do with Frank's spying.

The next day, when Frank gave me my dollar for our four hours of work, I told him I didn't want to hear about any more of his "cases." He was on his own from now on. I never heard what Mr. Brown did or didn't do, or what happened to Lloyd. But there was another dramatic consequence to my actions that only became clear much later.

Around this time, Dad came home and announced that we were moving to Vancouver. He was going to work in the shipyards—which had reopened to build ships for the war—and was going to make lots of money.

For the past year our parents had been more remote than usual, and their arguments had become more personal and vicious. Although neither of them said anything directly to us kids, we knew that Mum was seeing our bus driver on the sly and Dad was back drinking and gambling. The year before, he had made enough money gambling to buy a Chesterfield living room suite, a sawdust-burning kitchen stove and a full-size radio, and had even been able to send Mum and us kids to the farm in Princeton for a holiday. Things hadn't gone as well this year. When Hughie asked Mum why we were going back to the city when we were just getting on our feet in Youbou, she told him that Dad had lost our house in a poker game. It was a terrible shock. And then people wonder why none of us kids would ever gamble for the rest of our lives.

The night before we left for Vancouver, Hughie came home after supper very badly beaten up. He looked terrible, and he cried all night— the only time in my life I ever heard my older brother cry. Later he told me that Lloyd Sherman had beaten him up for no good reason that Hughie knew.

Thinking it over for these memoirs, it occurred to me that Lloyd probably beat up Hughie when he should have beaten me. Lloyd must have thought that the McGowan who had been spying on him was Hughie, not his little brother. I do know that if I had figured this out back then, and told Hughie the whole story, he would have beaten the hell out of me over and over again, as he had done many times before. By the time I realized all of this, though, my brother was dead of cancer in his early forties.

Deer-Killing Dogs

A final story from our time in Youbou concerns the fate of our dog Blackie. One of our neighbours, who lived about a quarter mile from us, had a German shepherd named Simon, who was a natural pack leader. One day he started coming round with two other dogs to pick up our next-door neighbour's big dog, Bingo, and off they would all go to chase and kill deer up in the mountains. Then Simon started coming over to pick up our dog, Blackie. Blackie was a thirty-pound short-haired dog, and up until then he had never given us any trouble.

It was quite the thing to watch Simon entice these dogs to go hunting with him. First he would come up and greet them happily, wagging his tail, rolling over and touching noses. Then it would be *Let's play!* and they would romp around until suddenly he would stop then walk a few more steps, looking back as if to say, *Aren't you coming?* Next thing you knew, away they'd go, following him no matter how much you tried to call them back.

At this time on Vancouver Island, the deer population was on one of its periodic cycles of high birthing, and there were deer everywhere. Consequently, the cougar population was also increasing. When we kids were up in the mountains behind town, it was common to find a freshly killed deer with its neck broken. The only thing the cougar had done was tear open the neck and lap up the blood or maybe eat the liver. There were so many deer, the cougars could afford to be fussy. Sometimes in the hills, or on the way to school, we would hear a cougar crying close by, but we knew they weren't hungry enough to attack kids—at least, we hoped they weren't.

One day, when we were a little way up the mountain building a tree fort, we heard a dog howling. Then a doe came bounding by with one of Simon's pack chasing it. We heard the other dogs yelping and wondered what was going on. I couldn't figure out how the dogs were able to chase down a fast-running deer, so I asked Smokey, a Native man who was a neighbour of ours. He told me that dogs were cousins of wolves and hunted deer the same way, taking turns chasing them in a large circle in relays until the deer was too exhausted to run anymore. Then all the dogs would attack and kill it.

Simon's pack would be away from home for as long as two weeks. When the dogs returned they were nothing but skin and bone, covered in wood ticks. We kids would bath Blackie in coal oil to loosen the ticks, pull them off with our hands and then tie Blackie up. But after two or three weeks, Simon and the pack would come over to chew Blackie's rope off, and away they would go for another two weeks. They say if a dog starts chasing deer, you can never break them of the habit.

One time, a couple of days after Blackie had returned home, Simon's owner came over and asked if we had seen Simon. Dad told him that we hadn't, and the man said, "Well, I guess the cougars got him."

A few weeks later, Bingo came over with the other two dogs to pick up Blackie. Bingo was now the leader of the pack. Off they went, and when they came back two weeks later, Blackie wasn't with them. Cougar food. We were all heartbroken.

Dad then went to Duncan and bought a purebred Springer spaniel pup that we named Lassie. We raised her carefully, but as soon as she was old enough, Bingo took her hunting. She came back in terrible shape, crawling with wood ticks. If we hadn't left Youbou shortly afterward for the big city, Lassie would have ended up like Blackie.

Playing Both Sides of the Street

Mum and we three kids landed in Vancouver without a place to stay. Mum contacted her oldest sister, Vi, who had reconnected with the family through our Grandma Jesse Hunter three years earlier. Vi lived in a tenement building in downtown Vancouver, on Homer Street, and she took us in temporarily. She had three older children, Jerry, 19, Elaine, 17, and Cyril, 15. Mum then managed to find us temporary accommodation on the top floor of an old three-storey house on Robson Street. It was a dump but better than nothing.

Dad didn't stay with us. He had a room downtown and was busy working in the Burrard Shipyards as an electrical draftsman. I guessed that mum and dad were working up to a parting of the ways, and we rarely saw him.

The Second World War was on, and Vancouver had pulled itself out of the Depression. The shipyards in North Vancouver and False Creek were going full blast, and Lulu Island had a large aircraft plant, employing thousands.

The guy who owned our apartment, Billy Bob, was a real character, like Fagin in Charles Dickens' novel *Oliver Twist*: charming, crooked and devious. He had many faces, and he lived by playing both sides of the street. One of his schemes was to find old cars that had been stored in garages during the Depression because people couldn't afford to run them. Now people were working and there was a demand for these vehicles, but because of the war, cars were not being manufactured for the public. Billy Bob would get these cars going by fair means or foul, selling them at an inflated price. He used to boast to us kids about the sneaky things he did to make the cars run.

Billy Bob had been a rum-runner, and he still had his old rum-running boat, even though prohibition had been over for a few years. The beat-up, unpainted little boat had a monstrous V8 motor in it, and when Billy took us out for a spin, he scared the daylights out of me with how fast it would go.

Like Fagin, Billy Bob ran two street gangs of kids who robbed stores and stole cars, bikes and boats. The two gang leaders would come over and talk with Billy Bob about their scores. He would spot the scores and take a commission on everything they stole. Surprisingly, another of his enterprises was to teach aggressive self-defence to the men of the Vancouver police force. This job may have grown out of his career as a professional wrestler. He would take us to watch him in the gym, where he and the man he was to fight that night would practise their moves.

Billy Bob took a shine to Hughie. In turn, Hughie thought the sun rose and set on Billy Bob and was slowly getting sucked into his orbit. At one point I broke the front fork on my bike, and Hughie said, "I know where you can get another one." He took me down to a house on Second Avenue. We went into the basement, where an associate of Billy Bob's had many boxes of parts and over three hundred bicycles hanging from the ceiling. The guy compared my bike fork to other forks, selected one, and asked for a dollar.

You may be wondering how I knew he had over three hundred bikes. Was I in the basement long enough to count them? No, but . . . surprise! A week later a picture of the man and his bikes was in the newspaper. The Vancouver Police had raided him and counted the bikes. After that, Hughie gave Billy Bob a wide berth; the sun no longer shone on him.

Rounding up the Japanese-Canadians

Just before school started, we moved into a rented house at 14th and Ontario. Soon after, I made a new friend who was Japanese-Canadian.

At this late date I can't remember his exact name, but it was something like Kyoshi Uno. I met him and his little sister because we all walked up Ontario Street to Simon Fraser Elementary School, and he was in my Grade Six class with Mrs. Cowan. Kyoshi was into making lead soldiers and so was I. His father had a big grocery store at 16th and Main Street, and the family had a big fancy black sedan and owned a nice two-storey house.

Two days after the Japanese raid on Pearl Harbour, we were at war with Japan. Two months later, there was a roundup of all Japanese-Canadians.

We were in class one afternoon when the door suddenly flew open and two men in strange uniforms came barging in. One of them loudly demanded, "Which boy is Kyoshi Uno?"

Mrs. Cowan pointed to poor little Kyoshi. He was sitting two seats from the front, and I was sitting at the back of the room. One of the men went over and grabbed him by the back of his shirt, lifting him right out of his seat, and carried him out the door. The door was closed and class resumed.

I was in a daze—what did he do to be treated like a criminal? After school I jumped on my bike and rode down to his house. I got there just in time to see the whole family, with suitcases loaded, herded into a van and taken away. We learned later that they ended up in the stables at Exhibition Park. Their nearly new car was sold for fifty dollars, their store was sold for $450, and I don't know what happened to the house. I'm sure that those who organized the roundup and sale profited handsomely. Greed and skulduggery thrived throughout the war.

Before Pearl Harbor, during the spring, summer and fall, many Japanese-Canadian men would fish for the canneries up and down the whole B.C. coast, and the women would work in the canneries. Each cannery had little company houses for them, and space where they could turn their animals loose to forage.

Now I heard that the Japanese-Canadian fishing fleet was being rounded up and escorted into Coal Harbour by the Canadian Navy. I was familiar with Coal Harbour and boats, thanks to Billy Bob, and

I decided I had to go and see this. It was a Sunday so I jumped on my bike, rode down Main Street to Hastings, and then down Pender to Coal Harbour. I should have brought my Baby Brownie camera.

There were hundreds of thirty-six-foot double-ended fish boats being escorted in or already anchored, plugging the entire harbour. Men, women and children were jammed into these boats, along with all their animals. Chickens were in cages on the decks; goats were suspended in slings from the long poles used for trolling, their udders and legs hanging down. The poles had been lowered, so the goats were about two feet above the water. However, these fishing boats had nearly round bottoms, and in a swell they would normally tilt forty-five degrees. You could imagine how this affected the poor goats: one minute they would be twelve feet above the water, the next minute submerged.

As the people in the boats came ashore, those officers in strange uniforms that I had seen in Mrs. Cowan's classroom were herding them into vans. All the Japanese-Canadians were confused, with kids and women crying. I don't know what happened to their possessions, including the chickens, goats and boats. I do know that in spite of all this, and wherever they were sent during the war, over the years these hard-working and industrious people rose to the top and became the best of citizens once again.

Hooray, Hooray, the First of May

"Hooray, Hooray! It's the First of May! Outside screwing starts today."

The war effort was in full swing. Shipyards and airplane factories were going all out. Vancouver was also the Pacific Command for Canada's Armed Forces, and personnel from the British Empire, as well as American sailors and airmen, were jammed into the city. In their downtime, these men were all looking for "poontang" and excitement. They were going overseas and there was a good chance they wouldn't be returning, so they did risky things they normally would never have done. Morality seemed to be selectively set aside during the war, and there was a lot of promiscuity.

Riding my bike around Stanley Park during this time with a friend, I noticed couples strolling into the park carrying two blankets over their arms. One blanket is nice to sit on, but what was the second blanket for? We soon found out.

Cruising to Lumberman's Arch, a great big grassy field in the park, we discovered what looked like a big sleep-in. There were about ten couples lying on one of their blankets, with the second blanket covering them. The movements under the blankets made it pretty easy to see what was going on.

The devil perched on my left shoulder, and I rode my bike quickly past each couple, from their feet to their head, sticking my foot out to push the men's bums down. Reactions varied from giggles to indignation, and we got out of the area in a hurry before somebody caught us and killed us.

I Am Not Your Wife

Hughie, Pat and I came home from school one day to find Dad talking to Mum. Both were excited. Dad had accidentally found two of Mum's sisters: the twins, Rose and Maple.

Dad was still at the Burrard Shipyards, and one day after work he dropped into a beer parlour off the corner of Main and the Cambie Street viaduct. Due to all the wartime work going on, the Men's side of the beer parlour was full. So Dad asked the bartender if he could sit on the Ladies and Escorts side.

Dad went in and spotted an empty chair at a large round table. When he looked across the table, he saw Mum sitting there and abruptly asked her, "Why aren't you home with the kids?"

She replied, "Just who do you think you are talking to?"

Dad said, "Why, my wife, of course."

She replied, "I am not your wife."

Dad replied, "Well, if you are not my wife, you are her twin sister."

Margaret McGowan and Lassie, 14th Avenue house, 1941.

One outstanding feature of all seven children from Mum's long-lost family was their dark red hair.

I personally don't know what Dad was thinking when he assumed he was sitting across from his wife. Mum would not have been caught dead in a beer parlour. She had never had a drop of liquor and, to my knowledge, had never been in a beer parlour in her life.

Eventually they straightened it out and discovered that Dad had found Mum's sister Rose. To cap it off, Rose had earlier found her twin sister, Maple. Rose had a husband and two children, a boy and a girl, and was living in Vancouver. Maple had two children and was living in Hedley in the interior of British Columbia.

After this, my mother started looking for her lost family, never giving up, and by one means or another, over the next forty years, she located all of them. Mum was over seventy-nine years old when she finally found her younger sister.

On a sad note, a few months later Rose came out of the same beer parlour and was run over by a car and dragged screaming two hundred yards up the Cambie Street viaduct before people could stop the driver—who was, strangely, an old boyfriend. She died, but he got only three years in jail.

Exploring the City on a Bicycle

Ever since we left Vancouver Island, Dad had been like a ghost. He wasn't around when we were living on Robson Street, although he did come to our house on 14th Avenue every now and then, making an effort to talk to us kids or to play cards with us. It was a strange time. Nobody discussed anything, and it was like living in suspended animation, waiting for something concrete to happen. Dad worked as an electrical draftsman and Mum was selling girdles, though she wasn't doing very well. It seemed like all the members of our family were doing things on their own and not as a family, including me.

Vancouver at this time was a wonderful place for a young kid with a bicycle. Other kids at school had family members working in the shipyards, and each time a Victory ship was launched, they would let us know. We would ride over and go down below the Christening Platform, where we watched as the men pounded out the holding blocks to launch the ship. Some were launched stern first, and some were launched sideways. It was exciting to watch such large ships being launched from our viewpoint down below.

I was also fascinated by fighter airplanes and would ride my bike out to the airport on Lulu Island, past all the neat Chinese garden farms, to watch the fighter pilots learning to fly. One group that came in from Australia was learning to fly Spitfires and Kittyhawks. They were stuck in camp and were dying for information about Vancouver. I talked to them through the fence because they were not allowed to come out. I went to the tourist bureau, downtown around Georgia and Richards, and got maps and brochures for them, as well as information on dances at the Military Service Centre on Burrard Street. They appreciated the information so much that they said I was their "unofficial mascot."

One time when I rode down to see the pilots, they were all talking about an incident that had happened the day before. A delegation of the local farmers had come to the base to complain to the Air Force brass that the pilots were flying too low. They were flying so low that when farmers were loading hay on a rack, the wash from the plane's propeller would blow all the hay off the rack. Apparently the farmers weren't too happy with their reception by the brass, so the next day one of the fighter planes came back with a pitchfork jammed up on the underside of the wing. The brass got the message loud and clear, and that stopped all the pilots' fun.

The pilots had another low-flying tradition that the brass frowned upon. When they received their flying wings, they celebrated and showed off their skill by flying under the Lions Gate Bridge. I got the distinct feeling that these Aussies were pretty tough characters, even though they were nice to me.

Unfortunately, I only had one year to explore wartime Vancouver and spend time with fighter pilots. In 1942, Grandma Hunter died, and Granddad, who was now eighty years old, wanted Mum to come back to the farm in Princeton to look after him. Mum agreed and moved to the farm, taking us kids. This was the end of my parents' rocky marriage. I don't know how acrimonious the separation was, but there was very poor communication with Dad from then on. And although he was making big money, in the next six years he sent us a total of just $136 dollars. Times were really tough for us.

Many years later, when I had grown up, Dad and I were out fishing and he started reminiscing about our early family life—the tough times and the endless arguments he and Mum had about nearly everything. He told me, "I've been married twice now and realize that I made some big mistakes with your Mum. If I could do it over again, I would have compromised and we would have lived a good life together."

From the time of the divorce, in 1942, to Dad's death in 1961, he never made a bad comment about Mum.

Forty years after the divorce, I was visiting Mum and Mitch, her second husband, in their trailer in Olalla, a small village in the Okanagan. Mitch was out, and Mum and I were alone in the living room when Mum suddenly blurted out the same sentiments that I had heard so long before from Dad. She was more specific about the wrongs on both sides, but she also admitted they could have had a good life together if they had known more about how to compromise and get along.

At any rate, in 1942 we left the big city and moved to Princeton and a very different life from what we had known to this point.

PART TWO

Life on the Farm

Our Adopted Granddad

Our grandfather, Hugh Hunter, was very tall, six foot four, and healthy, but he wouldn't get his hands dirty; he was an English Government Administrator and don't you forget it. Apparently he came from a good family in England, but he had made the mistake of being found in bed with the wife of the head of the Presbyterian Church. As a result, Granddad was one of the many so-called Remittance Men who were sent out to the Okanagan from England to escape whatever scandal they had been involved in.

He received a commission in the Northwest Mounted Police in 1885 and served across Canada, and in 1896 was appointed gold commissioner for the Granite Creek Gold Rush. Granddad's job was to collect the ten-percent gold tax from the two thousand men working the creek beds in the wilds of the B.C. interior. You can imagine the trouble he would have had collecting this money, or the equivalent in gold, from these tough miners.

He married Jesse Elisabeth Olding, a tall woman who was teaching Native children in the Lower Nicola Valley near Merritt, B.C. Grandma had come out west from Nova Scotia with her sister, who ended up teaching piano in Vancouver and never married.

After 1901, when the gold rush ran out, Granddad took the position of government agent in Princeton. He bought a beautiful ten-acre piece of bottom land three miles east of Princeton, on the Similkameen River, and built the first lumber house in the area. This land, and the section east of it, would be impossible to purchase today: all the Native

Chiefs for the whole Similkameen Valley are buried in a small fenced-off area right in the middle. It is sacred ground, but the Natives had to crawl through a barbed wire fence and traipse across a hayfield to get to their own cemetery. (I hope that this situation has improved for the Natives over the years.)

Granddad ran the farm like an English gentleman farmer, with a hired gardener, Len Yu, an old Chinese man who had been a gold miner. The house was built on a grand scale for the area, with ten-foot-high, embossed ceilings, big bay windows, a piano and organ, and a formal dining room. There were flower, vegetable and fruit gardens and lawns for croquet. There were barns, chicken houses, ice houses and a feed storage shed. It was beautiful, but after living in the city, all we kids could see was no running water, just the pump outside, and no flush toilet or electric lights. We couldn't even use our radio until we got a wet cell battery, and we were three miles from town without a car.

Granddad was on a tiny pension, so with all of us there, Len Yu had to be let go. We kids tried to picked up the slack, even though we didn't have a clue, and our gentleman-farmer granddad was no help. Mum

Hunter Farm in Princeton.

gave us some basic advice, but the rest was learned by trial and error. Granddad had sold the horse and cow, fortunately, so we didn't have to look after them. He'd also sold his car, because he could no longer drive.

We all learned how to light gas lanterns; cut kindling and wood; pack and fill the icebox; clean the outhouse; and feed, water and look after the three hundred chickens—and candle the eggs for sale in town. Candle eggs? What's that? Every egg you sell has to be put in front of a light to see if there are any blood spots in the egg. We also had to learn how to look after the garden: plant, water and weed it through the summer; then dig it up in the fall and store the vegetables in the root cellar for the winter. We made all kinds of serious mistakes but eventually learned what to do.

Some people would say we were city kids, and others would say we were country kids, but over the next few years we became a little bit of both.

In the meantime, Granddad developed dementia and lost all his money to a ruthless lawyer. He then got the idea to sell the farm from underneath us. Mum had to take her own adopted father to court and have him declared incompetent. This was sure tough on Mum in a small town, where everybody thought they knew everything. Shortly after this episode, Granddad died and Mum inherited the farm.

She also located another of her siblings. Mum got a long letter from Aunt Vi, telling us that she had found their sister Jean, in Vancouver. Mum started corresponding with her, and we ended up all good friends, visiting back and forth with Jean and her two children, a boy and a girl, Bob and Bev, over the years. (In the ongoing search for her six siblings, Mum had found her sisters Vi, Rose, Maple and Jean by this time, but was still looking for Alice and her brother Charles.)

The Toughest School in B.C.

Soon after we arrived on the farm, we found ourselves going to yet another new school. By now we had gone to so many schools that we let Mum know we could do this one on our own. We took the school bus in and registered at the office. I found the Grade Seven classroom and took a seat in the middle of the room. We had heard that this was the toughest school in B.C., but everybody seemed to be behaving normally.

Then a boy came in wearing a full set of logging clothes and a smart-alec look on his face. He was greeted with the nickname "Dink," and as he walked he made a strange scrunching sound. He suddenly lifted one of his boots to show everybody his new logging boots, spikes and all. What they were doing to the wooden floor, I shudder to think.

He then jumped up on a desk, did a little dance and ran along the tops of all the other desks, digging his spikes in. Just as he dropped off the last desk, right in front of the door, our teacher, Mr. Thorsteson, walked in. Mr. Thorsteson took one look at Dink's boots and hauled off and hit him, knocking him down. Dink spent the next two weeks sanding and painting all the desktops, which had multiple puncture holes in them. This was the toughest school in B.C., no doubt about it. What an introduction to a new school.

The next year, in Grade Eight, we had a teacher named Miss Snow. She was a tiny little thing and a good teacher, but she had a hair-trigger temper and a penchant for throwing chalk brushes. The Grade Eight schoolroom was on the second floor, on the south side of the building, beside the road.

One late spring day the sun was shining through the open windows, bringing in pleasant smells. My desk was near the back of the room, on the window side. Roy was sitting in front of me, and Bruce and Doug were in front of him. When Bruce started talking to Doug, Miss Snow looked up to see who was talking. Bruce had his head down, so she couldn't see him properly, but she figured it out and threw a chalk brush at him, yelling his name at the same time. She figured Bruce would pop his head up and get smacked in the face with the brush. But she had pulled this trick too many times, so instead of sticking their heads up, Bruce and Doug both ducked down, and Roy, peacefully reading his book behind them, got hit full in the face by the brush.

Now, Roy had been raised very tough, and school was the only time he wasn't working hard on his family's stump ranch or in their two-bit sawmill, cutting railroad ties. The school bus didn't go out there, so Roy had to walk the five miles to school every day on a lonely trail, even when the temperature was thirty below zero. Sometimes he made the trip with no gloves or jacket, and he didn't seem to mind it. He wasn't big, but he was extremely strong.

When he got that chalk brush in the face, Roy calmly got up, walked to the front of the class, bent down and picked Miss Snow up in his arms. He walked over to the open window, hung her outside for a few seconds, then opened his arms and dropped her to the ground, one floor below. We all rushed to the open windows to see her tangled in the large burr bushes, unhurt but screaming mad.

Roy turned and calmly said to the class, "I wasn't really learning anything anyway, so I guess that's the end of school for me. So long." He headed for home, never to return.

Five minutes later, Miss Snow came storming back into the room, eyes wild, looking for Roy. Man, was she a sight! Her fluffy pink angora sweater and her hair were covered in burrs.

Somebody started to giggle, and it soon spread through the class. Miss Snow stomped out and we had the rest of the afternoon off.

Entrepreneurship, Country-Style

As we settled in on the farm, we got to know our neighbours, including the Tennants, a family with two boys around my age and three younger kids, who lived on a farm about ten miles below ours and thirteen miles from town on the Hedley road. I thought that we were poor, but we couldn't hold a candle to the Tennants. They only wore shoes when they came to town, and their farm's log cabin had dirt floors. The old man was an ex-wrestler and built like a bear. He was mean, and when he was drunk he would throw his wife and kids around. When sober he had a hard time getting jobs, so very little money came in.

The Tennants lived too far away from everyone else for their kids to get any paying work, so Sonny, the oldest, developed an ingenious but highly illegal way to make some money. A quarter mile below their farm was a wooden bridge on Highway No. 3, a gravel road running from the U.S. border up through the South Okanagan to the Similkameen Valley. Usually only one or two cars went by every hour, many of them driven by tourists who didn't know the area.

Sonny figured he could puncture the tires on the tourist's cars and then charge them for repairs. He found some eight-inch spikes and drove them through a plank that could be nailed up under the bridge's own planking, with the nails protruding above the deck. He then positioned Red, his younger brother, down the road to watch for vehicles and to signal him when it wasn't a local vehicle but an unsuspecting tourist.

When Red gave Sonny the signal that someone suitable was coming, Sonny would temporarily nail the spiked plank up in place, with the nails projecting upward. The poor tourist would get at least one flat tire. The brothers would then remove the plank and follow the car. They usually found the stranded driver stopped, conveniently, nearly opposite their farm. Sonny would then offer to help him with the tires: "Hey, we have a pump and patches down at our farm. We could go and get them if you want . . ."

Business was going great until they forgot to remove the plank and accidentally punctured two tires on a neighbour's truck, which came to a stop beside a tourist's car with two flat tires. The neighbour put two and two together and came back with Mr. Tennant. That was the end of that little enterprise, and the two boys got a licking they would never forget.

A Very Brutal Father

Eventually, the Tennants moved from their farm to an old abandoned house in East Princeton. One nice sunny day in early spring, I decided to go fishing and headed over to their new home to see if the two oldest boys, Sonny and Gordon, wanted to go with me.

When I got there, Sonny was hiding in the woodshed. He peeked around the corner, motioning for me to come closer, and whispered,

"Don't go near the house." He told me their dad had been fired from his job as a logger and was drunk and taking his frustration out on the family.

I went up to the house anyway, looking for Gordon. *What the heck,* I thought. *He can't hurt me. I can run faster than he can.*

The front door of the house was open. When I looked in, I saw Mr. Tennant sitting on a kitchen chair in a living room empty of any other furniture. He had a case of beer under his chair, and he was throwing Gordon and little Red, in turn, against the wall, *thump, thump.* Mrs. Tennant and the rest of the kids were cowering in the far corner.

Mr. Tennant would call one of the boys to come over to him. Naturally, the boy was scared to go, so his father would threaten him. Slowly the boy would crawl over, crying. Mr. Tennant would then put his large arm around the boy, mumble something about the whole family being no good, then bodily throw the boy against the wall. He'd have another drink and then do it again to the other boy.

Mr. Tennant was just five foot eight but built like a brick shithouse. A former wrestler, he probably weighed 260 pounds and was as mean as he was powerful. It was an ugly sight.

Mrs. Tennant signalled for me to go away before her husband saw me. I had nightmares for days after, still hearing that awful *thump, thump.* Why one of them didn't pick up a gun and kill him is beyond me.

A few days later, on the school bus, Gordon told me the beatings were a common occurrence.

Fourteen years later, I was living in Kitimat, B.C., over seven hundred miles from Princeton, when there was a knock on the kitchen door. There stood little Gordon Tennant with a big grin on his face. He was now a bear of a man, six foot one and 250 pounds, with hands like boxing gloves.

He told me that when he was sixteen and had filled out, his dad made the mistake of trying to beat him up again. Gordon beat him to a pulp, and Mr. Tennant never fully recovered. Later on, he went blind and ended up in a care home. Gordon had a slight smile on his face when he told me this, and I couldn't blame him after what I had seen. You play with the bull, you're bound to get the horn sooner or later.

Gordon was now working for a core drilling company and had grown into a nice, responsible person. Older brother Sonny, who had stayed small and skinny, hadn't fared so well. He ended up dealing drugs on the streets of Vancouver and died when the police put a chokehold on him to force out a bag of drugs he had tried to swallow.

Old-Time Neighbours

We were flat broke, and there was no money coming from Dad, so Mum went to find a job. This was a hard decision for her. She was a proud woman and had grown up in Princeton as the daughter of one of the leading citizens. She had been the first student to graduate from Grade Twelve in the Princeton school system, and she had also taught Sunday school. It was embarrassing to have to admit that her marriage had failed and that her ex-husband was not supporting her. She could go to work or apply for welfare, but after being on relief for six years, putting up with "snotty relief workers" (Mum's own words), she chose not to go on welfare at any price.

Although Mum had no experience working in retail, the two old men who ran the Red and White store at the far end of town hired her. As we didn't have a car, this meant she had to walk four miles to work, stand on her feet all day, then walk four miles home. She started this job in August.

On the first day of school in September, Mum got us kids ready for the school bus and started walking up the road to town, as usual. The bus came and picked us up, and halfway to town we passed our own mother, walking on the side of the road. This is what we kids were dreading. Unless you have lived through an experience like this, where you are completely helpless to change the situation, you cannot understand how it scars you for life.

Bill Lucas, the school bus driver and owner, was Mum's age and had gone to school with her. He was a quiet, gruff man who hardly said a word. After all the kids got off the bus at school, Bill turned to Hughie, Pat and me and asked why Mum was walking. When we explained, he said, "You tell your mother that from now on she can ride the school bus, and to hell with what the school board would say."

So Mum rode with us on the school bus in the mornings, but she still had to walk home. This wasn't too bad in the spring, summer and fall, but in the winter, with heavy snow, wind and the temperature falling to thirty-five below, it was close to murder. Occasionally one of the neighbours would give her a ride if they happened to be going home at the same time, but mostly she walked. A good-looking young woman walking home alone in the dark had to be pretty brave and tough.

Margaret McGowan, Princeton farm, 1943.

Alan, Pat, Hugh, 1940s.

When it was way below zero, I can remember Mum rushing into the house and leaning over the kitchen stove for the longest time to get warm. Pat would serve supper, and as soon as we finished eating, Mum would rearrange the kitchen furniture for the evening. She would pull her big old wicker armchair over to the open oven. The wicker bottom of the chair was sagging, so Mum just kept piling more and more pillows in to be comfortable. She would put the gas lantern close by on the table next to her chair and would have a pot of tea and a cup within easy reach on top of the stove to stay warm. She'd get herself a good book, sit down in the chair, stick her feet in the oven, and settle down for the night while we kids did our homework on the dining room table. For a rare treat she would bring home a bunch of green onions, put salt in a saucer, and over the next two hours dip the onions in the salt, eating them all. To Mum at that time, this was living!

It turned out a lot of people were talking about Mum's situation. Among them was our next-door neighbour, Bob Taylor, who belonged to a small group of men who got together at the tailor shop in town every Saturday night to play poker and drink scotch. The end result of discussions by the poker group was a commitment to provide Mum with a ride home every night.

Bob Taylor and Gilbert Prideaux were the two main angels. It went on for four years—Mum taking charity from neighbours. Can you imagine the gossip of old ladies? Older men escorting a young woman home every night! But all of the men were married and had the support of their wives to help Mum. This was during wartime when gas was rationed, and they still gave up that precious gas and their time away from home for Mum and us kids. We had many kindnesses like this from neighbours over those rough years.

How to Blowtorch Your Mother

One of my jobs in the winter was to light the two fires in our large, cold house when we got home from school. The sawdust-burning cook-stove in the kitchen was easy to light and heated up quickly, but the big log-burning heater in the living room was a problem. I had to build a small fire of paper and kindling and then slowly, paying close attention, feed in larger and larger pieces of wood until I could push in a four-foot log or two. It took a long time so I developed a dangerous shortcut. I would open the front door of the heater, pour half a can of white gas on the paper and kindling, stand to one side in case of an explosion, then throw in a match and, *whoosh*! I would have a nice hot fire in no time at all.

On one winter day when it was thirty-five degrees below zero, I was in a hurry to get the house warm before Mum got home from work. This was before our neighbours had sorted out her transportation, and she was still walking the four miles from her job at the Red and White store. I knew she would be nearly frozen stiff.

Everything was going according to procedure until I threw the gas in. Instead of splattering over the paper and kindling, it shot under-neath, straight into the ashes, but today they weren't just ashes. Deep inside were embers from the previous night's fire, and suddenly there were dark grey gas fumes emanating from the ashes. Instead of putting my brain in gear, I continued with the standard procedure and threw in the lighted match. A second later, ten-foot flames shot out of the heater, straight at our front door. The only problem was the front door had been flung open, and there was Mum, framed in the doorway with a shocked look on her face, enveloped in flames.

She had never used the front door before, but because she was so cold that night, she took a shortcut to get into the house as soon as possible. Her timing couldn't have been worse. She had opened the door the moment I tossed the match. Fortunately, maybe because she was so cold, the flames only singed her eyebrows and front hair.

I stood there dumbfounded, making useless noises.

Pat heard the explosion from the kitchen where she was preparing supper and rushed in. She sized up the situation and helped poor, singed Mum into the warm kitchen.

Mum was in shock for a short while, but a cup of tea brought her around. Everyone took turns giving me hell, but by suppertime we all were laughing about it.

I never used gas to light the fire again. I used coal oil, which is slower burning but safe. And I still marvel at Mum's timing.

A Lifelong Passion

That first winter in Princeton, all the kids were talking about getting ready for the skiing season. I knew nothing about skiing but was curious, so when the snow finally came in late November, I took my bicycle and went out to the ski hill to see what it was all about.

The ski hill was four miles from town, on the opposite side of the river from our farm. There was a cabin at the foot of the hill. I went in and was greeted by Mrs. Irwin, whose husband, Pop Irwin, ran the hill. She gave me a cup of coffee and I sat on the porch and watched all these kids coming gracefully down the hill. Some of them were only eight or nine. I figured if they could do it, so could I, and I was hooked.

However, I had no money to buy skis, poles or boots. I solved that the next summer when I got a job on the neighbour's dairy farm (more on that later). In two months I made over eighty dollars. Mum took sixty dollars, and I bought wooden skis and poles from the Eaton's catalogue for thirteen dollars. With the remaining money I decided to do something we normally couldn't afford: I took my sister Pat to the movie theatre and then to the ice-cream parlour, where we ordered sundaes, floats and banana splits until we couldn't eat any more, then staggered down the road home.

The local shoemaker, Mr. Gallo, took my regular boots and made them into ski boots. He built a wedge between the heel and the sole, and cut a groove at the back of the heel for the Kandahar harness. I then discovered that my skis needed steel edges so I would be able to turn on the ice that often built up on the hill. Steel edges were expensive, but Pop Irwin said he had some old ones that he could fit onto my wooden skis. This took a lot of time and skill, and I really appreciated it.

My other big problem was getting back and forth to the ski hill. Pop Irwin, a crusty old guy with a heart of gold, had a one-ton truck that he would load up with kids heading to the ski hill, but this truck left for the hill from town, and riding a bike the three miles to town in the snow to catch the truck was a lot of effort for me. I developed what I thought was a better way to go. The ski hill was just across the river from our farm, and the river at this time of year was only fifty feet wide and two feet deep. So I would carry my bike the three hundred yards across the field to the river; take off my boots, socks, pants and long johns; stuff them in a packsack; and wade, naked from the waist down and barefoot, across the ice-filled river. Sometimes this was a little tricky, as the ice built up on the stones on the bottom of the river and made it slippery.

When I reached the other side, I would dry myself off with a towel, put my clothes back on, hike up to the road and ride my bike the rest of the way to the ski hill. The first time I did this, I thought I would freeze my legs off, especially at ten or fifteen degrees below zero, but packing a heavy bike through the snow to the road got me pretty heated up, and after a while I got used to it. Thankfully nobody ever saw me wading across the river. That would have been hard to live down, especially if I had run into the ski truck from town, with all my compatriots in it. (The next year I bought an old, very small punt for two dollars that I could pole across the river. This worked great.)

On my first day of skiing, I tramped twenty feet up the hill and came straight down. By the end of the first year I was climbing over fifty feet up the hill, but I had taught myself to come down in snow-plough turns. The other kids were going by me on the towrope, up to the top, and flying back down past me, but my slow progress didn't bother me too much because I was having so much fun.

One Sunday when I was up on the hill skiing, I looked down and saw one of my old Grade Seven teachers, Miss Nichols, who I had a crush on. She was going into the ski cabin below. I wanted to go down to see her, but I still hadn't learned how to stop properly on skis. I decided I would fly straight down the big hill and come to a stop by going up a small hill past the cabin.

Down the hill I went, and I was flying across the flat when who should walk out of the cabin and across the porch, stopping right in the middle of my narrow path through the trees, but Miss Nichols.

I had a big choice to make: hit her square on, hit the trees or hit the porch of the cabin. I chose to hit the porch. My skis went under the porch and I smacked into the corner post. The impact brought everybody out of the cabin to see me lying on the ground, trying to breathe. The end result was two broken ribs, a bruised jaw and a shattered ego. This accident also motivated me to learn how to stop properly.

By the end of my second year on the hill I was using the towrope, going two-thirds of the way up the hill and doing stem turns. In my third year I was stem-turning from the top of the hill.

What a wonderful thing Mom and Pop Irwin were doing. They offered an ingenious rope tow, when nobody in the province had anything like it; they needed only two main volunteers for the whole

Top: Alan and Cousin Bob, 1945. Below: Alan, Amber Ski Club, Princeton, 1943.

operation; and the price was right—one dollar a year for a season pass, plus an extra dollar if you wanted to go night skiing—which allowed anybody to ski. The number of vertical feet we skied in a day was probably ten times more than that on any other ski hill, and our sixty-person Amber Ski Club produced provincial, national and world champions, thanks to the Irwins.

Speaking of champions, Bert, one of our top-notch older skiers, came home on a two-month leave from overseas in 1944, just in time for our Amber Ski Club championships. For some reason, the Irwins had changed the downhill course, and it now had a sharp, dangerous, right-hand turn halfway down. Most of the skiers were forced to make speed-regulating turns on the way down. But Bert left the gate in the men's event and headed straight down the hill at a terrific speed, not slowing at all, and barely making the turn without crashing. With this daredevil move he posted a run time nearly half the next fastest time.

After the event, I went over to congratulate him and asked why he had taken such an awful risk. He looked at me, a naïve fourteen-year-old kid, and said, "Wouldn't you have done that if you had to go back overseas?" That gave me a lot to think about.

Thanks to the Irwins, skiing turned into a lifelong passion. I went to ski hills all over B.C. and Alberta, and introduced my kids to the sport when they were old enough to enjoy it. I only gave up skiing, reluctantly, when I was eighty-three, after I fell twice in one day and felt my balance was starting to deteriorate.

Mandy's Secrets

Along with skiing, I've always loved to fish and would go to great lengths to find secluded places to catch trout. Each fall, the whitefish migrate up the Similkameen River to spawn, and I heard that the Twenty Foot Hole was the hot spot for them. Never having fished for whitefish, I decided to try my luck.

When I got there, I was surprised to find about ten adults standing seven feet apart, all seriously fishing. An elderly Native woman was fishing two people up from me in the line, and by lunch she had ten fish, more than double the catch of anyone else. I figured if I was going to learn how to catch whitefish, I had better watch and learn from her, but when Mandy was baiting her hook, she would pull her jacket open, bend her head and, with her long black hair hanging down, hide what she was doing. The one thing I learned was that she tied a small knot in her line and kept the knot at the surface of the water. When the knot slowly went under, she struck. She caught twenty-five fish that day.

A year later I was fishing for trout on One Mile Creek, and who do I spot downstream but Mandy. I thought this was a good chance to spy on her. Luckily I had my granddad's old binoculars with me, and I hid above her, behind some bushes. She pulled in a nice ten-inch trout and took it off the hook, whacked it on the head and put it on her string in the water. She then pulled a snuffbox out of her pocket, opened the lid and laid a great big ugly white woodworm on a small board. She cut off a hunk of that worm and put it on her hook. Then the coup de grace. She pulled a long black hair out of her head and carefully wrapped it around the worm and hook. Aha! The secret! Normally you can't use woodworms for fishing because they're very soft and won't stay on the hook, especially for whitefish, which don't bite but gently suck the bait. But the hair kept them on the hook long enough for Mandy to set the hook in the fish's mouth.

I couldn't wait to try this method out; boy was I going to catch fish! Mum had beautiful red hair, and when she let it down it came nearly to her waist. She spent time each day brushing it. When I got home, she gave me five long strands and I carefully wound them around a spool. Then, after tearing apart stumps, bark and logs, I collected six large, ugly woodworms.

Early the next morning I excitedly rode my bike down to the Twenty Foot Hole. There was Mandy, along with five other fishermen, all standing in a row. I moved into a gap in the line beside Mandy and said hello. She looked at me, grunted and turned away. I set up my fishing rod and pulled out ten feet of line, took out a woodworm, cut off a hunk and put it on the hook wrapping it in Mum's hair, just as Mandy had done. Looking up, I discovered Mandy watching my every move with a small grin. I tied a matchstick to the line at surface level, threw the line in and started catching fish. Now all the grown men were watching me too.

Mandy got two fish for every one of mine, and by the end of the day she had twenty-five to my ten. She looked at me sideways with a big smile and a twinkle in her eye and said, "You sure learned a lot, hiding behind that bush on the One Mile, didn't you?" The sly old fox. She never let on that she knew I was watching her.

Three years later I finally beat her at catching whitefish. As we were walking away, she said quietly to me, "Fishing is mostly with the eyes, and now I can't see the line as good. Guess I'll have to quit fishing."

On second thought, knowing her, maybe she was just funning me and had no intention of quitting. She was a great lady.

My First Buck

My other great love was hunting. When I was thirteen, Hugh bought an old army rifle, a .303 Mark 1 from the First World War, with money he earned as a fireman at the local coal-fired steam-electric power plant. (By the time he was fifteen, Hugh was acting up in school, playing hooky, drinking and staying in town nearly every night. His marks were so poor that Mum made him quit school and got him a good job at the power plant. Hugh never forgave Mum for this. And when I say never, I mean not even before he died many years later.)

Even though I was only thirteen, I would borrow this rifle every chance I got and tramp the hills with our dog, Lassie. I didn't know anything about hunting, and with no Dad around I had to teach myself. Lassie was supposed to be a hunting dog, so I thought maybe she could teach me, and I did learn a lot by closely watching her hunting moves. If the grass was short, she went through it quickly because she knew that grouse couldn't hide in it. But if the grass was long she would move slowly, watching and sniffing and, sure enough, there would be a grouse hidden there, which would burst up into the air. I learned to be aware of large animals downwind from us when Lassie began aggressively sniffing the wind and growling. I managed to get a few grouse with my grandmother's old single-shot .22 target rifle, and we saw lots of does in our travels, but no bucks.

Then, late in October, Lassie and I were on top of Holmes Mountain when we came out of the trees onto an open slope and woke a four-point mule deer buck that was sleeping. I was as surprised as he was, but he reacted quicker than I did. With leaps over thirty feet long, he bounded down the slope and into some trees. I charged down the hill after him and ran full-bore into the trees, where I lost his tracks. By then it had started to get dark so Lassie and I headed home.

The next day, bright and early, I was back up the mountain to see if I could find that buck. I went right to the spot where he had disappeared in the trees and finally found tracks, which showed he had looped around behind me and stood in the bushes fifty feet back of where I had jumped him. From there, he must have watched me thrashing around in the bush below. I was learning.

About a week later I was wandering around on top of this same mountain. As I came over the brow of the hill, a herd of deer appeared, slowly ambling up from the Five Mile Creek two thousand feet below. A little spike buck got wind of me, and the whole herd took off.

I couldn't wait to get back up there. I figured that deer were something like cows; they liked routine and would be coming up that same draw every day at the same time until the weather changed. But now that I had learned about being upwind or downwind, the next time I went, I positioned myself behind some bushes upwind, where the herd couldn't smell me. Sure enough, up they came, slowly grazing. It was the same herd with the little spike buck.

I sat there for a while, idly watching all of them. As they came closer, I took up my gun and aimed at the spike buck, even though he was too young to shoot. In less than a minute he started raising his head, ears twitching and tail coming up—all signs that he sensed danger nearby and was nervous. I slowly lowered the gun and looked away from him. His agitation diminished, and within two minutes he was back eating.

Could he actually sense that he was threatened? I took the gun up again and aimed at a big doe. Within a minute she became alarmed, looking around nervously. I turned the gun from her to the buck, and again he started getting nervous.

Wild animals' survival instincts are so sensitive, I realized, they can sense not only when they are being watched, but also when the watcher is planning to do them harm. If I casually watched the deer without killing thoughts, they didn't become as agitated as when I was thinking killing thoughts. I believe that humans have the same ability, but it has been dulled by urban life. During these years when I was spending a great deal of time in the wilderness, that instinct or sixth sense became more and more acute. When I go back in the woods now, I'm sad that I've lost that instinct.

Lassie and I kept hunting all the way through into December, when the snow on the mountains was nearly two feet deep, which made for heavy slogging. One day as I was ploughing along the edge of the mountain, two thousand feet above Five Mile Creek, a four-point buck jumped up out of the snow fifteen feet in front of me. I stood dumbfounded for a second, then struggled to get my gloves off, shoved a shell in the chamber, raised the rifle and, what do you know, the iron sights were clogged with snow.

Desperate, I aimed down the barrel, jerked the trigger and nearly fell over from the recoil. I was only thirteen and had never shot a high-velocity rifle before—you couldn't afford to practise with the war on and shells being rationed. The buck just stood there.

I fired another shot, and the buck fell over backward with his legs straight up in the air, horns planted in the snow.

Lassie jumped on his chest, heading for the throat. The buck bent all four legs, then suddenly straightened them out, and Lassie went eight feet in the air, yelping. Down the bank she went, about thirty feet. She snarled and came scrabbling back up, grabbing the buck by the side of the neck.

I rushed over, placed the gun against his head and put him out of his misery.

Alan's first deer, 1944.

I bled and gutted him, but decided I couldn't drag him out to the farm by myself, so left him behind and headed straight home, where I told the family proudly that we had venison to eat for the winter. Hugh was jealous because I had got the first buck, but the next day he reluctantly gave me a hand to haul it home. A neighbour with a truck helped us too. We hung the buck in the ice house and skinned it.

Because it was so cold, the carcass remained frozen all winter. Every time Mum needed some meat, I would go out and cut off what she wanted.

Mum could cook venison better than anybody I knew. If she left it in the warming oven for a day or two, it would be dark brown and tasted like candy. Some nights before bed I would wander by the stove and peel off a dry stringy bit; nothing tasted better.

Cruising Down the River

A few months later, in the spring, my schoolmates and I were walking over to the Tulameen River every day at lunchtime, watching as it rose higher. The Tulameen and the Similkameen Rivers come together just below Princeton, and you can normally walk across them at a riffle. That spring, though, both rivers were up over twelve feet deep, and uprooted trees, branches, debris and logs swirled in the current. Townsfolk of all descriptions stood on the bridge, watching the water overflow its banks.

One of our schoolmates, Kevin, came down the side of the river, his clothes covered with tar and dirt. He reported that he and a bunch of the boys had found some timbers and railroad ties up at the old coal mine on Allison Flats and were building a couple of rafts. They planned to raft down to the Sterling Creek Bridge, just above Hedley.

I thought, *Hey! Hedley is twenty-four miles downriver. What an exciting thing to do*!

Forgetting all about school, a bunch of us headed upriver. Sure enough, there the boys were, building two rafts with old railroad ties and spikes. We gave them a hand and made some long poles to use for steering the rafts. When they were finished, some of the guys looked at the dirty, fast-flowing river and chickened out. That left seven of us.

Bruce, who was the main raft builder, Kevin and I helped the other four guys launch one raft, and then we launched ours. We had a bit of trouble, and by the time we got going, the first raft was a quarter mile away.

Out we went into the middle of the stream, the three of us standing up happily, moving at a fast pace. We were carried swiftly downriver to Princeton, where our classmates gawked at us from the railing of the bridge, like a flock of crows. There we found that the other four rafters had gone ashore. We three had just enough time to yell "Sissy!" before we shot under the bridge and away. We should have yelled "Smart!"

We joined the Similkameen River, getting used to manoeuvering the heavy raft, then passed my family's farm and other local landmarks, having such a grand time that we never gave a thought to how we were going to get home. A while later, as we went by the bluffs at Bromley Rock, we saw a large rock directly ahead of us, sticking four feet out of the water. We hit it at full speed. Bruce and Kevin were thrown into the river; I held on for dear life.

The raft kept going at high speed. I had lost my pole, so I couldn't steer when the river made a sharp turn to the left. The raft shot to the right into a fast-moving side channel that was overgrown with brush, trees and logs. I had to jump over some branches as the raft flashed underneath; other branches I had to duck under, and I got smacked in the head and body when I missed. As I came around another bend, I saw a three-foot-thick log lying across the stream right in front of me, half in the water and half out, with branches sticking in all directions.

The raft smashed into the log, tilted up and then shot under it, breaking off branches in the process. I tried to leap over the log but was stopped by two branches. Then I fell backward and was going under the log, feet first, when the front of my belt caught on the stub of a branch on the bottom side of the log.

There I was, underwater—unable to go forward under the log because my belt was caught, but also unable to pull myself up onto the log because of the pressure of the current pushing against me. Desperation gives you extra strength, and I managed to grab one of the upper branches and pull myself around the log, releasing my snagged belt. My legs were still under the log, but now I could breathe, and I was eventually able to roll myself up onto the log.

I lay there for a few minutes, gasping for breath and trying to figure out what to do. I was marooned and soaking wet on the far side of the river, with no road or people for seven miles. And where were my two friends who had been thrown into the Similkameen? To make matters worse, I had lost my favourite hat.

I finally stood up and made my way along the log to dry land, then climbed up onto the long-abandoned right-of-way for the old Kettle Valley railroad. I started walking, and who should I see coming toward me but Bruce and Kevin, soaking wet but alive. They both had managed to swim to shore, which seemed like a miracle to me. God looks after fools and drunks!

We began walking down river toward the Sterling Creek Bridge to get to the road side, our shoes squishing with water. It was getting cold, and soon it was dark as well. Boy, were we going to be in trouble with our parents and the school.

After a while, away up ahead, we could see a light. As we got closer, we saw the light was in a farmhouse. We knocked, and a man cautiously opened the door and led us into a nice, warm house. Miracle of miracles, he had a party-line phone. We asked him to phone our parents and the police, thanked him and then kept walking. By the time we got to the Sterling Creek Bridge, local members of the BC Provincial Police were waiting to take us home. Soaking wet, cold and hungry, we were dropped off at our homes in time for a well-deserved scolding. The whole town knew about our misadventure, and the next day at school we were treated like stupid heroes, if there is such a category.

Mob Thinking

About a year and a half later I got caught up in another bright idea that didn't end quite as well. It was Halloween night in 1944. I was fourteen years old and full of piss and vinegar, hanging out with my peer group. The group grew larger as more kids joined us. Time went by and impatience built.

"Come on, let's do something."

Someone spotted an outhouse and started to push it over. Somebody else went to help. Somebody said, "This is not right." Somebody laughed. All of us snickered or laughed nervously, more went to help push.

A leader yelled, "Let's go push over more shit houses."

"Yay!" said the mob. Resistance to moral wrong grew less, and the damage escalated. The mob was now united, ready to follow a leader.

A member of the group saw something more damaging to do. Now came the frightening part. The whole mob instantly saw the "something," and all reacted together. Leadership flicked from one to the other, but as the damage escalated, the leadership shifted to just one. Along the way, various members came to their senses and disappeared until there were twelve left with the older, stronger, leader, Albert, who now said, "I know where there's a D-8 Caterpillar tractor. Let's push it over a cliff into the river."

The mob yelled, "Yeah! Let's go!"

We hiked up to the ballpark and there sat the Cat. Albert went over to it and we all crowded around him. We didn't have a clue how to start it, but Albert fiddled with various parts, attempting to get it going. This took about twenty minutes while the rest of us stood by.

A strange thing happened during this time. The mob unity went out of us and we all realized the stupidity of the damage we had done and were about to do. Six of the twelve remaining in the mob made excuses and left for home.

But then Albert got the Cat started and climbed aboard. The five of us remaining stood back, suddenly realizing the enormity of what we were about to do. But nobody said anything.

Albert drove the Cat over to the edge of the cliff, but we didn't follow him. He set the Cat in gear and jumped off. Over the cliff it went. On the way down it completely turned over and landed back on its tracks, heading for the river where it high-centred itself with the tracks still grinding away.

We were all played out and looked at our leader as if he had coerced and intimidated us into doing his bidding. What was left of the mob broke up, and we went home separately. Eventually, six of us were charged and received one-year suspended sentences. A month later I found out that our fearless leader had a personal grudge against the owner of the Cat and was using us. That didn't feel very good.

When you see some young fellow accused of mob violence, and he looks like he's been hit in the face with a flat board, you might understand why. It can happen to anyone, in the right mood, around the right cause, and at the right time. I've been there, and I believe we are no different than birds in a flock when we are in a mob. We twist and turn, synchronizing instinctively with the direction of the flock.

Hiring On

When I was thirteen and starting to put on muscle, I thought maybe I could get a man's job to help put food on the table, as there was little money coming in. I spent some time visiting one of our neighbours, Jack, who had a large beef and dairy ranch, to see if I could do the work. Then I tentatively brought the subject up with Mum. She encouraged me, so I got up enough nerve to ask Jack if he would hire me. He agreed so quickly I suspected that Mum had paved the way. After all, she had known Jack's wife all her life. Jack and I made a deal that during Easter, Christmas and summer holidays, he would pay me forty dollars a month or $1.25 a day.

I still had my chores to do at home, but now I was earning real money, with thirty dollars a month for Mum and ten dollars for me. I found the work interesting and challenging. As a hired farmhand, you do what the boss tells you to do, regardless of your personal feelings, and you are often given the toughest jobs.

There were a pair of dogs on the farm, Queenie and King, that earned their pay patrolling the property and herding and finding lost cattle. They had a pup, Kelly, who turned out to be totally useless. Even his parents knew something was wrong with him. When we were getting ready to round up some cattle, Queenie and King would be raring to go, but Kelly would come creeping out of the large kennel, take one look, then slink away and hide. The breaking point came when Jack, the boss, caught him with a free-roaming chicken. Jack told me to take Kelly out and shoot him.

Every farm has cats—usually one housecat, two barn cats and maybe a feral cat or two. They earn their keep catching mice and rats, but cats breed as fast as rabbits. You can castrate the males, but Toms will come from miles around to do the job. So every six months or so, the farmhand has to cull the cats.

Then there was Old Bessie. I milked Old Bessie, currycombed her, fed her, took her to the bull and helped her with her calves. She'd been a good cow for many years, and I had grown fond of her. But Old Bessie wasn't producing milk anymore; she had come to the end of her usefulness. The slaughterhouse didn't want her because she was too old and too tough, so my job was to load her onto a truck, and away she went to the mink farm to feed the mink, which aren't as fussy about their meat as we are. You hate to do it, but that's life as a farmhand.

Of course, there were some bright spots too. One of the many scheduled events on the farm was the weekly Wednesday delivery of three tons of used malt from the local Princeton Brewery, which made Highlife beer with a seven percent alcohol content. The malt was primarily given to the dairy cows—it made them very healthy, with lovely soft fur, and the placid, semi-inebriated cows epitomized the slogan about "milk from contented cows"—but everybody who got a taste enjoyed it: cows, pigs, chickens and horses. Paddy, one of the old workhorses, and Marie, the undisputed leader of the cows, were the biggest fans.

Every Wednesday, an hour before the regular delivery time, Paddy would come over to the malt bin and wait for the truck. How he knew it was Wednesday was a mystery to me. The truck would stop at the farm gate and, three hundred yards away, Paddy's ears would flip forward and his old tail would start swishing in anticipation.

The malt bin was a large wooden structure built six inches above the ground. Over the years, Paddy had dug a two-gallon hole beside it. As the malt settled in the bin, beer would seep out and flow into the hole Paddy had made. He stood beside his hole, guarding it from other animals. Marie, the cow, stood on the other side of the bin, where another trickle seeped out into another, shallower hole.

Slowly, both holes filled up. Marie would drink a gallon or so and leave, letting other animals have a drink. But Paddy wouldn't share. He sipped his beer, enjoying every swallow. This went on for hours. Then you would notice a marked difference in his demeanour: eyes nearly closed, tail lethargic and hanging straight down, ears slack, legs splayed out front and back and sideways, trying to keep his balance. Paddy was drunker than a sailor.

Just for fun, I sometimes would put my shoulder under his chest, lift and push. Paddy would stumble sideways for ten or fifteen feet before he regained his balance and stopped. He would stand there, looking stupid, and a few minutes later he'd stagger back to his hole to continue sipping. After three hours he slowly staggered away.

Was he an alcoholic? I would say yes. And was he in good shape for work at twenty-four years old? Yes. Did he have the softest, thickest coat from all that beer? Yes.

Coyotes, Calves and Cougars

Some cows, when they are ready to give birth, will go into the wilderness, find some heavy brush and drop the calf. When the calf is a few days old and able to run a bit, the cow will bring it back down to the home ranch. This is a fight between ancient instinct, dating back to when cattle ran wild, and logic. Logic has the cow and calf safe and sound in a nice warm barn. Instinct has the cow in the bush, at risk from the wilds of nature. As a rancher, you need to go and find her quickly, before the predators smell the birthing blood.

One day I was out looking for a pregnant cow that hadn't come home. I was riding along the side of an open grassy hill, and way up ahead I could see two coyotes beside a bush; one was snapping at the head of the cow, trying to provoke her so she would lunge at him and leave the calf unprotected.

Before I could get there, the coyote succeeded in getting the cow to lunge; at the same time, the second coyote streaked into the bush and ripped the calf's throat. Then came the worst part of all. The coyotes both sat on their haunches, opened their mouths and yipped at the poor cow, which was now bawling plaintively. It was as if they were making fun of her. My hatred for coyotes increased tenfold.

I was too late to save the calf, but the cow was unhurt, so I strapped the little carcass behind my saddle. The coyotes weren't going to have the satisfaction of eating this calf. From then on I carried a rifle whenever I was out looking for cows.

About a month later, Lassie came into heat and was attracting male dogs from all over. I got an idea for revenge, and on my next trip to find lost cows I took Lassie with me. We did a big twenty-mile loop, and Lassie ran way out front. Mr. Coyote got a whiff and came in to start romancing Lassie, jumping up and down, rolling over and wagging his tail, touching noses and wanting Lassie to play with him; it was their usual mating stuff, similar to that of young humans.

I gave a whistle, and Lassie came running toward me. By now, Mr. Coyote was drunk with lust and followed her in. I took aim at him and *crack*! (Joe, the rancher's five-year-old chestnut gelding that I was riding, was so calm and steady I could shoot a rifle from his back and he wouldn't turn a hair.) Now I had one dead coyote, plus a seven-dollar bounty on his cape and three dollars for his fur. I made good money over the next two weeks, and the cows were a lot safer for a while. They say all is fair in love and war.

On a cold, miserable, rainy spring day, Jack asked me to go up on the range to find another pregnant young heifer who had gone missing. I took off on Joe and headed into heavy tree country, where the cow might have had her calf. After twelve hours of fruitless searching, I decided to head home, tired, wet and weary, before it got dark. By then the fog had moved in, and visibility was only about thirty feet.

If you haven't ridden a horse all day in the rain, you have never really known misery. You're sitting there, hardly moving; the rain is coming down between the back of the saddle and the seat of your pants. It is also coming down between the pommel and your crotch area. In other words, your ass is wet, as if you peed yourself. On top of this, because you aren't moving, you get cold. To warm up, you have to get off the horse and walk awhile in the mud. The horse also isn't too happy to be out in the rain and behaves accordingly.

At this point I was on top of Bald Mountain, which was about 1,500 feet above the back of the ranch. The descent from here was a very steep, grassy slope, with no trail. But even though it could be muddy and slippery, I knew it would be safe if I took my time. Joe had new, cleated shoes, so I thought we would be okay.

As we approached the brow of the mountain, the wind came up from below and blew a hole in the fog and there, about fifty feet away to my right, I saw a great big old male cougar with grey on his muzzle. He saw me at the same moment and let out an ear-splitting scream, clawing at the air. Instantly, Joe and I were airborne, and I was in for the ride of my life. Horses are scared of cougars, and Joe took off straight down the mountain as fast as he could go, slipping, sliding and crow-footing, with clumps of wet clay flying in all directions. To hell with the notion that real cowboys don't grab the pommel—I grabbed and held on for dear life.

At the bottom, Joe shifted to a full gallop, and in nothing flat we were back in the ranch yard. Jack looked at me and Joe, covered with mud, and asked, "What the hell happened to you?" I tried to explain, but I don't think he believed me.

Renegade Range Bull

One early spring day, Jack said to me, "One of the neighbour's range bulls broke loose, and he's up on the range somewhere, raising hell with the cows. You'll have to go out, find him and bring him in."

What he really meant was this range bull was impregnating the cows too early in the season, so the calves would be born in the middle of winter and die. The bull had to be taken off the range as soon as possible. I wasn't the only one looking for him, as all the ranches had to help for the common good.

I was only fourteen, and these 1,200-pound range bulls can be mean and dangerous, especially if there is a cow in heat around. I saddled Joe, got an old lasso and rode up onto the range. I was in luck and spotted the bull ambling across the side of an open mountain. He saw me and took off, and the chase was on. Joe was going along in a lope, but because of the slope it was tough riding, and my saddle was going side to side as well as up and down. The next thing I knew, I was underneath the horse, half lying on the ground, twisted around and looking up between Joe's back legs. My work boots were jammed in the twisted stirrups. To my amazement, Joe didn't kick me to death or stomp on me; he stopped dead with his back legs splayed apart.

I managed to get my boots free while Joe stood still, and then I rolled out from under the horse, cursing the old cowpuncher who a few days before had shown me a new quick-release fold knot for the cinch. It had come loose, along with the cinch, and that's why the saddle and I slipped around under the horse's belly. I swore I'd never use that knot again as Joe stood patiently and I turned the saddle over and cinched it up with the proper knot.

By then the bull was half a mile away, but I caught up to him. He definitely didn't want to go back to pasture, and he headed straight for a small mud lake in nearby Deer Valley. I guess he thought if he got out into the lake, I couldn't get to him.

He kept going farther and farther into the lake, looking back at me as I came closer. Joe and I stood in the mud on the edge of the lake, and by then the bull was up to his belly, sixty feet away. Joe and I stood there watching him, trying to figure out what to do. We waded out a ways, but Joe started sinking and we panicked and got back to shore. The bottom of the lake was quicksand! I figured I wasn't going to get stuck in quicksand for some stupid old range bull.

As we stood there watching, the bull was slowly sinking. He started bawling his head off, his eyes as big as saucers, looking at me. The water came up over his back, with only his head now showing. Then, ever so slowly, nearly all of his head went under the water until just his horns, nose and two bugged-out eyes were showing. I hated to see him drown, but I wasn't going to risk Joe's and my lives to get him out of the quicksand.

Then Burt came riding up. He was the old-time professional cowboy who had taught me the quick-release cinch knot, and he was also looking for this range bull.

Burt took stock of the situation and said, "Looks pretty bad, but I think we can get him out."

Still smarting from my upside-down saddle, I said, "Well, if you're so bloody smart, tell me how, before he drowns. If he sinks two more inches, that will be the end."

Burt said, "Hook your lasso onto my pommel and the other end on your pommel. I'll wade out and try to lasso his horns."

Both Burt and I tightened up our cinches, and then Burt said, "If I start getting stuck, or sinking, you pull me out."

He slowly rode his horse into the lake to the full length of my lasso. Then he made a long throw and hooked the bull's horns. He wrapped his lasso around his pommel and yelled at me to start pulling, and between the two of us we pulled the bull up to the surface. Once he was floating, he lay on his side, and we pulled him to shore like a beached whale.

Mr. Range Bull was now as docile as a little lamb, and we let him rest while Burt had a smoke. The bull then slowly got to his feet and away we went, back to the home ranch, with the bull between us. Burt kept the rope around the bull's horns, but he wasn't resisting anymore.

Sex on the Farm

Molly, one of the cows on the ranch, was heavy with calf, and we could see that the calf had dropped into the birthing position. Molly was trying to push him out, but he wasn't coming. The next day she was lying down, still trying, and she was not looking very good.

Jack said to me, "Well, Alan, it looks like you got a job to do." I didn't have a clue what he was talking about.

Jack explained that the calf's legs were broadside to the birth canal, blocking the calf from coming out. And even if the legs straightened, Molly didn't have enough strength left to push the calf out. Jack wanted me, with my smaller arms and hands, to reach up her birth canal, straighten the calf's legs and loop a small rope around its feet. Jack would then gently pull the calf out with the rope.

I said, "You mean you want me to shove my whole arm up inside her? Won't she fight back and break my arm?"

Jack explained that, at this stage, Molly knew we were trying to help her, or at least he hoped she did, and that if I didn't try what he suggested, we'd have to shoot her.

That convinced me to give it a try, as Molly was a good milker. I took off my shirt and greased my right arm. Jack placed a sack on the ground, and I lay on the sack on my side, gently pushing my arm inside Molly. She turned around with wide eyes, ears twisted forward, and looked at me. I kept pushing until nearly my whole arm was inside her. At that point she went into a contraction and I thought she was going to break my arm, the pressure was that great.

Then she relaxed, and I slowly pushed the calf back, unhooking the feet that were wedged sideways against her hip. I withdrew my arm, took the rope in my hand, went back in and looped it over the feet, tightened the loop, and withdrew my arm. Jack took over and gently pulled out a cute little heifer that was very weak. Molly was back on her feet the next day, but the calf took a few days of special care before she was able to stand up.

* * *

That wasn't my only experience with the nether regions of animals on Jack's ranch. Shortly after I helped Molly with her calf, Jack decided he wanted to breed Suzy Q, one of his young mares, who had come into heat. A neighbour, Bert, brought his old stallion, Bud, to the ranch in a truck. Bert said he wasn't going to charge for the service, because Bud was getting old and sometimes couldn't get a good hard erection. Bert had agreed to give him a try because Bud loved his screwing; he hadn't had any in a long time, so now maybe he could do the job.

Right off the bat, Bud caught a whiff of Suzy Q, who was 150 feet away in the breeding chute. His ears went forward and his nostrils flared and he whinnied. We put Bud in the pen with Suzy Q, but nothing happened.

Jack turned to me, and with a grin on his face he said, "Well, Alan, I guess you have got yourself a job as a go-between." He wanted me to hold Bud's cock up so he could push it into Suzy Q.

I said, "No way." I had been around before when the range studs bred the mares, and the final thrust was always extremely violent, sometimes nearly breaking the mare's back. There's no way I wanted to put my arm between them. But Bert and Jack assured me that Bud was a gentle lover, not a "wham, bam, thank you, ma'am" kind of stud.

Bert then explained that Bud didn't like spectators, so the others were going to have to stand back away from us. I was on my own. Bert said, "If you need help, just yell," and he started laughing as he walked away.

Bud took his time, snuffling Suzy Q's rear and gently pawing her backside. Finally he started getting an erection, and slowly and gently he mounted her. His penis was shaped like a man's, but it was about twenty inches long and as thick as a baseball bat. It was nearly erect when I reached between the boards and gently lifted it up to where the head touched Suzy Q's vulva. At this point, Bud must have felt the heat, and he gently eased it in, to its full length. By then I had taken my arm out of there; you're talking about two 1,200-pound animals coming together.

I stood back and watched. You could see Bud surely did love his screwing. I'd watched the stallions out on the open range, and they were extremely rough when they were breeding. It was more like rape and was all over in ten seconds. Bud was a lover. He was licking Suzy Q's ears, licking the side of her neck and gently moving his rear end. He would lay his head alongside her neck and close his eyes. Suzy Q was obviously enjoying it. Finally, after about four minutes, he was tired and he withdrew and dismounted. Suzy Q stood looking back at him, swishing her tail, as if to say, *Isn't there more?*

Sad to say, Suzy Q didn't get pregnant. I guess that Bud, at his age, was only shooting blanks.

Jack could be quite a gossip, and I made him swear he wouldn't say anything to anyone about what I had done that day. I knew if the kids at school ever got wind of this, I would be a laughingstock.

* * *

Jocko, the Jersey bull, had to be fed, watered and looked after year round, just for the six-week breeding period in late summer when he earned his keep by mounting up to fifty cows. However, for the two months before this official breeding time, he had to be locked in his pen because some of the cows would come into heat too early and he could smell them. If the cows were bred too early, their calves would be born too early and would die.

During the springtime, when he was locked in his pen, Jocko grew meaner and meaner, and you could see his scrotum swelling up. When he smelled some of the cows that had come into heat, he got even meaner.

One day I noticed him standing with a swayed back and his legs spread out. His head was stretched up and he was making strange, small, rapid, grunting noises. Then his pink, javelin-shaped penis emerged. He gave a thrust with his hips like he was mounting a cow and *Kerpow*! Out shot a jet of sperm that hit the ground ten feet in front of him. He relaxed, his penis withdrew and he casually went to the trough for a drink of water, job done. That solved the swelling problem for Jocko.

* * *

One morning I found two of the ranch guests, spinsters from New York City, hiding behind the fence at the calf shed. They were close to the breeding chute and were watching the breeding procedures through the slats in the fence. Jocko obliged them and mounted the cow. Wham, bam, thank you, m'am, and he was done. You could have knocked the ladies' eyes out with a stick. They babbled on about the violence of the performance, but I think they also found it titillating, because they were waving their arms and talking a mile a minute.

* * *

Jessie, a good-looking brunette, thirty-two years old, whose husband was overseas in the army, was a guest at the ranch one summer. She stepped in to help around the farm, collecting eggs and stuff, but she started making me uneasy because she always seemed to be watching me with an intense gaze, or coming by when I was working.

One day at lunch, she asked Jack if she could go with me onto the range to get the dairy herd in the afternoon. Jack said it was okay and told me to saddle a horse for her. Just as we were ready to leave, she appeared with a rolled-up blanket, which she tied behind the saddle. What was she going to do with the blanket?

She wasn't a bad rider, and we made good time to Deer Valley, where I figured the herd had wandered. She said, "You go find the cows. I'm going to lie down up in those trees and have a rest. You can join me after you find the cows." With that she took off up the mountain and disappeared into the trees.

I went down the mountain to find the herd, stopped and listened, and sure enough, I could hear the large bell on old Marie, the lead cow, clanging away.

Luckily, all forty cows were together, so it wouldn't take long to round them up and be on our way home. I left them and went to find out what Jessie was up to. When I came around a clump of bushes, there she was, lying on the blanket, her horse grazing nearby. I rode right up to her, not saying anything and looked straight down at her.

She smiled up at me, patted the blanket and said, "I'm a little tired, get down, and we'll sit a while before we start back."

I wasn't too sure what was going on, but I thought, *This is a married woman, nearly as old as my mother, who is obviously lonely. I am a fourteen-year-old boy. No way am I going to have anything to do with a married woman.* I mumbled something about having a bit of trouble rounding up the cattle and took off out of there.

When I had rounded them all up, I gave a yell. She came out of the woods as cheerful as ever, and we drove the herd home. She left a couple of days later and never bothered to say goodbye.

During the war there were a lot of lonely wives. I often thought of this little episode over the years and concluded that I had missed an opportunity to learn something that might have prevented the stumbling, fumbling embarrassment I experienced later in life when dealing with the fair sex.

Trying to Keep Chickens

Even when I was working for Jack on his ranch, I still had chores at home. Our main source of income on the farm came from a flock of Leghorn chickens that ended up as my sole responsibility when I was fourteen. Hugh, my older brother, used to share this job with me, but after he quit school and went to work at the power plant as a fireman, and started paying room and board, he felt he didn't have to do chores anymore.

So every morning before I went to school or went to work on the ranch, I would get a pail of wheat from the feed shed and go down to the chicken house to feed the chickens. At night it was the same, with the addition of collecting the eggs.

Looking after a large flock of chickens with no experience or help, I faced a steep learning curve. When the first batch of spring chicks from brood hens grew to half size, they started flying over the fence of the chicken yard to get at the nice green alfalfa outside. Before we knew it, they were roosting in the large ponderosa pine trees, behaving like crows and not returning to the chicken house at night. They flew all over the place, farther and farther from home, getting wilder and wilder.

Then they started falling prey to hawks, feral cats and coyotes. What could we do? How do you re-domesticate a flock of wild white Leghorn pullets?

Mum contacted one of our neighbours, Old Tom, who was originally from Kentucky. He came to the farm, took a long look at all these white birds, away up in the pine trees, smiled and in a slow southern drawl explained that we had to clip the leading feathers off one of their wings. With one wing clipped, if they tried to fly they would only go in small circles. Grounded, they would put on weight, and when their feathers grew back, they would be too heavy to fly.

When I asked how we could catch them, Tom said we had to feed the flock only in the chicken house, not out in the yard. That way, we might be able to catch a few. Otherwise we would have to wait for a rainy day. Chickens do not like rain and it would force them into the chicken house, where we could get at them.

Over the next few days I managed to grab and clip a few that came in to eat. Then we had a nice steady rain and, sure enough, they all came home to roost. Just as Tom said, the clipped chickens couldn't fly over the fence, and when their feathers grew back the birds had reached a size where they were too heavy to fly at all.

This wasn't the end of my problems, though. A few months later I noticed that there were fewer eggs than usual. With 350 chickens, it is pretty hard to tell when one is missing. I tried to count them, but that was impossible.

The next night, as I was following my usual routine with a pail of wheat in my hand, I started to open the chicken house door toward me. I got it about a foot open. The next second I was knocked ass-over-teakettle onto the ground, covered in wheat. I looked over my shoulder and glimpsed the ass end of a coyote going up the driveway at high speed.

Mr. Coyote had been taking my chickens! But how had he been getting into the chicken house? I noticed that one of the small panes of a window four feet above the ground was missing. Sure enough, there were coyote hairs caught in the frame, and paw scratches inside and out. That smart coyote had been leaping up, squeezing through that small hole and slipping inside in one clean movement. He then killed the chicken and either stood on his hind legs to push it through the opening or leapt up with the chicken in his mouth and went back out through that small hole.

I sealed the hole with a piece of plywood and, with Hugh's help, herded all the chickens into the feeding room. Then I opened the small passageway between the two rooms and herded the chickens through one at a time, counting them carefully. There were 250 birds. That bloody coyote had stolen 100 chickens. He and his family had been living at the top of the heap for a long time.

Every day from then on, I took a gun with me when visiting the chicken house. I lay in wait for Mr. Coyote for a few days, but he never showed up again. I would have given anything to have nailed him.

Does a Skunk Really Smell?

One sunny summer evening I went to feed the chickens and collect the eggs. We kept it pretty dark in the laying room; the chickens liked it that way for laying eggs, sleeping and hatching chicks. It was so dark I could just make out vague shapes. After following the routine for years, I found I could go from one nest to the other in the dark: find the nest, reach in and feel around for the eggs, carefully pick them up, and put them in the basket. If a hen was still sitting in a nest, I would gently pick her up by the back and put her on the ground.

Sometimes I ran into a hen that had started brooding (that is, she was sitting on eggs to hatch them) at the wrong time of the year, and I would have to take her clutch of eggs away from her. Otherwise the chicks would hatch in the middle of winter and freeze to death. I could always tell a brooding hen by feel because her temperature was much higher than normal, and when I put my hand under her in the nest, it was very warm.

This particular evening I had collected nearly all the eggs, except those in one of the dark corners where we stacked nests three high. I took a few eggs out of the top nest and then reached into the second nest, where I felt a chicken who was brooding and warm. She had collected twelve eggs to sit on. I grabbed her by the back and attempted to lift her off the nest. Man, was she heavy! I tried again and managed to lift her up to about shoulder height.

Sometimes when you disturb a brooder she will get mad and open her beak and spit at you. Well, this one made a hacking sound, twisted around and really spat. She got me in the face and down my shirt.

I dropped the hen on the ground and gathered the eggs, but as I straightened up I noticed that my shirt was sticking to my chest and my eyes were hard to open. I thought, *That was a lot of spit for one hen.* I picked up my pails and left.

At the house, the kitchen door was open due to the summer heat. I was still forty feet from the door when Hugh came charging out and yelled at me, "For God's sake, get away from the house! You stupid runt! You've been blasted by a skunk."

I couldn't smell a thing, but he ordered me to stay away from the house until they could figure out what to do. I sat on a pile of wood with my basket of eggs, totally confused and hungry. I later learned that being sprayed by a skunk, especially at close range, can temporarily destroy your sense of smell.

Mum finally came out and, yelling from the porch, ordered me to go into the garden, dig a large hole, take off all my clothes, put them in the hole and, layer by layer, cover them with soil. She said that in a month we would dig them up. By then, she hoped, the moist earth would have removed the skunk smell.

After that, she and Hugh and Pat moved the bathtub outside and brought out two large cans of tomato juice. Mum told me to cover myself completely in tomato juice, let it soak for twenty minutes, then wash it all off on the ground. After that I was to have a proper bath with lots of soap. Doing all this out in the yard, while Hugh and Pat snickered, was embarrassing, but I did as I was told, protesting throughout that I couldn't smell a thing.

They gave me my supper outside, made up a bed on the front porch and gave me a set of clean clothes.

In the morning, when I ventured into the kitchen, Hugh greeted me with "You stink!" As if it was my fault. But they let me eat with them. Mum made me promise that if anyone complained at school, I would come straight home. Pat was worried I was going to take the school bus, but I said I'd ride my bike. I figured if I really did smell, riding the bike might blow it away.

My first class was English literature. The teacher asked us to open our textbooks. She told us that we were each going to read a piece out loud. Warren had left his book at home, so she said, "You can sit with Alan." Why me, of all the class?

At first everything was going fine, but eventually Warren started sniffing and looking around. Finally he leaned over and whispered in my ear, "Some son of a bitch in this room stinks." I got up and headed for the door, chuckling all the way.

I spent the next three days having a grand old time, hunting and fishing. The following Monday at school you could say I was the off-centre centre of attention. Word of my encounter had gotten around, and everybody gave me a wide berth.

Back home, we now had the answer to two things that had puzzled us for a few months: chickens had been found dead, and the egg count had been down. Hugh decided that the skunk was to blame. He took a shotgun to the chicken house and lay in wait. The skunk showed up, right on schedule. When he saw Hugh he promptly turned around, raised his tail and prepared to blast him. But Hugh blasted the skunk first, right smack in the scent glands. Bits of gland, blood and fur flew all over the walls of the chicken house. What an awful bloody stinking mess.

We cleaned and whitewashed the inside of the entire chicken house, but years later, on a damp day, you could still smell skunk. The smell was so strong it went right into the eggs—when we broke open an egg, we had to leave the room. This meant we couldn't sell the eggs for a long time, which wasn't funny because we relied on the egg money.

As for the skunk, from eating all those eggs it had the softest, silkiest, most luxuriant coat you have ever felt. I know this because it fell to me to bury the body, as I still couldn't smell it.

There are not many people who can claim they have picked up an eight-pound skunk by the back and let it spray them from head to toe. It took about a month before my sense of smell came back.

The Slick Pigeon Caper, or Live and Learn

Living on a farm is tremendous for young people who get a sudden passion to raise dogs, ducks, geese, rabbits, pigeons or whatever. At one time or another, I tried them all. Large ducks and white geese were great fun and excellent watchmen; if anyone came near the farm or flew over it, these birds raised a ruckus. Plus, they were excellent eating.

Rabbits were a disaster as they bred like, well, rabbits. We started off with six, and before we knew it we had sixty full-grown rabbits that nearly ate us out of house and home. We ate some but couldn't keep up with them. Finally I turned them loose in the alfalfa field by the old barn. The coyotes solved the overpopulation problem when winter came.

At one point I thought raising pigeons would be a fun hobby. I had heard of a boy my age in town who was an avid pigeon fancier, so I went to him to buy some pigeons without knowing the first thing about them. The boy advised me to buy only females first. He said that if I had a male, the birds would start breeding before I had learned anything about pigeon husbandry. Later on I could get a good breeding male.

I took his advice and bought four females at two dollars apiece. He said to keep them locked up for a month until they accepted my place as home.

I built a monstrous wire-enclosed pen, six feet off the ground, and as the month slowly passed I visualized eventually releasing the pigeons and watching them up in the sky, flying around the farm and then coming home to roost.

Finally the great day came and they tentatively took flight for a little while before coming back to the pen. I was happy and locked them in for the night. Each time after that, when I let them out, they flew for longer and longer. On the sixth day, only three of the four came back, then only two, then one and then none.

I went back to the pigeon fancier and asked if any of my pigeons had returned to his place.

He said, "Not that I know of. After all, I have over one hundred, and it's hard to tell. If they disappeared one at a time, the hawks must've gotten them."

Trusting him, I bought two more females and kept them penned up for over six weeks this time. But when I turned them loose, the same thing happened, so I decided to give up on pigeons.

About a year later, I was talking to a guy who had bought his birds from the same breeder and had the same experience. He had then studied up on the subject and found out that if you take a mother bird away from her young, she will always return to the home nest, no matter how long you keep her locked up. Apparently our expert selected these mother birds to sell, knowing full well they would return to him, and he could sell them again. With a mind like that, he probably became a successful businessman.

Lassie and Bonnie

Hugh decided that he was going to make some money by breeding our purebred Springer spaniel, Lassie. She gave birth to a litter of five pups, and Hugh sold four for ten dollars each. He kept one bitch with beautiful markings for future breeding, and we named her Bonnie. As Bonnie grew up, though, we realized there was something wrong with her; she had no hunting instincts and was constantly getting into trouble.

One day I came home from school to find the chicken yard covered with blood, feathers and twenty-four dead, mutilated chickens. It was springtime, and the chickens had been out of their pen for the first time to get some fresh greens.

Lassie was there, with her head and tail hanging low. She knew there had been wrong done, but I checked her out and found no signs of blood on her; Lassie knew better than to do anything like this. Bonnie, on the other hand, was covered in blood and was happy to see us and proud of what she had done.

When Mum came home, we held a family council. What to do? Mum phoned our old reliable neighbour Tom, the farmer from Kentucky, who had given us farm advice before. He came and saw the sad ugly mess and shook his head.

Tom's recommendation was to shoot Bonnie if we didn't want any more trouble. Once a dog kills, he said, they will do it again and again,

Hugh and Bonnie, Alan and Lassie.

no matter how much you beat them or tie them up. The only other solution, he said, was really gruesome, took up to three weeks and required us to be united in our purpose: we would have to wrap a dead chicken in wire mesh, tie it to an eighteen-inch steel cable and then attach it to Bonnie's collar. The chicken would have to stay attached to Bonnie until it rotted away.

Eager to save Bonnie's life, we jumped on this solution with enthusiasm. Hugh made up the contraption and tied it to Bonnie's collar. At first she tried to get away from it, to no avail. She tried walking with it between her front legs, which forced her to waddle. Then she developed a method of walking partially sideways, dragging it beside her, which worked quite well.

After a few days the chicken started to stink, so nobody would go near her. Poor Bonnie. Even Lassie, her own mother, didn't want anything to do with her.

Slowly the days passed, and pleas were raised—hasn't Bonnie suffered enough yet? But I was adamant. After all, they were my chickens she had murdered.

Finally the chicken disintegrated, and we took the cable off. Bonnie was one happy dog.

Later, Bonnie was in her doghouse, fifty feet away, when I noticed there were five chickens loose between her and me. This was an excellent chance to test her, so I called to her and she started coming straight toward me, wagging her tail. But when she saw the chickens, she stopped dead in her tracks, then turned and made a large circle around them to get to me. Problem solved.

Hugh eventually bred Bonnie, and she had four beautiful pups. However, after only a couple of days she came into heat again and abandoned her pups, taking off with three male dogs.

Bonnie's doghouse was about fifteen feet away from Lassie's. Poor Lassie. She could hear the little pups mewing for their mother, and you could see that it really bothered her. We tried feeding them warm milk, but they would throw it back up. They were so small and weak.

After three days of listening to them crying, Lassie couldn't stand it anymore and moved into Bonnie's kennel. Within a few hours there was no more crying. Lassie finally came out to get fed and—surprise!— she was lactating, and the pups were happy.

A few days later, Bonnie finally came home and went straight to her kennel to reclaim the pups. Lassie snarled and threatened to attack her. We ended up selling Bonnie, and Lassie raised the four pups.

A Long Overdue Fight

I feel very sad to say this, but my older brother, Hugh, bullied me throughout my childhood. For some reason I didn't understand, he would pick on me. Out of the blue, he would haul off and hit me. If I ran away, he would threaten to beat me when I came home. Mum never took a stand on this, and when the police brought me home, my dad never took my side. Hughie was the apple of Dad's eye.

I seldom initiated a fight with anyone, but if cornered, I would fight to win. In the case of Hughie, though, I wouldn't lift a hand in my defence. He was bigger and stronger, and I loved him—after all, he was my older brother. But he made my life miserable.

Now here we were, nearly grown up. Hugh was sixteen and working at the power plant, and I was fourteen. As I mentioned earlier, Hugh figured that, since he was paying room and board, he didn't have to do his share of work around our farm. I ended up doing my work plus what used to be his work. But around this time the fence along the road running by our farm was falling down, and Mum wanted Hugh and me to put up a new one. Hugh grudgingly agreed. He wouldn't work with me, so we divided the job: I would do ten posts and he would do the other ten.

The work involved finding trees that could be cut down and made into fence posts; cutting, limbing and bucking the trees to size; dragging them to the site; peeling and planting them; and then stringing the barbed wire on them.

One day, as I was finishing my part of the job, I heard Mum and Hugh arguing about when he was going to do his share. He then came over to where I was working and told me to finish the job and do his ten posts or he would kick my ass.

I told him that I had finished my share and the rest was up to him. Then I turned to go back to the house to clean up. He reached out to grab me and swing me around, so I hit him square in the nose. The fight was on.

I guess my rage from all those years of being picked on came out, and I pounded Hugh down onto his knees. His hands were covering his face, but I kept hitting him until I was pulled off by two of my friends who had come down the road to visit. I had been doing hard work on the neighbour's ranch for over a year, and I hadn't realized the strength I had built up compared to the town kids my age.

I left my brother there, kneeling on the ground and blubbering, and went off with my friends. When I came home at suppertime, he was outside waiting for me.

Oh-oh. What now? I thought. *Are we going to have at it again?*

My rage came back, and I was ready to fight. I asked, "Are you looking for more?"

He replied, "No, I don't want to fight. I want to apologize."

I was flabbergasted; he had never, ever, treated me as an equal. We shook hands, and from then on we were good friends, sometimes hunting and fishing together. My only regret was that I had not become stronger earlier. I might have avoided all that hurt and hate.

In reviewing my life in such detail for these memoirs, I finally realized why Hugh had so much contempt for me. I believe it came from my fear of water and his discomfort about this. One particular incident may have triggered it. I was very young and our family had gone to English Bay in Vancouver for a picnic and a swim. As usual, I refused to try to swim or even to go in the water. My dad, who was a great swimmer, called me a terrible word for all to hear: "Come on, Alan, don't be a big PANSY."

In our household there was nothing worse than being called a "pansy." I believe that when Hugh heard Dad condemn me as a "pansy," he felt he had a good excuse to express his contempt by hitting me. This was further intensified when I embarrassed him by being too scared to go in the water in front of other kids. As I said before, I wish I'd known the reason for my fear of water earlier so I could have overcome it, but over a period of many years I have nearly conquered the fear. And at least I had a good relationship with Hugh from that time on.

Hunting Stories

The next year, Hugh bought an old convertible Model T Ford and took up duck hunting. I got my second buck, but he pooh-poohed deer hunting. According to Hugh, "A real man's sport is duck hunting." However, I could see that he was still jealous of me for getting the first deer, and eventually he announced to the family that he was going to try deer hunting. I was to take him out. Not show or teach him, but just take him out. So, early in the season, off we went to climb Holmes Mountain to my favourite spot.

We were about to come up over the brow of the mountain into a large sloped clearing when I spied a herd of about twenty-five deer. I signalled to Hugh, and *click, bang*! At 150 yards he dropped a four-point buck. The herd took off at full run across the slope and *bang*! Hugh dropped a two-point buck. Both were shot through the neck; two shots, two deer.

Hugh turned to me and said, "This deer hunting is nothing. It's like shooting fish in a barrel."

I could hardly believe it. I couldn't have done that in a hundred years. I had to give Hugh credit; he was now the great white hunter. Target shooting, I could beat him every time. But live action shooting, he was the best. He later ran a thriving sporting goods store in Merritt and wrote a weekly hunting and fishing column in the *Vancouver Sun*.

We were both deliriously proud and happy that we had shot the first two bucks of the hunting season. We tagged them, dragged them down the mountain and, as was the custom of the day, mounted them on the front fenders of the Model T. Then we drove them up and down the main street of Princeton and parked right in front of the Travelers Café for all to see. Proud as punch, we drove home to show Pat and Mum. They were both pleased that we were going to have lots of venison for the winter.

Mum told us that while we were parading all through town, the neighbours had been phoning. Surprise! It was traditional that whoever got the first deer of the season had to share it with their neighbours. We spent the next few days dressing the deer and delivering roasts to everyone. It felt pretty good to give something back after all the help our neighbours had given us when we needed it.

* * *

I decided one Sunday to go hunting for bear with my friend Sonny Tennant. Country folk figure bear meat is as good as any meat. It's a bit stringy, and if cooked too long it's dry. But Mum could cook a bear roast so that, other than the wild taste, you thought you were eating a beef loin. I've never hesitated to shoot a bear for food, regardless of what others might think.

Sonny and I managed to get a bear, but where we shot him there wasn't a road within three miles. After we bled and gutted him, we needed to figure out how to get our three-hundred-pound prize home. Horses won't go near a bear, not even a dead one, but mules sometimes can be persuaded, so we decided to hike back and get Old Whitey, Sonny's skinny, ugly old pure white mule.

Sonny sat on the pack saddle, and I got on behind, but I didn't ride very far. The mule's backbone stuck up so high it was like riding on a narrow piece of board. We traded places, each walking a couple of times over the distance.

As we approached the bear, Old Whitey's head went up, his ears went forward, his nostrils flared, and his eyes widened and fixed on the bear. Then he wouldn't go any farther.

You've heard the expression "Stubborn as a mule"? This is wrong. Mules are not stubborn; they're smart, and they can reason. A horse will react instantly to a new situation, but a mule stops and reasons it out.

Knowing this, I dropped the lead rope and walked over to the dead bear, kicked it and stood on it to show it was harmless. Then I slowly walked back to Old Whitey and stood directly in front of him; he bent his head down and smelled me all over.

We did this a few more times, getting closer to the bear each time. Eventually Old Whitey began to settle down and figure out the job that needed to be done. He let us heave the bear carcass onto his back, and we arrived home with this snow-white mule now bright red, with bear blood dripping all over him. After unloading the bear, we took Old Whitey down to the creek and washed him carefully so the horses in the barn would still associate with him.

* * *

Gordon, Sonny's younger brother, told me that the farm they used to live on, twelve miles down the Hedley road, had old fruit trees on it and in the fall, deer and bears would come down just before dark to eat the ripened fruit. So we decided to play hooky from school one afternoon and get us a deer or a bear. I took the old family .303 Mark 1 rifle apart and wrapped it in a sack to hide it. Being only fourteen, and without a hunting licence, I needed to be careful. Gordon and I then stood out on the road hitchhiking. A middle-aged man stopped and picked us up. When we were in the car, he asked us where we were going.

Before I could say anything, Gordon blurted out, "We are playing hooky and are going down to our old farm to shoot us a deer or bear."

Mr. Driver then inquired, "And what are you going to shoot them with?"

By then the cat was out of the bag, so Gordon told him we had a rifle in the sack. We travelled along, chitchatting nicely after that, with the man asking us a lot more questions.

At the farm, we started to thank him for the ride when the man said, "You kids are sure lucky. I was the game warden for this area until two weeks ago, but I've been moved to another region. So good hunting, and don't shoot yourself."

Wow, what a scare! That was too close for comfort.

We picked out a nice spot downwind of the fruit orchard and waited around, but no game appeared. And when we were hitchhiking home, we hoped the new game warden wouldn't pick us up.

* * *

One Sunday in the fall, I decided to go hunting up Darcy Mountain, about seven miles from our farm. I was riding Joe, the chestnut gelding who had been on many adventures with me. I've never met another horse like Joe; he was so steady that when I spotted a grouse I could stop him, raise my rifle and pull the trigger—*bang*!—and even his ears wouldn't move. Hunting by horse also has a great advantage because game is less scared of horses than of humans.

With Joe, it didn't take too long to wade across the river and climb the big zigzag trail up to the top of the mountain, two thousand feet above the valley. It was beautiful horseback-hunting country, with trees spaced wide apart, thick heavy grass and patches of brush.

I had already picked off three blue grouse with my long-barrel .22 pistol when I spotted a three-point buck quite far away, down in a little valley. I dismounted and tried to get around to the other side of the valley for a clear shot. The buck sensed something was wrong and moved away, into thick brush. We played ring-around-the-rosy for over an hour, until I realized it was starting to get dark.

I rushed back to Joe, who was grazing on the lush green grass, and swung up onto him, hoping I could find the zigzag path in the dark, or even the logging road that was the long way home. I searched fruitlessly for a few minutes and started to panic. With an overcast sky and no moon, I could see barely ten feet in front of me. How was I going to find my way home? Joe sensed my confusion and flicked his ears, which is a clear sign that a horse is alarmed. I forced myself to calm down and start thinking.

I remembered that an old cowpuncher had once told me horses could see quite well in the dark—and that if I ever got lost when I was on horseback, the horse would take me home. I decided to go for it. I tied everything down, tightened my windbreaker, pulled my hat down tight, tied the reins to the pommel and, with some trepidation, gave Joe a gentle kick in the sides.

Joe stood still for a minute, then turned his head to look at me as if to say, *You mean I'm in charge?*

He took a few steps, stopped and looked back at me again, as if to say, *Aren't you going to use the reins?* Next he started walking, then trotting and finally loping off home under his own direction.

I was nearly knocked off a few times by low-hanging branches, so I kept my head down as he bashed through small trees, branches and bushes as if they weren't even there. At one point, Joe crow-footed straight down the steep side of the mountain, nearly throwing me off. There were many times I grabbed for the reins, but Joe's confidence in where he was going assured me he knew what he was doing, and I left them alone.

In just forty minutes we were back to the river and across from our farm. I couldn't believe it. When I walked into the house I had no hat, pine needles were sticking all over me, and one pant leg was ripped.

Mum took one look and asked, "What on earth happened to you?"

I replied, "I was worried about getting home late, so I hurried." No boy of fourteen ever tells his mother the whole awful truth.

PART THREE

Growing Independence

Sawmilling

At the start of the summer of 1944, I decided I'd try to get a job at the sawmill across the river from our farm. I had been happy working on Jack's farm and earning forty dollars per month. But Jack had hired me when I was only thirteen, and now I was fourteen and wanted more money. I felt guilty leaving him because he was a good boss, but the last summer Hugh had been earning fifty cents an hour at the sawmill, which was a tremendous difference.

I carried my bike across the alfalfa field to the river, took off my boots, slung them around my neck, picked up the bike and waded across to the road. Then I pedalled the last mile to the sawmill office and asked Mr. Taylor for a summer job.

The sawmill was pretty small, with just nine employees—eight men and one woman, Rosie, the slab-truck driver. When Mr. Taylor hired me, he put me to work with Johnny Kupchak, a cheerful thirty-five-year-old. Our job involved loading logs, cutting slabs for firewood, and piling lumber. Some of the large planks weighed two hundred pounds, and Johnny and I would carry them from one part of the mill to another. They didn't have rollers to move logs around like today; everything was "bull power."

The job also included going into the bush with a truck to get the raw logs. Logging trucks in those days had no power steering, power brakes or power equipment. Operating them was all physical effort. The old Ford logging truck we used had fourteen speeds ahead, and Johnny could double clutch those gears without grinding or revving the motor. Even though he was much older than me, when we were getting the logs at the camp, Johnny would climb high up on the pile to adjust the slings and then jump down like a young man.

One hot day after lunch, as we were sitting around before going back to work in the sawmill, Johnny said, "Man, is this heat ever making my leg itchy." He pulled up his pant leg and, surprise! He had a wooden leg. He'd lost his lower leg in a farm accident. Prostheses in those days were very crude, and the itching, infections and pain must've been terrible. But Johnny didn't limp or show any sign that he was different from any one of us. With no insurance and a wife and kids to support, he did the same work as any man without complaint.

Cat Skinning

One day Mr. Taylor was short a cat skinner at the logging camp up on Darcy Mountain. Cat skinners are the men who take a team of horses into the bush to collect logs, clearing a trail for the horses and then hooking the logs onto the harness so the horses can pull them out and onto the ramp for the logging truck to pick up. I had driven a team of horses in my previous job, so Mr. Taylor thought I could fill in.

Johnny drove the logging truck up to the camp, which was one small shack and a barn. Harvey and Chris, two middle-aged Native men, came out of the shack to greet us. Johnny told them what I was there for. They looked at me and then they looked at each other and smiled. Harvey said, "Barney and Queenie are in the barn over there. Harness them and bring them out."

I discovered that the horses were huge Percherons, so tall their backs were higher than my head. I had only ever handled horses half their size. I found the harnesses hanging on the wall and tried to lift one off but couldn't. It must have weighed 170 pounds. As the lowest man on the totem pole at the sawmill, I was learning about the sly, sometimes cruel humour of the workingman, and I got mad.

I walked out to Chris and Harvey and said, "Which one of you clowns is going to give me a hand? Mr. Taylor sent me to do some work, not fool around." They both laughed, and Harvey helped me with the harnesses.

In the camp they were doing what is called selective logging, taking one tree here and one tree there, leaving everything in between. A few years later you would hardly notice the area had been logged, and if more trees had grown to marketable size by then, you could log it again, ad infinitum.

After I found some logs that looked ready to be brought in, I spent two hours clearing a trail to them through the brush. Then I located a pair of skidding tongs hanging in the barn. Skidding tongs are long, curved hooks, bolted together like a pair of scissors, with a cable attached to the loops. You clamp the hooks on the log, and as the horses pull on the cable ring, the hooks dig into the log. The harder the horses pull, the deeper the hooks dig in.

With the heavy skidding tongs in one hand and the reins in the other, I drove Barney and Queenie down the newly cleared path. When we got to the first log, I tried to lead them around to the right and back them up to the log, but they stood still, facing ahead, with their ears straight up, refusing to move.

I looked over and there were Harvey and Chris, hiding behind a bush, watching to see what I would do. I knew I couldn't force those two big horses to do anything, so I faced them and said, "All right, how do you want to do this? After all, you have been doing this all your life, and I know squat." I hooked the reins over Barney's collar, stood back and yelled "Giddy-up," and, slick as a whistle, Barney and Queenie turned to the left, not the right. I picked up the doubletree and they backed up to the log, sweet as apple pie. I put the tongs on and then snuck a look over my shoulder in time to see the loggers turning around and heading back to work. No more fun for them here.

Barney and Queenie couldn't be that smart, could they? I was in charge, not them. But later they were still ignoring my directions when we approached the loading ramp. The ramp was on the far side of the road, and the log had to be pulled up to a ten-foot-high skidway. When the horses came close to the road, they suddenly speeded up, nearly knocking me off my feet, and in twenty seconds they had the log in a perfect position up on the ramp. They had used momentum to make the uphill pull easy.

I was wondering what exactly my job was, and at lunchtime, Harvey and Chris confirmed it for me: "Barney and Queenie know what they're doing, and you don't, so let them alone."

From then on, I let them lead the way. They would pick the logs they wanted and choose their own path back and forth from the ramp, keeping a nice steady pace. I just hooked and unhooked the tongs as they worked. What a nice, easy job!

Firing Coal in a Steam Locomotive

Around this time, Mum had a boyfriend. Jerry was a CPR fireman, a tall, charming, good-looking man. In the farmhouse, Mum didn't have a bedroom of her own. She slept on a large horsehair chesterfield in the dining room. To give her some privacy, we kids used the hallway off to one side to get from the kitchen to our upstairs bedrooms.

One Sunday morning I got up early to go hunting and, without thinking, opened the door to the dining room to get to the kitchen instead of going around by the hallway. Mum was lying in bed with her eyes wide open, clutching the bed sheets around her neck. Through clenched teeth she said, "Get out, for God sakes, get out."

I glanced around, wondering what was the matter, and saw twelve bare toes peeking out from under the long, heavy drapes that closed the dining room off from the living room.

Mum came into the kitchen a little later and asked me not to say anything to anyone about what I had seen. I agreed. Mum was a good-looking young woman and deserved more in life than just work and looking after us kids, but she had been raised very prim and proper, and she would have been extremely embarrassed if the old biddies in town knew about Jerry. My sister and brother and I were not against her having a boyfriend, but we didn't want to see her get hurt.

Mum also said she thought that Jerry and I should get to know each other a little better, so I was thrilled, about a week later, when Jerry offered to take me to work with him on the old steam train that hauled ore from the Copper Mountain mine down to the concentrator in Allenby. Jerry and Charlie, the engineer, filled the boiler tank with water and began to build up a head of steam to climb the 1,600-foot grade in the fourteen miles to the mine. The long boiler was above the firebox in the front of the open cab, and the coal tender was behind the cab.

Jerry opened a valve that blew air through the fire-pit embers, just as a bellows blows air into a blacksmith's forge. He then grabbed the coal shovel, swung his upper body and legs around, and scooped coal from the tender. As he swung back around toward the heavy steel fire-pit door, he stepped on the floor-mounted, steam-operated button that opened the door a split second before the shovel and coal entered the fire pit. He flipped the shovel, and the coal spread out evenly over the large fire pit. Quite the synchronized movement! You could see that he had perfected it over many years.

By now we had built up steam and were climbing the first seven hundred feet to the mill in Allenby. Halfway up the hill, Jerry pulled a long, steel poker out of the coal tender and raked the coal bed to get more heat and steam. I moved around a bit from my seat by the coal tender and promptly burnt my pants on the still hot poker. Both men laughed, and Jerry threw a cup of water on the smouldering cloth and told me to get used to it.

We collected empty ore cars at the mill and proceeded to climb a further eight hundred feet to the mine. We were now travelling well above the Similkameen River, on a narrow railroad track that had been blasted out of solid rock. The roadbed was on the side of the mountain, with about a seventy-degree slope. The drop into the valley below was at least a thousand feet nearly straight down, and it was a little scary.

We arrived at the mine's large crusher and storage silo. At this point, the engine had to be turned around, which Jerry and some other men did using a large turntable. Then we backed up and hooked on to the full ore cars.

When Jerry asked me if I would like to try firing, I said yes without any hesitation. After all, I had dug ditches and post holes and shovelled chicken, cow and horse shit, as well as sawdust and snow, so I figured I should be able to shovel coal.

The first shovel went in perfectly, but I didn't flick it to spread the coal. After a few more tries, everything seemed to be going well, but then I got careless and hit the closed door with a shovel full of coal— *Ker-splat*! The coal went everywhere and I had to sweep it off the floor, much to the delight of Jerry and Charlie.

When we got back down to the Allenby mill, we unloaded the ore cars and then turned the engine around again. This time they let me help. We eased the engine onto the turntable, and Charlie juggled it back and forth until it was balanced perfectly. Then the two of us pushed that great old heavy steam engine around, using only our own strength. What a thrill! Down the hill we went, and I was given a stern warning not to tell anybody about my big adventure.

Unfortunately, Jerry turned out to be a bit of a rounder. We discovered he had girlfriends in each town in the valley and a wife in Penticton, so his relationship with my mother didn't last long.

If You're Big Enough, You're Old Enough, or The Art of Shovelling Ore

One day in the fall of 1944, with the war still on, a friend of mine, Warren, mentioned he was working at the ore concentrator in Allenby, shovelling ore for cleanup and making sixty-five cents an hour. That was big money, so I got on my bike after school and pedalled up the mountain to see Mr. McKay, the manager. He looked me up and down and finally said, "Well, you're big enough, so you must be old enough." They were so short of manpower due to the war that they would hire anyone. He then said, "Report to Frank, the Bull Gang boss, sharp at eight o'clock Saturday morning."

On my first day at the mill, the Bull Gang boss, Frank Smith, an older, heavyset man with a tough-looking face, put all the members of the Bull Gang to work, then finally turned to me and said two words, "Follow me." Not "Hello, glad to see you. My name's Frank." Just "Follow me." We climbed up through the mill, which was built on the slope of a hill, past railroad tracks and boxcars, the filtering process floor, the flotation process floor, the large noisy ball mills, and the crushing plant. Still farther up the hill, we came to a line of immense piles of raw ore. The chunks of ore had fallen from the ore cars as they passed along the trestle above our heads. Frank pointed to a shovel, a wheelbarrow and a chute where I was to dump the ore. "Get to work," he shouted at me and walked away. No instructions, and no details on hours of work or where the lunchroom or toilet were located, etc.

I put down my lunchbox, picked up the shovel and the wheelbarrow, and went over to the first pile. Someone had been there before me and made a small dent in the pile, and there was a three-foot-square sheet of steel that I could push against the pile to make shovelling easier. I took the pick and loosened enough ore to fall down and cover the steel sheet. Then I shovelled the ore into the wheelbarrow, wheeled the barrow over to the chute, dumped it and repeated the process, ad infinitum—or, more accurately, ad nauseam.

This was the most boring job I had ever had. It was like trying to bail out the ocean. I only worked Saturday, one day a week, but the trains came seven days a week, dumping more ore on my piles. At sixty-five cents an hour, though, the best money I had ever made, I decided I could stand a bit of boredom.

By working hard and steadily for three months, I had the satisfaction of eliminating the first two piles. Then Frank put me to work with Warren. We would go around and clean up other spills around the plant. This was a lot better; I had company and variety.

At one point Warren asked me, "Do you know how to shovel crushed ore?" Well, I had shovelled everything related to a farm, so I figured I could hold my own. Was I mistaken.

We approached a large conveyor belt. A thirty-ton pile of crushed ore had spilled off the belt and had to be reloaded onto the conveyor. Warren said, "I'll take this side, you take the other." Two hours later he had completed his half, and I was only halfway through mine, which he helped me to finish. I had discovered that crushed ore is very heavy.

Warren showed me how, for long-term shovelling, you have to do most of the work with your legs. Within a month I was keeping up to him. We had a good thing going, and the big boss trusted us, or nearly trusted us. After doing cleanup for six months, I was promoted to the position of operator's assistant in the crushing plant, where I did all kinds of oddball jobs.

I ended up working at the mill for two years, shovelling various ores and helping the operators. I sometimes worked three shifts on a weekend and shared my earnings, 75/25, with Mum. As a single-parent family, we needed every cent we could scrounge.

Crushed Dead in an Ore Bin and Other Dangers at the Mill

Above the concentrator mill were eight large bins full of coarse ore. Each bin was twenty feet across and forty feet deep. The ore would drop out of the bins onto the conveyor belt to be carried through the mill for processing. Occasionally the ore would get compacted around the sides of the bin, opening up a five-foot-wide hole in the centre. As a result, no ore would come out of the chute onto the conveyor below. These holes were called "hang ups," and to fix them you had to climb inside the bin holding a long steel bar, stand on the compacted ore and use the steel bar to pry the ore loose from the sides so it would slide down into the chute.

This job was difficult and dangerous because we had no safety belts or ropes. If the ore collapsed while you were standing on it, you would fall into the hole and be buried by the ore, and it would be a while before anyone noticed you were missing.

When I started at the mill, I learned that a couple of years earlier a fellow named Bud had gone up to the top of one of the bins to deal with a hang up, but the side he was standing on gave way under him. He went down headfirst and was buried. The ore started coming out of the chute onto the conveyor, but then it stopped again, and the gang leader noticed blood dripping out of the chute. When the gang investigated, they discovered Bud's head was jammed in the chute. They had to remove the whole chute/gate mechanism to get the body out without burying everyone else in ore.

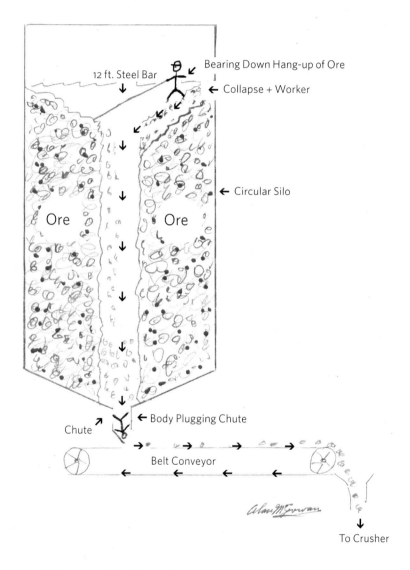

Sectional elevation of ore bin and "hang up" of ore, Allenby Ore Mill.

At the mill we were never given formal training of any kind, but the old-time operators would tell new employees about the hazards of the job. The stories were usually very gruesome.

Some of the hazards I learned about first-hand. For example, I noticed one man, Jerry, who spent his days wandering around, oiling the machinery. He never seemed to talk to anybody; his movements were slow, and he was nothing but skin and bones. He came into the lunchroom one day, and when his head passed in front of the light bulb, I was shocked to see that he was translucent! I could see the bones of his nose and jaw, and when I looked more closely, I could see the bones in his hands.

After he left, I asked Henry, the gang leader, what was wrong with Jerry. Henry told me that Jerry had silicosis and was slowly dying. He explained that the dust we were breathing in the mill contained a high concentration of silica, produced when rocks containing ore are ground down and when the ore is crushed. When we inhaled silica, it was drawn into our lungs. Every single particle attached itself to one of the thousands of follicles that absorb air in our lungs. With the moisture present, it cauterized the follicle permanently, making it no longer able to absorb oxygen. When enough follicles were blocked, you had a permanent, incurable, deteriorating condition called silicosis. Men working in hardrock mines, concentrators and rock-crushing plants accepted this lung disease as part of having a job. In the ore mill, and in many other similar workplaces at this time, there were no fans or dust collectors to limit the amount of silica in the air, nor did we have face-masks or filters to protect us. However, anyone who bitched about the danger would be fired or branded a troublemaker.

Well, my questions came fast and furious, partly driven by compassion for Jerry, and partly selfishness because, after all, I was working in these conditions! Henry explained that the government did not recognize silicosis as an industrial disease, so there was no Compensation Board money available to allow Jerry to stop working, nor to provide for Jerry's widow when the time came. As a compassionate compromise, when a worker was diagnosed, he was given lighter and lighter jobs as the disease progressed. Jerry was now an "oiler," which was the last job before a worker died.

Jerry lived in one of the company houses with his wife and three young children. When he died a few months later, everybody chipped in a dollar apiece for the widow. After the funeral, the superintendent took Jerry's last paycheque, our donated dollars and a bouquet of flowers to the widow. He also handed her a written eviction notice. She was to vacate the company house before the end of the month, as it was needed for another workman's family. The widow was left with nothing. No pensions, no compensation, no nothing.

Twenty years later, when I was long gone from the mill and was having a routine health examination, an x-ray technician took one look at my lung x-ray and exclaimed, "You used to work in a hardrock mine! Your x-ray shows silicosis scar tissue on your lungs. But it's not serious."

All I could think was "Thanks a lot!"

I saw a graphic example of another safety hazard one hot summer afternoon when I was sweeping up above the floatation floor, where the finely crushed ore is added to large floatation tanks. These tanks have water and cyanide in them to separate and collect the copper from the ore. Some cyanide is lost in the filtration process, so the men working on the floor frequently added more cyanide powder to the tanks. The cyanide was stored in large green cans.

I watched as an operator, as usual, walked over to the cyanide drums, which were sitting on a wooden pallet. He picked up a crowbar and snapped the lid off one of the cans. A large cloud of green dust puffed up directly into his face. Next thing I knew, he was lying on the concrete floor, twitching, covered in green dust.

I yelled for help, trying to be heard above the continuous noise. Finally the foreman came out of his office. He took one look and, as if he'd seen this before, yelled at me to get out of there, turned around and went back into the office to phone someone. By then, the man on the floor was no longer moving.

I went upstairs to the crushing floor lunchroom and told a couple of the guys what had happened. They shrugged and went back to work. That night, on the jitney bus that took mill workers back down into Princeton, I was sitting next to the foreman. He told me that the pallet loaded with cyanide cans had been sitting out in the sun for hours before it was brought up to the floatation floor. The heat had compressed the air inside the can, which caused the dust cloud when it was suddenly opened. If the can had been left for a few hours to cool down, there would not have been a build-up of air pressure. Conversely, it should have never been left out in the sun.

There was no investigation or other follow-up after this death, or if there was, I was never called as a witness. It took me a while to get over this incident.

Shift Work and Horseplay

When I was promoted to operator's assistant on the crushing floor, my job was to fill in for operators when they took their breaks. This area was full of dust and loud noise, and the work was dreary and routine. Everyone engaged in horseplay to break up the monotony.

On one afternoon shift, I was sitting on a chair beside the raw ore conveyor belt, grabbing foreign objects—such as dynamite, blasting caps, drill bits and other mining equipment—that had got mixed among the chunks of ore. These foreign objects could damage the crushing and grinding equipment if they got through, so it was an important task, but it was also incredibly boring. I nodded off frequently.

I was awakened by a yell. One of the guys was standing on the walkway opposite me, frantically pointing at the conveyor belt.

Coming straight at me was a lit fuse, attached to a stick of dynamite! Sparks were shooting from the fuse, and it was rapidly burning down. I knew I was supposed to pick it off the conveyor when it came to me, before it exploded, but I didn't know what I was going to do with it once I grabbed it. So I bailed out of there and hid behind the crusher. I waited, but the dynamite didn't explode.

When I looked up from my hiding place, five guys were perched on the railing opposite me, like so many crows, laughing their heads off. It turned out the fuse was a clever fake, with cuts every two inches so it would keep throwing out sparks.

Another practical joke was much more deadly. After spending a few hours on the crushing floor, everyone was covered with thick dust from the ore. Before entering the lunchroom, the guys would blow the dust off each other with a high-pressure air hose. One day, a couple of years before I started working at the mill, one guy bent over in the middle of this process, and another guy stuck the air gun up his rear, just to be funny. The air pressure killed him.

Not all horseplay was lethal. Our lunchroom was small; six men would sit shoulder to shoulder on the benches, around a narrow table. When Frank McKenzie, who was a bit nuts and didn't believe in washing, came in, most of us left, eating our lunches outside to avoid his stink. To solve this problem, the crew lay in wait for Frank one night in the bunkhouse, grabbed him and locked him in the shower, fully clothed. They then turned on the hot water and nearly scalded him. But Frank came to work the next day with a big smile on his silly face. I guess he enjoyed the attention. It didn't solve the problem, though, because a week later he stank again.

Another time, Frank was on a walkway about thirty feet away from me, standing beside the conveyor. He waved to get my attention, then sat down on the stairs, spread his legs, pulled his huge testicle sack up over his belt and let it hang away down between his legs. Then he started bouncing his balls around. I had never seen anything so grotesque in my life. I later learned Frank had been in the First World War and had contracted a venereal disease. His balls swelled to the size of cantaloupes, permanently stretching his scrotum.

Never Drink Bootleg Beer

There are times in life when you feel you have the world by the tail on a downhill pull. I had that feeling the spring after I started working at the mill. It was Saturday night on the Easter long weekend, and the weather was warm and sunny. Alvin had just got his driver's licence, and his dad had given him the truck. Lenny's dad, who worked at the local brewery, had arranged with the night watchman, Chris, to hide a case of beer at the back door of the brewery for us teenagers.

Alvin drove past the brewery a couple of times to make sure nobody was around, and then he backed up to the rear door. I got out and went inside. There was our case of beer. Good old Chris. But next to it was a thirty-two-quart keg of beer, labelled "eleven percent overproof and fogged, not for sale" whatever that meant. I looked at our little case of seven percent beer and then looked at that large keg. What the heck, let's go for it! I picked the keg up, carried it outside, put it in the pickup box and threw a tarp over it.

In the cab, Lenny explained that the keg I had stolen was meant for Stan the bootlegger. Stan and Chris had an arrangement. Fogged beer has developed too high an alcohol content. There is nothing wrong with it, but the brewery can't legally sell it, and the fogged beer is supposed to be dumped. Instead, Stan sold it bootleg to people with empty containers and then returned the empty keg. This had apparently been going on for years, and nobody was the wiser.

We drove through town, right down the main street, and headed for Alvin's farm because his mum and dad had gone to visit relatives, and all four of his siblings were out. We were going to have fun, just like the grownups.

We figured since Lenny's dad worked at the brewery, Lenny would know how to open the keg. Were we ever wrong. We placed the keg on its side in the middle of the kitchen floor. Lenny got a butcher knife and a hammer, and drove the knife into the keg. The beer came out in a geyser, spraying the ceiling, walls and floor, and making a disaster of Alvin's mother's impeccable kitchen. Somebody got glasses, we started drinking and the mess we had made turned into a big joke that we thought was extremely funny.

I blacked out after this and came to three days later, with the sun in my eyes, lying in the mud beside a small lake on top of Jura Mountain. Alvin was lying in the grass next to the truck, and the truck deck was swimming in sticky, almost-dried beer. The cab was not much better. I couldn't have felt worse. Alvin remembered driving Lenny home on the first night of our bender, but neither of us remembered what happened after that.

Luckily Mum was at work when I got home, but Pat was there and filled me in. We had been reported missing, and the one and only policeman in town had talked to Lenny and been out looking for us.

When Mum came home from work, she said, simply and without raising her voice, "It was a very foolish thing that you did." She explained that we had worried everybody who knew us.

After two days I was fully recovered physically, but the repercussions I felt, and the apologies I had to make as a result of this event, went on for months. Sixty-five years later, I'm still ashamed of it. To this day I have never had another drop of beer and can't stand the smell or taste of the stuff—although I will drink wine or whiskey.

Crown Fire

July 1945 was a hot month, and the weather had been hot for a long time. Smart, eligible men who could be conscripted to fight forest fires were mysteriously absent from the main street and the beer parlours. Times were good, and there was lots of work at high wages. Firefighters got lousy food, lousy wages, heat, smoke, dirt, exhaustion and danger, plus they were away from home for weeks on end.

Finally the bomb went off; there was a large fire up the Coquihalla Canyon. The provincial ministry of forests closed both the mine and the mill and conscripted all five hundred men and boys working there, including me, to fight this fire. We were divided into ten-man crews, with one experienced firefighter as gang leader for each crew. Our gang leader was Larry, a quiet, middle-aged man. We were lucky to have Larry, because he had fought many fires. There are times when the knowledge of your leader means the difference between life and death, as we were to find out.

The only way to get near the fire was by the CPR train, so the forests ministry commandeered the train, and off we went, dumped at various camps along the way. We were taken to a tent, given a bunk and issued water bottles and grub hoes. Then we were ordered to clear a line of brush on a sidehill to try to stop the fire that was above us and coming down the mountain.

The area had big virgin timber with thick underbrush, and it was nearly impossible to clear a firebreak. The task was made even more difficult because as we laboured to root out brush and roots, we were soon panting and gasping for air, which meant we were inhaling dense smoke from the fire. But on our first day, fresh and eager to get back home, each of the ten-man gangs cleared a line over a mile long.

At 7 p.m. we trooped back to the camp, bone tired. I ran into three schoolmates who had fought fires the previous year. This time they had volunteered as cooks and flunkies, looking after tents and bedding. They called me a sucker for doing the grunt work. Next time out, I thought, I'll know better.

The next morning, Larry, our gang leader, told us that during the night the fire had jumped over our firebreak, so we had to repeat the previous day's process farther north. The next night, the same thing happened. This time the fire had climbed up one side of a steep, two-thousand-foot mountain and was coming down the other side. Larry said this might be our only opportunity to stop the advance of the fire, because fire will go up a mountain fast, but come down slowly.

We started the new firebreak about three hundred feet from the bottom of the burning mountain, in a steep ravine with a little creek running down the centre. The ravine was between two steep mountains, both heavily forested with large timber. The temperature in the ravine must have been 120°F, with thick smoke. We worked like dogs all day, hoping our line would stop the fire. The next morning, Larry told us the fire was slowly creeping down the mountain. We would have to widen our firebreak.

By two o'clock the heat was unbearable, and if you worked hard, you breathed hard, which, with the smoke, made you cough. The fire had crept down to five hundred feet above the creek when Larry came running over, very upset, and told us to get the hell upstream as fast and as far as we could. He kept yelling, "Crown fire, crown fire." Whatever that meant.

All the crews on our side headed up the ravine. The crews on the lower side headed down the ravine. We got about a quarter of a mile away from the fire before Larry called a halt and we all sat down.

I asked, "What the hell is going on?"

Larry explained, "Combine heat, smoke, bone-dry virgin timber and a steep ravine or valley, and it spells crown fire."

Just as he said this, all hell broke loose. The fire on the south slope jumped over the ravine to the north slope, setting the tops of the trees alight. Then it started rolling up the mountain in a massive ball, from tree top to tree top, with a thunderous roar. The wind came rushing down the valley from behind us, nearly blowing our hats off, and feeding oxygen to the fire. That rolling crown fire climbed from the creek up 1,500 feet to the top of the mountain in about two minutes. It sounded like a freight train.

Larry then explained that if we had been under the fire when it leaped across the ravine, we wouldn't have been hurt or burned, but we would have died of oxygen deprivation in the vacuum that was created. Thank God there are people like Larry to look after us ignorant sheep in the forest, and luckily nobody got hurt.

A few days later, rain finally came and extinguished the fire. We went home, and a skeleton crew put out the remaining spot fires. Since that time, I have heard that only one in ten forest fires is put out by human efforts. The others burn out for lack of fuel or are rained out.

A Multi-Millionaire Drunk

H.H. McBain, a multi-millionaire builder, was coming to our little town to hunt a giant grizzly bear that had been spotted up the Coquihalla. We'd all heard about this rich man and his shenanigans. He had thrown a pile of paper money from his hotel window onto Georgia

Street in Vancouver, causing a traffic jam as people chased after the dollar bills that floated down to the street and sidewalk.

McBain took over a bunch of rooms in the Princeton Hotel, rented the local theatre and got all the students an afternoon off school to see a movie of the big dam he had built back east. He then hired a couple of local guides, cooks and flunkies, and they took off hunting up the Hope–Princeton Trail.

They returned a week later with the huge grizzly displayed on the back of a one-ton flatbed truck. The bear was huge, lying on its stomach with its four legs hanging over the sides of the flatbed. Rumours flew in all directions about this expedition: two questionable women had been hired, the trip was one big drunk, one of the guides actually shot the grizzly bear.

One day when McBain was still in Princeton, I went downtown as usual during school lunch break with my friends Alvin and Lee. We were on the opposite side of the street from the Princeton Hotel when a window flew open on the second floor, and McBain stuck his bloated red face out and yelled something unintelligible. We stopped to see what he wanted. He then threw two handfuls of coins out the window at us: pennies, nickels, dimes and a few quarters. The coins hit the street and bounced and rolled in all directions.

Alvin and Lee got down on their hands and knees, trying to pick up as much money as they could as quickly as they could. I stood there dumbfounded. These were my closest friends; both of them came from families that were much better off than mine. Both had good allowances, and here they were, down on their hands and knees like beggars in their hometown.

At that time I was working in the mill, making a man's wages, and this drunk wanted me to scrabble on the ground for pocket change. I bent down and picked up a small handful of coins, walked halfway across the street and threw the coins in his face, nearly breaking one of the windows. The look on his face was really worth the effort.

Alvin and Lee couldn't figure out why I did what I did. Maybe it had something to do with being poor for so many years, and the shame that can bring. Unless you have been there, you cannot understand. Living in poverty gives you a different perspective on life.

My First Motorcycle

Our little town had only two motorcycles. One was a 1928 Harley-Davidson, with a 74-cubic-inch engine, and the other was an old Indian with a sidecar. Art, the man who owned both of these bikes, looked so cool riding down the main street, and I wanted a motorcycle so bad I could taste it. I had been working all year in the ore mill and had been giving Mum most of my wages, but had still saved $130, which I figured would be enough to buy a bike. There were only three obstacles that stood between me and my dream: I had to persuade my mother to let me buy a motorcycle; I had to convince Art to sell one to me; and I had to get a driver's licence at fifteen years old.

Mum with Harley (1928 74-cubic inch).

I begged and pleaded with Mum, who argued that I was only fifteen, that I needed the money for clothes and that I would kill myself. I said I could get a special driver's licence because we lived on a farm, that I'd do without new clothes and that I'd be really careful. She finally relented but said she wouldn't pay for any repairs if it broke down. Whoopee! One down and two to go!

I rode my bicycle uptown to see Art. He had just got married and needed money but wasn't too happy about the idea of selling one of his motorcycles, particularly to a kid. He also couldn't decide which bike to sell. After I had pestered him three times, he finally decided to sell me the Harley-Davidson. We settled on a price of $115. He took me out on the road and taught me the rudiments of operating a motorcycle. He also showed me how to ride a motorcycle on a washboard gravel road without flying all over: you adjust your speed to the particular type of washboard so that your tires clip the tops of the ruts, making for a smooth ride.

Now for the last hurdle—I still had to get "the powers that be" to give me a licence. Mum and I went to see the government agent, Mr. Burns. Mum explained the situation, and Mr. Burns turned to me and asked, "Well, young fellow, can you ride this machine?"

I replied that I certainly could and added, "Would you like to go for a ride with me?"

Mr. Burns backed away from the counter, held up his hands and said he'd take my word for it. He filled out the licence, asked for one dollar and said, "You drive careful. Your mother is counting on you."

I thought I would help Mum out by giving her a ride home each night from the Red and White store where she worked, but that was a disaster the first time out. My mother was of the old school, where a proper lady did not wear slacks (the first winter she worked in the store, she walked the four miles home wearing a skirt until it was thirty-five degrees below zero, at which point she finally put on heavy slacks, but just for the walk home. As soon as the temperature went up again, they came off), and she insisted on riding sidesaddle. At home, she got off and looked down at her precious, rationed silk stockings. The heat

Lassie on the Harley.

from the exhaust pipe had melted a big hole in each of them. That was the first and last time she rode a motorcycle.

Racing the Game Warden

In the fall, right after I got my motorcycle, I went grouse hunting. With Lassie on the buddy seat, I drove to the foot of Holmes Mountain, and we hiked up the trail to the top. I got three blue grouse before I remembered that the season for grouse didn't start for another week.

I sat down on a log overlooking the valley below to have lunch and then took out Granddad's old field glasses to look around, as it was a beautiful sunny fall day with the trees starting to change colours. High up, way across the valley, I spotted a flash of sunlight reflected off another set of field glasses—and they were looking right at me. Away down below, by the river, sat a green truck, which I recognized as belonging to the game warden, Jim Smith. Because I wasn't yet sixteen, I didn't need a licence to hunt, but I was supposed to be accompanied by an adult over twenty-one. With no father available, I always ignored the latter part of the law. My family needed meat.

I reasoned that at that distance, Jim wouldn't know I had shot the grouse unless he could catch me. And if he wanted to catch me, he would have to go down the mountain and back up to Princeton before he could cross the river and drive down to our place. By that time I would be home. I only had to go three miles to get there from my side of the valley, and he had to go nine.

I took off, running straight down the two-thousand-foot mountainside in leaps and bounds. Halfway down, I looked across the valley and saw Jim doing the same thing. Lassie and I reached the motorcycle, and I put her on the front seat and took off.

On the other side of the river, Jim's truck was running neck and neck with my motorcycle. He kept looking over at me, and I kept looking over at him. I swung into our farmyard, parked the bike, hid the grouse in the chicken house where his hunting dogs couldn't smell them, and went into the house, where I told Mum about the game warden chasing me, but not about the blue grouse.

When Jim finally arrived, I was sitting in the kitchen, drinking a glass of water, and Mum was cooking: a peaceful family scene. Jim asked Mum if I had been hunting. When she told him that I had been, but didn't get anything, he said, "Mrs. McGowan, I know you are having a tough time making ends meet. If Alan does get a deer or two, please just keep it to yourselves."

Later, when I presented the blue grouse to Mum, was she ever mad at me for making her unintentionally lie. Still, the grouse tasted great.

A Creepy Feeling

One of my favourite hunting spots was on the top of Holmes Mountain, which has featured in a few of my hunting stories. It was a beautiful place with a magnificent view of the valley below. Cox and Euhler, two old English gentlemen had settled there, but had died several years before I started hunting, and their farm and small silver mine were now abandoned.

I had many adventures on that mountain, but one memory stands out. I was up there hunting blue grouse. When lunchtime came, I was in the middle of a thickly forested area and decided to have a nap. I snuggled down against a log but couldn't relax or go to sleep. I had an overwhelming feeling that something horrible had happened here. I got up and went about four hundred yards due north, past the thick trees, and the uneasy feeling went away.

A couple of weeks later, I returned to hunt with a friend. Without saying anything about my weird experience, I suggested we sit in the forested area and rest a while. After a few moments, my friend got nervous and suggested we keep hunting. Over the next few years I tried this on three other people—including Hughie, my big brave older brother, and my cousin Bob, just out of the army, who was staying with us on the farm—with the same result. I came to believe that some terrible tragedy or injustice occurred on that spot.

Wrong-Way Charlie

Bruce was a friend of mine, and Charlie was a friend of his. Bruce was full of stories about the adventures that Charlie had gotten into.

Charlie was a strange-looking dude, six foot four and skinny as a rail. His long skinny arms came down nearly to his knees, and he had enormous hands and feet. To top it off, he had a tiny round head, with pale grey eyes, on top of a skinny neck. You would never guess it, but anybody who mixed with Charlie found out the hard way that he was also extremely strong. He was one year older than me and had quit school during Grade Eight to go logging.

One day I noticed that Charlie's hand was swollen and all bandaged up. Bruce told me that a rattlesnake had bitten Charlie when he was logging. Apparently Charlie had been sitting on the end of an old hollow log with his long arm hanging down beside the hollow. Mr. Rattlesnake had his home in the log. He didn't like Charlie's hand waving in front of his nose and struck at it. Charlie couldn't figure out who or what had bitten him, so he got down on all fours and looked into the end of the hollow log. When he saw the rattler, he got mad and started punching it with his bare fist. Naturally the rattler bit back until he was dead; by then, Charlie had at least seven bites.

A couple of weeks later, I asked Charlie how his snake-bitten hand was doing.

"It's all cleared up," he told me, "but I have other fish to fry."

He wanted me to give him a lift on my motorcycle the twenty-four miles to the Hedley Beer Parlour. When I pointed out that he was underage, he said Hedley was different and that he went to the beer parlour every night with his logging crew.

Not knowing what I was getting into, I agreed to take him down. We must have looked strange on the bike, with Charlie's big legs bent nearly to my shoulders.

When we got to Hedley, the beer parlour was nearly empty, with only one man nursing his beer, plus the bartender. We sat down, but the bartender seemed to be very busy, doing everything except waiting on us. We waited about ten minutes, and finally Charlie shouted, "Bartender, two beers over here." The bartender still didn't respond, so Charlie yelled again, "Are you deaf? I want two beers right now."

Finally the bartender, a fair-sized man who looked like he could handle himself, walked over, without any beer, and said to Charlie, "First off, you're underage, and I'm not supposed to serve people under the age of twenty-one. Secondly, you got into a fight with our waiter, who's still recovering at home. If you don't leave peacefully, I'll be forced to call the Provincial Police, like I did last time, but I really don't want to do that unless I have to." All this was news to me.

Charlie brought a fist up from the floor and sucker-punched the poor bartender on the side of the head with his big fist. He went down like a pole-axed steer, out cold. I sat there dumbfounded.

Charlie casually stepped over the body and said, "Well, I guess I'll have to get my own beer. Do you want some?"

I declined but he filled two glasses anyway, came back to the table and sat down, had a few sips, then casually poured some beer on the bartender's head.

The bartender slowly came to and crawled away from our table, stood up and went behind the bar. Without raising his voice he said, "Charlie, the police will be here in ten minutes." Then he scooted out the door. I started looking for an exit in case I had to beat a retreat, and spotted a side door to the lane.

A little later, somebody yelled, "Here comes the cop!"

I took off through the side door and was running full tilt down a dark alley when I slipped and fell head-first into a large outdoor grease pit, nearly knocking myself out. Gasping for breath, I crawled out, covered from head to foot in old grease and with a spring break in the bone of my right forearm. I hid in a shed until everything quieted down, sneaked around the front to my bike and then left for home in a hurry. I decided to give this so-called friend a wide berth from now on.

Bruce told me later that Charlie had been arrested in the same beer parlour a week earlier for being underage and having a fight. Halfway back to Princeton, the cop had kicked him out of the patrol car and told him to walk the rest of the way home to cool off. This was pretty generous of the officer, but Charlie had taken it personally and had plotted revenge against the cop. The day I drove him to Hedley, he was arrested by the same cop, who made the mistake of not handcuffing him. On the drive to Princeton, Charlie overpowered the cop, took off all his clothes and turned him loose on the side of the road. Then Charlie took the car home and went to bed, leaving the police car in front of his house.

Three years later, Charlie was out of jail but managed to get in the headlines again. The Hope–Princeton Highway was under construction, and two out-of-towners on the work crew, who were playing a lot of pool at Rosie's pool hall, noticed that Rosie had a regular habit of going to the bank every Friday afternoon to get a large amount of cash, which he put in the safe in his office. He did this because everybody was working a six-day week and couldn't get to the bank to cash their paycheques, as the bank was closed on weekends. Rosie was using the money he withdrew to cash workers' cheques for them. He had windows all around his office, and from the pool hall you could see him handling large amounts of cash. Rosie had been doing this for years with absolutely no problem.

The two guys decided to steal Rosie's safe. They did the job in the middle of the night, and by 3 a.m. had managed to get the large heavy safe, on rollers, out of the office, down the hallway and through the front door. When they came to the two front steps, they couldn't hold the safe, and it crashed down the steps, flat on the sidewalk. The two guys couldn't lift it up to get it into the box of their pickup, which was backed up to the sidewalk.

Who should come staggering down the sidewalk at that moment, blind stupid drunk, but our hero, Charlie! He gave the two thieves a hand lifting the safe onto the truck, and two days later, when the police discovered the remains of the open safe in a field, it had Charlie's fingerprints all over it. He went back to jail for three years.

Fortunately, a year later, the police caught one of the real safe robbers, who verified that poor old Charlie had just been giving somebody a helping hand when it was really needed. Charlie was released on probation, but I have often wondered how he made out in life.

The Long Road to Vancouver

By the summer of 1946, the war was over and the Wartime Prices and Wage Board, which had frozen prices and wages during the war, was dissolved. Seizing the moment, our union at the ore mill started negotiating for better wages and working conditions. In retaliation, the company closed both the mine and the concentrator. Along with five hundred other men, I was out of work. There was no chance I'd get another job in town, so I decided to drive to Vancouver on my motorcycle to look for work.

I was only sixteen, and Mum was worried about me travelling such a long way on the bike, but she eventually agreed, reluctantly. She then cautiously asked if I was going to see my father when I was in Vancouver.

This was a loaded question. Since they had divorced, whenever I did something wrong, Mum would say, "You're just like your father." I didn't know what that meant, as I hadn't seen Dad in years, but it hurt. So now I told her, "Yes, I am going to see him. You keep saying that I'm just like my father, and I want to see what he's really like."

Poor Mum. She just wilted right in front of me. The past five years must have been incredibly hard for her. Dad had sent us almost no money since they separated, and a year earlier things had reached the breaking point. Hugh was acting up, and I was no better. Between caring for the family, working all the time and having no life of her own, Mum had become very depressed. She held a family meeting and said she had considered abandoning us to welfare, but had changed her mind. She decided that she could work and provide for the family needs, but she couldn't also provide us with supervision. From now on, we were on our own; we could do what we liked and she would not say a word about it.

At the time, I thought, *Hey, this is going to be great—I can play hooky from school, fish, hunt, get drunk, stay out late.* I did all of that and much more, and Mum kept her promise and never mentioned what she thought of my behaviour. I still feel embarrassed thinking about those days.

At any rate, Mum said I should get in touch with my father before I headed off, so I phoned Dad to tell him I was coming. He didn't sound too enthusiastic, but Mum talked to him about his need to take some responsibility for me. He was now married again, to Eleanor, and living right in downtown Vancouver.

In preparation for my trip, I tied a cardboard box to the rear fender platform on my bike and loaded up my work clothes and tools, two old army blankets, a piece of canvas, an old frying pan, a loaf of bread, apples and two cans of spaghetti. Then I got up early on a sunny morning and said goodbye to everybody. They didn't seem too happy to see me go. Who would look after the flock of chickens, cut the firewood, light the gas lamps, take out the slops and bring in the fresh water? (Hugh still felt that, since he was paying room and board, he shouldn't have to do any chores at home.) However, I needed to make some money, and since it was summer holidays, and school was out, now was a good time to go find a job.

The first fifty miles was an easy winding gravel road, and I started to feel like I had the world by the tail. The next forty miles brought me back to reality. I came around a corner to find that a highway crew had just laid six inches of sand on a patch of road. I was going forty miles an hour, and when I hit that patch, the bike ground to an instant halt. I flew over the handlebars, landing in the sand face first.

Miraculously, I wasn't hurt. I picked myself up and rushed over to the bike. It was lying on its side, still running, so I shut it off. I didn't realize that the bike had pumped out about a quart of oil and sucked in some sand through the carburetor. I did notice a four-inch tube buried in the sand and immediately identified it as the carburetor's venturi. How in hell did that ever get out? I pulled out my tools, replaced the venturi and started up the bike. It didn't run quite right but was good enough to get going.

Rolling along, I saw three horses grazing on the left side of the road up ahead. The sound of the straight pipe on the Harley scared them, and they suddenly shot across the road right in front of me—so close that I just missed the rear end of the last horse. I didn't think too much of it, but when I stopped for coffee at a café in the tiny town of Spence's Bridge, the waitress who came to take my order looked at me strangely. In the bathroom mirror I saw there was blood all over my neck and on my shirt collar. I washed the blood off my neck and discovered three thin, five-inch-long slices right across the front of my throat. How did they get there? When I went to put my helmet back on, I found a long black hair caught in the buckle of the chinstrap. Did I come so close to the running horse that it cut my throat with its tail?

I fired up the Harley and took off on what was now an asphalt road. What a treat after riding on nothing but gravel ever since I got my bike and licence. Away we go! The Fraser Canyon was very narrow at this point, and I came to a two-hundred-yard section of wooden road, built with planks that were fastened onto the rock wall of the canyon about thirty feet above the river. This section of road was old and rickety with only one lane. Fortunately there was hardly any other traffic.

Just past here the Harley's motor seized up. I let it cool down and limped into Boston Bar, where I bought three quarts of oil, stopped at a park, started a fire and ate my spaghetti out of the frying pan.

Later, I was cruising along on the south side of the Fraser River when I turned a sharp right-hand corner and came face to face with the toll booth at the old Alexandria Bridge. The attendant charged one dollar per vehicle. I argued that I was a bike, with a motor, not a vehicle. He laughed and let me across for fifty cents.

A few miles north of Yale I decided to stop for a pee break. As I walked around, stretching my legs, I saw a middle-aged Native man on a log sitting by the river with a fully harnessed workhorse beside him. A thick rope ran from the horse's harness to a thin log floating in wide circles away out in a back eddy. On the far end of the log I could see a large spike, with a line going into the water. When I asked the man what he was doing, he simply said, "Fishing," and turned away, focusing on his line.

A few minutes later he said, "Time to put more bait on the hook."

As I watched, the horse pulled the log, the line and a large hook out of the water. The man re-baited the hook with chunks of rotten meat and then began to push the log back into the river. I gave him a hand, and then he explained that he was fishing for sturgeon. When I asked, "How big are the sturgeon?" he gave me a patient look and replied, "Big enough to need a horse to pull them out." I found out later that there have been sturgeon pulled out of the Fraser weighing well over 1,200 pounds.

By the time I arrived in Chilliwack, it was getting dark, so I pulled onto a side road and camped in a hayfield. I slept like a log but woke up to a driving rainstorm, soaking wet, cold and itching all over. I ate a shivering cold breakfast of water and two slices of bread.

There's nothing more miserable than riding a motorcycle without a windshield in the cold rain and without rain gear. I arrived at New

Westminster on the two-lane Number 1 Highway to be greeted by another toll bridge. Big-city people, no argument; I paid the full dollar fare. From there I went through New Westminster, up Kingsway, down Main Street, along Hastings and up Burrard to Dad's place in downtown Vancouver, opposite the Hotel Vancouver, where I parked in the alley.

Meeting My Dad Again

I found Dad's apartment—Suite 16 (kind of a cute number)—and knocked on the door, dripping water all over the hallway rug. A very plain woman answered my knock. I guessed she was Eleanor, my dad's new wife. She was nervous and shaking and stared at me strangely. I must have looked like a drowned rat.

I introduced myself and asked if my dad was home. He heard the kafuffle and came down the dark hallway. We looked at each other for a long time; after all, we hadn't seen each other since I was eleven. We coolly shook hands, and he invited me in. It was an emotional moment for me. I didn't know whether I should give him a hug or haul off and hit him. Over the past five years he had sent us only a lousy $138 and no letters, and then there was Mum's often-repeated comment.

When I took off my soaking wet clothes so I could put on dry ones, I discovered I had broken out from head to toe in large sores with pustules that were coming to a head. Dad said they were hives, from sleeping in the hayfield, and we would solve that problem with his favourite remedy. Dad had spent nine years in the British Army—one year on the front lines during the First World War as a machine gunner, and eight years as a member of the occupying troops in Germany. Each soldier had been issued a vial of permanganate of potash, "P and P," a strong disinfectant, highly poisonous if ingested, that was used for trench mouth, trench foot and any other infection.

This brought back vivid memories of when I was five and had a severe case of trench mouth. I was in bed with a raging fever for over a week, but we didn't have money for a doctor. This was 1935 in

Joe McGowan and Eleanor Evans, 1948.

Vancouver, the middle of the Depression, and Dad hadn't worked for four years. My parents fed me with an eyedropper because touching my mouth with food was extremely painful. Dad finally cured me with repeated gargling of P and P, after convincing my mother that if I didn't swallow it, I wouldn't die. He watched me like a hawk to make sure I spit all of it out after gargling.

This time around, Dad made up a hot bath for me and added a

large dose of P of P that turned the water a dark purple. I soaked for over an hour. By the next morning the hives had subsided, but I was purple from neck to toe. This episode let Dad and me bond again. My resentment of his failure to help our family during the tough times disappeared, at least for the time being.

After breakfast, Dad told me I needed a haircut. He was a meticulous dresser (it must have come from his army years), and his grooming rituals had fascinated me when I was a child. He had two hairbrushes that he filled with brilliantine hair oil, and he would spend a solid five minutes each day brushing his wavy black hair, one brush in each hand.

Up to now, Dad or Mum had always cut our hair, but this time he took me to his favourite barbershop, the Willows, at the north end of Granville Street, where they had four barbers. He introduced me and asked them to give me the works. He seemed proud that he could introduce one of his sons to people he knew.

Art, Dad's barber, washed and cut my hair. Noticing my purple neck and hands, he asked Dad what had happened. Dad told the story of my coming down the Fraser Canyon on my own and sleeping in a hayfield. I think he was proud and embarrassed at the same time, because he ended by saying, "Well, you know, boys will be boys." Afterward, Dad bought me lunch and took me to the Labour Exchange on Cordova Street, where I got a job with a roofing company at fifty cents an hour, starting later that week.

Dad and Eleanor's apartment wasn't very big, and Eleanor had her mother, "Ninny," living there with them, as well as an older female boarder. I was sleeping on a cot in the hall.

That second night I heard Dad and Eleanor quietly arguing in their bedroom. Eleanor said that she liked me, but there was no room for me, even if I was only staying until school started in the fall. Ninny, who was sleeping in the living room, was scared to get dressed because there was no door for privacy, and the boarder was upset because she had to go by my cot at night to get to the bathroom. Dad told her not to worry, that we would work something out.

But then Eleanor said, "I've never had any experience with a young man, but do they all squirt juice on the sheets? It's vulgar. Do I have to wash the sheets every time this happens?"

Overhearing this was both funny and embarrassing; I couldn't help what happened when I was sleeping!

The next morning I got up early, slipped out of the apartment, went to a phone booth and called home. I explained the situation to Mum, and she said she would contact her sister Jean, who was also living in Vancouver, and see if she would take me in. Mum phoned back later to tell me Aunt Jean would help me out. Aunt Jean lived in Kerrisdale, a good neighbourhood, and had a nice little house with a spare bedroom.

Dad was relieved when I told him I was moving on. He was living in Eleanor and Ninny's apartment, so he had little control over anything.

A-Logging We Will Go

I was an hour late for work the second day of my roofing job because the motorcycle wouldn't start and, surprise, they fired me.

Aunt Jean suggested I look for work on Vancouver Island, where her son, my cousin Bob, was. I went down to the logger's hiring hall at Cordova and Carrall Street, on Vancouver's "skid row." They hired me on as a "choker man," whatever that was, and gave me a pass for the ferry to Nanaimo and a bus pass to Campbell River, where the logging camp jitney would take me to the same camp where Bob was working. I was sort of glad to be leaving the cold hard city.

I was also looking forward to seeing Bob again. When he came home from serving in the army during the war, we had taken him in on the farm for six months for rehabilitation, and I'd gotten to know him then. We'd had a lot of fun fishing and hunting together. Bob was a strange dude, very quiet but very good looking. All the local farm girls were hitting on him, but he said they were a bunch of cows and he wasn't interested.

I took my motorcycle to Fred Deeley's motorcycle shop on Broadway and had a talk with Mr. Deeley, whom I knew from ordering parts. He said he'd fix the bike and store it until I got back from logging in the fall.

Going down to Pier C and taking the old Princess Elaine brought back memories of living in Youbou and all the trips that we had made from there to Vancouver or Princeton and back. On the boat were some old-time loggers, who told me that the choker man's job was to take a cable and tie it around a log so the donkey engine could pull it out of the woods to the loading deck. They also told me about the logging boots I'd need to buy, as good boots were more important to a logger than anything else. There were times, when you were climbing on slippery logs, that your very life depended on the traction of your boots.

From the ferry, a jitney took us to the camp, which was by a lovely lake about thirty miles into the bush from Campbell River. It had over three hundred men housed in eight-man cabins, with separate quarters for the married men and their families. We had arrived too late for supper, but the cooks had laid out cold food, and the company store was kept open for us. I bought a good pair of logging boots for forty dollars. My wages were one dollar an hour, so one week's wages was shot before I even started. But I ended up using those boots for the next seven years for every kind of job. I even took the caulks out and put hobnails in them for mining and exploration work. They were made of the best leather, and if I looked after them properly, they never leaked.

I found my cabin, stored my gear and then asked the Head Bull Cook, who was in charge of all the cabins, washrooms and mess hall, where I would find cousin Bob's cabin. I was looking forward to surprising my cousin and hoped he would help me fit in at the camp and on my job. There was no answer when I knocked on his cabin door, so I opened it to find Bob on his bed reading.

He leapt to his feet and said, "What the hell are you doing here? Did my mother send you up here to spy on me? If she did, you can go to hell. You stay on your side of the camp, and I'll stay on mine. Now get the hell out of my life."

Confused and hurt, I left the cabin. That seemed no way to treat a cousin, but I respected his wishes and stayed away if I saw him around the camp. We never did make up, but his sister, Bev, became a life-long close friend.

Because of the hot, dry weather and the danger of sparks from the machinery starting forest fires, we began our shift early each morning when there was dew on everything, which lowered the fire hazard. There was also a smoking ban in the bush, so everybody was chewing snoose.

To wake everyone up, the Head Bull Cook or one of his flunkies swung a long, thick, steel bar in circles around the inside of a triangle made of railway steel, suspended on a chain. This "gut hammer" was very loud and woke up the entire camp; I'll bet it even woke up the married quarters over four hundred yards away. Then it was dress, wash and hurry to the mess hall, six men to a table; porridge, flapjacks, eggs, bacon, toast and coffee on the table, help yourself; then to the lunch shack to pick up a variety of sandwiches, fruit, cake and coffee.

Our big boss, Fred, a "hook tender," was an old-time logger wearing pants cut off below the knee, a green plaid jacket, red shirt and old gray felt hat. Our crew boss was Rudy, a Native man who lived with his family in the married quarters. I piled into a boxcar with Rudy's crew and met Joe, a choker man, who Rudy said would show me the ropes. Joe was maybe forty years old and looked like he had just got off a long drunk, which I later found out was true. Joe believed he had taught far too many young punks already, so only taught me something after I had muddled through on my own and messed it up. This put me in danger of being killed almost every day, but Joe didn't seem to care.

Over the next month I had two very close calls. I later learned that during the 1940s the B.C. logging industry killed an average of 335 loggers a year. The number of loggers permanently injured was never released.

Rolling logs were what almost killed me in that camp. One day our whistle punk, a university student up logging for the summer, was sitting on a stump, teasing a squirrel, when he fell over backward and accidentally pulled the whistle wire. The operator started the mainline, and Joe and I were caught between two huge logs lying on a sidehill;

we had just hooked up the chokers. When the two logs started rolling together and down the slope, we ran like hell. We managed to get out from between them just before they smashed together.

We both knew what had happened as soon as we heard the whistle blow because we had been watching this educated idiot fooling around with the squirrel before we went down to hook up the logs. Without saying anything to each other, Joe and I headed for the whistle punk. He saw us coming and took off. We never saw him again; he was either fired or was moved to another logging show.

The Camp Bully

After the first day of work, I was tired and very hungry. After getting cleaned up, I went to the mess hall and sat down at a six-man table, salivating as the flunkies brought us huge platters of vegetables and potatoes—all of it smelling fantastic. Then they placed a large platter with twelve steaming-hot pork chops in the centre of the table. By this time I was ready to eat a horse.

Before we could serve ourselves, a huge French-Canadian faller, sitting at the other end of the table, stood up, reached over, took the whole platter of pork chops for himself and sat down, circling his large muscular arms around it.

There was a deadly silence at our table.

The big fellow said to all of us, "None of you guys want pork chops, do you?" He then stared at the two men nearest him on his right, waiting for a reply. Each meekly said no. I couldn't believe it!

He then looked at me, at the far end of the table. I was blazing mad. I couldn't believe anyone could be that much of a bully.

I stood up and yelled, "You are a crude, rude, greedy son of a bitch."

There was a long moment of silence, during which I realized what I had done; it was either fight or flight. Given his size, I chose flight and ran out of the mess hall, into the woods.

Much later, as it was getting dark, hunger drove me out of the woods, and I sneaked into the lunch shack. Nobody was there except one of the flunkies, who had heard what had happened. He advised me to avoid the mess hall and get all my food at the lunch shack from now on, and to stay as far away from the bully as possible, which I did. This lasted two days. After that I returned to the mess hall, sitting at a table as far away from the bully as I could get.

Two weeks later, we heard that the bully had fallen on his chainsaw, which at that time was a big, heavy, two-man machine, responsible for many injuries in the woods. The saw had cut three fingers off each of his hands and ripped him open from chest to stomach. He was hurt in the early afternoon, but the company wouldn't take him back to camp right away, as that would cost them extra money and tie up the train that transported all the loggers out of the woods. So he was forced to wait in a boxcar until the end of the shift.

Sadly, I did not feel sorry for him at first. But later, when I talked to one of the men who sat at our table, he told me that a few days after my outburst, the bully had just laughed about it. Then I felt sorry for him. We never heard how he made out. If he survived, he would have had a hard time being a bully again or even making a living. He probably ended up on skid row with the rest of the burned-out loggers.

Close Encounters

The washroom in this camp was a large, open room, with open showers, washbasins, laundry tubs, clotheslines and a large, circular table where up to twelve men could sit playing poker. Also, right out in the open, by the far wall, was the crapper. It was the crudest and most ingenious crapper I had ever seen—a large V-shaped trough that was over thirty feet long, two feet high and three feet wide at the top. The entire trough was on a slope so the water could flow through and also so taller folks could take the high end and small folks the lower end. There was a rounded two-by-four on the front edge of the trough that you could hang your rear on, with toilet paper available on a nearby post.

At the top end, high above the trough, was a wooden five-hundred-gallon water barrel. A hose ran into the top of the barrel, continually filling it with water. When the barrel reached capacity, a trap door at the bottom sprang open with a bang, and five hundred gallons of cold water filled the trough to the top and charged down the slope at a terrific speed, pushing all the waste through a hole in the washroom wall and into an open cesspool at the bottom of the hill. All in five seconds flat.

The barrel was so large, and so high above the trough, it was impossible to know when it would flush. This made having a crap seem like a game of Russian roulette. If it flushed when you were there, and if you got caught hanging too far into the trough, you had your rear washed for free. And if you were careless, or shocked by the rush of water, you could fall over backward into the trough and be flushed through the wall and down into the cesspool.

Fear of these horrors made me pay serious attention to what was going on with the level of water in the barrel. While I hung my rear over the two by four, I would listen to the water dropping into the barrel and try to determine if the sound level was low, signifying low water in the tank, or high, indicating the barrel was nearly full.

If I miscalculated and suddenly heard the water coming like an avalanche, it was Abandon Ship! I'd try to stand up with my pants around my ankles, panicked about falling backward. Then, after I'd managed to get away in time, I'd worry that the guys at the poker table were watching me, laughing at how I'd made a fool of myself. But then I realized that, no, they were too interested in their game to even care.

Camp Politics

The logging camp had rigid rules that you did not break without facing dire consequences. There wasn't a rulebook, so someone either told you the rules or you learned the hard way. Two rules I learned from an old-timer:

- Never get caught in the married quarters after dark.
- Professional gamblers are not allowed in camp.

If someone in camp turned out to be a professional gambler, they were treated very harshly.

One night I was in the washroom, doing my laundry, while a card game was in progress. Suddenly two loggers walked through the door and pointed at one of the card players, saying, "That guy is a professional gambler, and he's cheating us. That's why he's winning so much. We found all these marked cards in his cabin."

Without saying a word, the players jumped on the accused, dragged him outside, tore all his clothes off and hog-tied him to a timber they attached between two train cars loaded with logs that were waiting to go to the coast sawmill in the morning. The men then came back into the washroom and picked up their game as if nothing had happened. Every now and again, somebody stepped out to check on the cheater.

The next morning, the train and the naked cheater were gone. He must have been very sore, riding that timber over a rough track for thirty miles. I assume somebody untied him when the train arrived at the sawmill, and maybe scrounged him some clothes.

There were other rules I learned the hard way. We worked a forty-eight-hour week and had Sundays off in the camp. I got to know two young fellows my age, and when the weather was hot, the three of us would go swimming and sunbathing on the diving float. Two girls, Sue and Joan, who were home from school for the summer and staying with their parents in the married quarters, would also swim out to the float and lie in the sun. Sue and Joan were seasoned veterans of camp life and camp etiquette. They were both homely as a mud fence, but because of the scarcity of single women and the great surplus of single men, they behaved like they were movie stars and got away with it.

One day, a notice was posted in the camp store: there would be a dance in the small community hall on Saturday night. I was sixteen and had little experience with girls but really liked to dance, so I was looking forward to it. We three naïve young men went to the dance early, hoping we could get a dance or two before the older men arrived. The women, including Sue and Joan, stood on one side of the hall by the kitchen, and the few men who had arrived stood on the opposite wall by the door.

The small band fired up, and I went over and asked Sue, the blonde, for a dance. We were the only ones on the floor. After the dance, I rejoined the men, but nobody was dancing the next few songs, so I went back to ask Sue to dance again. She hesitated, looked at the other women, and with a mischievous smile said, "Sure, what the heck." She knew the score, but I didn't.

After that dance, one of the older guys came up to me with a serious face and whispered, "You had better get out of here."

I asked, "What the hell for? I haven't done anything."

He told me that I had just broken a camp rule. Nobody was allowed to dance twice with the same woman, and Sue had a boyfriend, Derek the Chaser, who was built like a two-hole shithouse. According to my advisor, Derek was now honour-bound to beat the crap out of me.

I was having a good time, so I didn't pay him any mind and went and danced with Joan. A while later, a bunch of men arrived through the kitchen door. They were loud and alcohol primed. A good-looking Native fellow put his arm possessively around Sue. I assumed this was Derek. One of the women said something to him, and he kept looking over at me. Finally, with a slight stagger, he headed my way.

I like to think discretion, or fear, is the better part of valour, so I took off. I ran out of the hall, stumbled down the steps in the dark and ran across two sets of railroad tracks into the woods—for the second time that month. This was becoming a habit.

I heard Derek charging down the steps behind me. Since they called him a chaser, I figured he could run like a deer, but so could I. I glanced back and saw some of his friends, backlit, peering out the open door of the hall, but I couldn't see Derek. I kept going farther into the bush until I eventually stopped, knelt down and waited.

I couldn't see anything from where I was, and all I could hear was the music from the dance. I waited fifteen minutes. Nothing. I waited a little while longer, then slowly crept out—still nothing. I wondered where Derek was hiding. Eventually I decided to sneak back to my cabin, so I walked in the pitch dark along the train tracks past the dance hall, feeling my way with my feet.

I stumbled over a body. Bending down, I could see in the dim light that it was Derek the Chaser.

What the hell had happened to him? I touched his face and felt something slippery on my hand—blood? He must have stumbled and hit his head on one of the steel rails. In the dark, without thinking, I wiped the blood on my white shirtsleeve.

The trains sometimes ran at night, so with a lot of effort I pulled Derek off the tracks and onto the footpath outside the hall. I left him there and went into the hall.

Everybody was surprised to see me, and someone who noticed the blood on my white shirt asked what had happened. Being a smartass, I replied, "If you really want to know, go see Derek. He's lying out on the path." I then took off, not wanting to push my luck.

It turned out Derek hadn't been badly hurt. He had a large bruise between his eyes and was at work Monday morning. I saw him around camp a few times after that, but he just looked at me with a puzzled expression.

My Breaking Point

Right after the episode with Derek the Chaser, Rudy, our crew boss, started singling me out for verbal abuse and extra-heavy rotten jobs. Whatever I did, I was too slow, stupid or clumsy. There wasn't a single curse word he didn't use against me, and the crazy thing was that the more he yelled at me, the more confused and clumsy I became. I overheard the crew telling him to take it easy on me because I was just young and trying to learn. He told them to mind their own bloody business. I hated coming to work in the morning, and I wasn't getting much sleep, but I was damned if I was going to quit for some jackass boss.

One day we were retightening the stabilizing cables that run from the top of the spar tree to the stumps around it. I had a long steel bar with a very sharp point in my hands and was prying the heavy cable down around the stump so it could be spiked in place. Rudy stood right in my way and yelled, "You're a stupid clumsy bastard."

I had had enough. In a fit of rage I yanked the bar up, aimed its sharp point at Rudy's chest and drove it forward.

Fortunately, Joe was standing right behind me. He grabbed the other end of the bar and pulled it down so it went over Rudy's shoulder instead of into his heart.

I stared at Rudy, and Rudy stared at me. Whatever went through his thick skull, he didn't say anything and walked away.

The realization of what I had nearly done knocked the breath out of me like a physical blow. I turned around and thanked Joe for intervening.

I understood then that anybody can be pushed to the point of murder, and I never let myself come that close again. You can always make changes, no matter how painful, to avoid being sucked into a whirlpool of hate.

Rudy kept his distance after that, and a couple of days later the camp was shut down due to extreme risk of forest fire. I picked up my cheque and discovered my compensation for all the work and stress, with deductions of $40 for the boots and a dollar a day for room and board, came to a grand total of $122. Fortunately there were no tax deductions as I was still a student.

Travelling back to Vancouver, I fell into conversation with Mike, an old-time faller, who was still using a two-man crosscut saw. You should have seen his arms; they were huge. Mike had spent all his life in the woods and told me he was seeing a lot of changes. For one thing, he knew the invention of the power saw was going to put him out of work. But he had saved his money and would be okay. Another change was that while most loggers in the past had lived in camps and been single, now that working people could afford to buy cars, loggers were starting to live in town and commute to logging camps. They were also getting married, having kids and buying houses. Mike had a wife and home in Burnaby.

As we chatted, I told Mike about Rudy's bullying and confessed how close I had come to killing him. I told him I couldn't understand why Rudy had it in for me. Mike knew the whole story and revealed that Rudy was the uncle of Derek the Chaser. Apparently Derek had been ashamed that a young punk like me had got the best of him in a fight. Rudy, as his uncle and my supervisor, was honour-bound to get rid of me.

When I told Mike the secret of my so-called fight with Derek, he had a great chuckle and asked if he could tell Rudy what had really happened. I agreed, as logging and I were never going to get together again.

Mike and I were leaning on the rail as we approached the pier in Vancouver. I saw a large group of women on the wharf, and the men on board were waving enthusiastically at them. I thought the women must be their wives, but Mike explained that the relationships were purely professional. When "their" man came to town, these women lived with him through the drinking and gambling or whatever he wanted to do, and he would give her money. But when his money was gone, he'd be out, and she'd move on to another man. Sometimes, when the man was too old to log anymore, and the woman was too old for her trade, they would end up living together permanently.

Mike and I got off the boat, shouldering our duffel bags, and said goodbye.

California, Here I Come

Back in Vancouver, I was only five blocks from my dad's place, but I didn't want to give him any more problems. So I took the bus up to Fred Deeley's motorcycle shop. Fred greeted me warmly and told me they had discovered the problem with my bike. I had put the carburetor's venturi in backward. Fred had fixed it, changed the oil and adjusted the mechanical tappets. For twenty-five dollars, the bike was ready to go.

I stowed my gear on board and bought groceries. Now where should

I go for the night? It would just complicate Dad's life with Eleanor if I stuck my nose in there. I phoned Aunt Jean and told her I was back from logging and was going home to Princeton tomorrow, but there was no invitation to stay the night. Before I hung up, I told her a white lie: "As far as I know, Bob is doing okay."

I studied my map and realized it was pretty much the same distance home to Princeton if I went down into the United States and headed across that way. And it would be all U.S. paved roads instead of Canadian gravel. So I took off and headed down the Coast Highway. After making supper in a park near the border, I discovered that I had lost my two army blankets. It was getting dark, and I was feeling desperate, so I asked a family camping in the next site if they had any spare blankets. They reluctantly handed over two old burlap sacks. I put one sack under me and one over me, along with my old piece of tarp, and had a very cold night.

At that time the border was just a two-lane highway with one lonely U.S. customs agent in a small building. The next morning I pulled up

Peace Arch from the Canadian side, White Rock, B.C.

on my motorcycle, and the agent came out of his little office and met me in the middle of the road. I greeted him with a cheery "Good morning, sir."

He responded with a grin. "And where do you think you're going this fine morning, young man?"

I told him that I was heading back home to Princeton, B.C., via Snoqualmie Pass because the roads were paved, and ours weren't. He seemed to think that was a pretty good reason and then asked how old I was.

I looked him in the eye and replied, "Sixteen, sir."

He said, "You're pretty young to be travelling on your own. How much money do you have?"

"I have twenty-five dollars in my wallet, and twenty dollars in my headlight," I replied.

He said, "You seem to know what you're doing." With that, he waved me through, wishing me a nice, safe trip home.

I thanked him, fired up and headed down the highway. I missed the turnoff to Snoqualmie Pass and ended up in Mount Vernon before I realized what had happened. Then I decided to keep going south and take Stephen's Pass, the next route heading east toward home. This would take a little longer, but I had nearly two weeks before school started.

Heading farther south, the highway was now going right alongside the ocean; the day was sunny, and the scenery was spectacular. I pulled into a gas station and filled up, and was pleasantly surprised to find that gas was only eighteen cents a gallon (in Canada it was twenty-one cents). I was feeling great, and the devil was riding on my shoulder, telling me to keep going south instead of heading east. Finally I decided, since I still had nine days before school started, that I should take a little holiday—California, here I come! Mum wouldn't be expecting me so wouldn't know I'd taken a detour until I got home. I stopped at the war surplus store in Seattle and bought two army blankets for two dollars to keep me warm at night. Then I headed south.

After six days rolling down the beautiful Washington, Oregon and California coast, I started to get lonely for someone to share it with. I turned inland toward Bakersfield, a fruit-growing town, and camped in an orchard, but it was so hot I couldn't fall asleep until midnight. Lying there, listening to all the things that go bump in the night, was not good for someone with an imagination.

In the morning I had a cold breakfast, picked up some fallen apples and headed into town for gas and a good cup of coffee. In the café toilet, the drains of the urinals were filled with the biggest black cockroaches I had ever seen. I guess they also wanted to stay cool.

By 10 a.m. it was so hot I figured it was time to head back home to cool Canada.

Flat Tire Rip-Off

I was working my way north on a narrow, two-lane, semi-deserted highway when I developed a flat front tire. This was real trouble. I was miles from anywhere, and there were no cars coming. I started pushing my 750-pound bike in the heat. To where, I didn't know. About two hours later, and still no cars, I could make out what might be a gas station a mile ahead. I thought I was in luck.

When I'd sweated that last mile, the building turned out to be a little store/gas station, with a garage and tools. A big fat ugly bald man was sitting on a stool behind the counter, sweating and staring silently at me like he thought I was going to rob him.

I was so thirsty that I bought a nice cold coke and tried to get a conversation going. No way. He just looked at me, then looked away. I told him I had a flat tire, but he didn't respond. When I asked, "Can you fix it?" he waited five minutes before replying, "Fix it yourself." I told him I'd never fixed a motorcycle tire before. He snarled, "Learn!" When I asked how much he would charge if I fixed it myself using his garage, he said, "Five dollars." Shocked, I said that was an awful lot of money for a patch. But he didn't respond.

I pushed the bike into the garage and looked around for tools, hunting and finding what I needed. The man sat on that stool, looking at me through the door, never missing a move to make sure I didn't steal anything. I hoisted the front wheel and blocked the bike, took the wheel off and, with much straining, got the tire off and the tube out. He had the hot hatch type of tube repair equipment, which I didn't know how to use. My frustration seemed to amuse him, and I caught him with a smirk on his ugly face.

I finally figured it out and repaired the leak. Now came the painful part—having to pay five dollars for a job that a tire man would have charged only a dollar fifty to do for me.

I said to him, "I don't have much money, and I have a long way to go to get back to Canada. Seeing I repaired the tire myself, could you reduce the cost?"

He just held out his left hand and said, "Five dollars."

I was about to protest when I looked through the glass countertop and saw that his right hand was resting on a great big .45 revolver. I paid up and got out of there. Welcome to the wonderful U.S. of A.

American Hospitality

I spent the rest of the hot day driving steadily north through flat, uninteresting desert country. Later I found myself in cattle country and spotted an old deserted barn where I spent the night. I noticed that the bike was getting harder to start, and the lights were growing dim. The next day I took a look at the generator and found a wire that had been torn off.

I drove down the road a bit, rolled into The Dalles on the Columbia River and found a small motorcycle repair shop. I explained my problem to the mechanic, a slim young fellow named Ralph. We got talking as he was checking out the bike. He found out I was nearly broke and needed to get back to Canada. He said he needed help tarring the roof of his shop—if I would help him for two days, he would repair my bike for free. Sold to the man in the bright red suit!

Ralph's wife gave me supper, the best meal that I had on the whole trip, and then we sat on the front porch, overlooking the Columbia

River, and talked until dark. They were a great couple, but it was unbelievable what they didn't know about Canada.

I slept on their front porch, and for the next two days worked on the shop roof. Ralph then fixed my bike, and I bid them adieu and headed north.

I took a small detour and went through Yakima, then turned northeast to visit the new Grand Coulee Dam. This was the one and only dam on the Columbia River, and I was keen to see it. I went on a free tour and was impressed by the size of the dam and the number of men who had been killed building it; twelve were buried in the concrete.

I spent my last night on the southern outskirts of a sleepy little town called Omak. I could have made it the last seventy-five miles to the border, but it would have meant driving in the dark, and I wasn't in that much of a hurry to get a tongue-lashing at home. I spotted an old house and barn beside the Okanagan River; Omak was right on the other side of the river. I turned in, prepared to ask the owner if I could sleep in his barn because it looked like it was going to rain.

On the porch, sitting all alone in a rocking chair, was a very old, very dark, African American man.

Getting off the bike, I said, "Evening, sir."

He looked confused and a little scared and said, "Good evening, suh." He had a pleasant Southern accent that made me chuckle; I had never spoken to anybody from the deep South before, and his accent reminded me of the way people spoke in movies I'd seen.

I said, "You have a nice quiet place here by the river. Would you mind if I slept in your barn tonight?"

He was slow to answer and finally said, "Come on up on the porch and sit awhile, and we'll talk about it."

I came up on the porch and sat in another rocker, realizing this was going to take some time. He had to check me out before he said yes or no. It was getting dark quickly, and I still had eleven dollars, not counting my headlight money, so I figured if it didn't work out, I could go into town and get a bed in a fleabag for a dollar.

The man stood up and went into the house, fussed around for a while and came out with tea and biscuits. He said, "Hep yoself if you don't mind eating with a black man." I didn't know what that meant so I kept my mouth shut.

I had read about the problems that black people had in the States, but I hadn't a clue about the subtleties. Having missed supper, those biscuits looked awfully good, and I didn't hesitate to dig in.

As I ate, I explained to him where I had been and where I was going. He seemed relieved, told me his name was John, and we drank tea in peaceful silence, with the sound of the river in the background.

He seemed to be a very lonely man, and when he finally spoke, he said, "Yo'll are from away up north in Canada, and you don't know nuffin about our troubles. You can put your motorcycle in my barn, outta sight. And you can sleep in my barn. But you've got to be off'n my property in the morning before it gits light, so the white folks don't see you."

I didn't know what this was all about, but I decided to go with the flow. We sat in silence for a while more, and then I bid him good night, pushed the bike into the barn, checked for pigeons, selected a stall with some nice soft hay, made up my bed and set my alarm for 4 a.m.

When I woke up, there was just enough light from a street lamp across the river for me to wash up. I didn't want to wake John, so was pushing my bike across the front yard without starting it when he came out and said, "Breakfast is ready." I was in the house in one minute flat. We had a big breakfast of bacon, eggs, toast and coffee. I thanked him and was on my way in the early dawn, through the rain and the little town of Omak, which was still asleep.

I headed up to the border and was waved through—home again in Canada. It felt good and I gave a sigh of relief. I hit the long gravel road and was home by noon. It was Saturday and Hugh was working, but Mum and Pat were home. Both were, I think, more relieved than happy to see me home safely.

True to her promise from that family council, Mum never raised her voice or complained about my behaviour, but she did say quietly,

"It would have been thoughtful of you to let us know how long it would take you to get home." Apparently, after I had come out of the camp and phoned Aunt Jean, she had phoned Mum, so they had been expecting me days earlier.

We went in the house and had lunch. Pat was peppering me with all kinds of questions, but Mum wasn't saying anything. Finally Pat left the room, and Mum asked how Dad was. I filled her in on Eleanor and Dad and how they lived.

PART FOUR
Some Hard Lessons

Looking After Dick

In 1947, when I was in Grade Eleven, Mum quit her job at the Red and White store and moved Pat and me back to Vancouver. One of her friends in the city had died, leaving her job open, and I guess Mum was fed up with farming life and the drudgery and long hours working in the store. Hughie was making good money as a fireman in the steam plant, so he stayed in Princeton to look after the farm.

Mum's new job was taking care of an elderly man, Mr. Black, and his thirty-eight-year-old son Dick, who had Down's syndrome. Dick was short and tubby with a large head; small, protruding eyes; and a pleasant disposition. He and his dad had a nice old house one block off Kitsilano Beach, and we lived with them, so Pat and I now went to Kitsilano High School. We all helped look after Dick, which was challenging but enjoyable. As long as everything was routine, he had a wonderful attitude toward life. Anything new and complicated, and he could get upset, confused and angry. To teach him something new, we found we had to repeat it patiently many times before it would stick, but once he got it, he would be proud of himself and never forgot it.

For example, Dick long ago had learned how to set the table cutlery in a very precise way. For the fun of it, we sometimes moved a fork one inch out of alignment while he was busy with some other little project, like bringing in the mail from the front door. As he rushed by the dining room table, he stopped dead when he spotted the error. He would then reach over and adjust the fork before continuing on his way, never suspecting it had been moved by someone else.

I tried to teach him to cut kindling with an axe but soon gave up on

Margaret McGowan, Vancouver, 1945.

that. He had poor coordination, and I realized he would end up cutting off some fingers. I then painstakingly taught him how to catch a softball. He was proud of this newfound skill and would bug me endlessly to "go play catch."

One day, feeling adventurous, I decided to take Dick fishing for flounders at the far end of Kitsilano Beach, near where we were living. He didn't know what fishing was and wasn't sure if it was something he could do. I explained that it was something that everyone could do. We went into the backyard and dug up some worms and put them in a can. I got my trusty old rod, found another in the basement, and away we went.

We had to walk the full length of the beach to get to the fishing spot, which was under the Burrard Street bridge. On the way, we ran into two of my friends. I was surprised at their reaction to Dick. One of them asked, "Why are you taking this nut out fishing?" When I replied that I thought he would enjoy it, he said, "Well, help yourself. I wouldn't be seen dead with him."

I knew Dick understood what had been said, but he didn't comment. I bought each of us an ice cream cone, and pretty soon he was his cheery old self again. People sure can be ignorant and cruel.

We got out to the point, where there was deep water, and set up our fishing rods. Demonstrating, I explained to Dick over and over again, "If you feel a pull, or a jerk on your rod, lift the rod slightly to set the hook."

Dick turned out to be a patient fisherman. An hour went by with no bite on our lines. But suddenly Dick felt a jerk, and did he ever react! He yanked a large flounder clean out of the water, high into the air and onto the beach, nearly breaking the fishing rod. The fish flopped around violently, and Dick was jumping up and down; I stood there laughing. Dick was worried the flounder would flop back into the water, so he kept standing between the water and the flounder, but he wouldn't touch the fish. Finally I went over and put it out of its misery.

We fished for a while more with no luck. When we were ready to walk the mile home, I pulled the fish out of the water, where I had fastened it to stay fresh, and gave it to Dick to carry. Man, was he proud! He had to show off his fish to everybody we ran into. He would say, "See my fish, I caught that," and there were plenty of people out on the beach that day to admire Dick's fish.

When we got home, he insisted that we have it for supper. He nearly drove us all crazy repeating over and over, "It's good, isn't it? I caught that fish!" We had to reply each time, "Yes, Dick, it's a great fish."

The Fine Art of Shovelling Coal

At the end of the school year, Mum and I had a meeting with the school counsellor. He had reviewed my grades and told me I had barely managed to pass into Grade Twelve. Kitsilano High was more advanced than the country school back home, and this had placed me at a disadvantage. I had also lost interest in my education, feeling adrift in this huge new school with its two thousand students and indifferent teachers. The Princeton school had been a small, close-knit place where I knew everybody, everybody knew me and I could get help if I needed it.

The counsellor recommended I drop academics and transfer to Vancouver Technical School, where I could major in automotive mechanics and prepare for an apprenticeship. I had taken mechanics courses by correspondence for three years when we lived in Princeton, and I had earned good marks, so we all agreed this was the best route for me.

Then Mum dropped a bombshell—she was giving up her job and was going back home to Princeton with Pat. She had spoken to Dad, who was still living in Vancouver with Eleanor, and he had reluctantly agreed to pay for my room and board while I went to Van Tech. This was a big deal, as Dad was of the old school that believed anything after Grade Four was a waste of time for common folk because that's all he ever had.

After we set this up, I went back to Princeton for the summer with Mum and Pat. Hugh had got me a job working in the steam-electric power plant on the Bull Gang, which was the heavy labour or "bull power" work gang. On my first day I was teamed up with Mike Popovich, a middle-aged, silent, almost sullen Polish man with a solid, powerful build. In his deep voice, Mike told me to grab a shovel and follow him. When I asked, "What kind of shovel?" Mike replied, "It don matter." I found a rack of various shovels and, seeing we were in a coal-fired plant, picked out a large coal shovel. When I rejoined Mike and saw he had picked up a gravel shovel, I rushed back and traded my coal shovel for a gravel shovel.

For the next four hours we walked around the grounds, climbing up inside the plant, peering into coal bins and working our way back down to where the coal cars were unloaded. I thought we were finally going to start working. But no, we went back to the lunchroom.

"When are we going to go to work?" I asked Mike.

He looked at me long and hard, and said quietly, in a thick accent, "We don have no work. If the big boss see us, he will tink we are workink, and he will leave us alone. Do you unnerstan?"

I didn't say anything but I thought this was crazy. Four years earlier I had worked hard on a farm with fourteen-hour days for one dollar a day. Now I was getting a dollar an hour for doing nothing.

After lunch the boss finally gave us a job shovelling pulverized coal into a chute. Mike took one side of the monstrous pile and I took the other. Pulverized coal is very light, and we had big shovels, so I assumed this would be a fast, easy job. Up until now, I had figured I was a pretty good man with a shovel, having shovelled nearly everything there was to shovel, but I quickly saw that Mike's side of the pile was shrinking faster than mine. Being young and strong, I worked harder and faster to keep up. But Mike just rolled along, no fuss, no muss, and was shovelling over half again more than I was. After a couple of hours, I was exhausted, so we sat down on the coal for a break. Under my persistent questioning, Mike revealed that since the age of fourteen he had done nothing but shovel coal, first in coal mines and now in the steam plant, so he really knew how to shovel coal.

I was proud of how well I could shovel, and how much, but I had met my match with Mike and coal. Mike said he would teach me how to shovel coal properly so he wouldn't end up having to do my work for me.

"You in high school but not very smart," he said. "Don't they teach you anythink? You work all time with arms and not with legs. I show you, using legs."

He demonstrated. I tried. He demonstrated again. Slowly I caught the overall movement, using seventy percent legs and body, and thirty percent arms, and after a while I got the rhythm.

It wasn't too long before I kept up with Mike, and after that he treated me with respect. We became good working friends, and he even allowed me to wash his back in the showers—now that's trust! We didn't talk much, but we went throughout the plant shovelling whatever needed to be shovelled.

Training the New Kid

One day they sent Mike and me to get some gravel from the nearby riverbank for a construction project in the plant. Our job was to fill up a three-ton dump truck every half hour. We worked like dogs because river gravel is as hard as concrete. It has been sitting there since the beginning of time, pushed and shaken around by ice, and moved and settled by the flow of the water in spring floods. You have to loosen every square inch with your pick before you can shovel it, and it is especially hard to shovel up and over the seven-foot-high sides of a dump-truck box. After filling the truck, we had a fifteen-minute rest while the driver delivered the gravel to the construction site.

After lunch, the big boss came down to where we were shovelling and sent Mike off to another job. He then introduced me to Gordon, a sullen fifteen-year old boy he had brought with him. The boss said, "Alan, Gordon is going to replace Mike this afternoon. Teach him how to shovel gravel, and make sure he does his share. If he doesn't do his share, you let me know." This was not a very good recommendation from the boss, who apparently knew Gordon.

Gordon looked about as enthusiastic as a cat facing a bath. I had no idea what was going on but figured this kid must be the troubled child of someone, and the boss was looking after him.

"Have you ever shovelled anything?" I asked Gordon once the boss had left. When he said no, I started to demonstrate. After a few minutes I looked up to see him sitting down, playing with a couple of small stones, not even looking at me.

Well, I thought, *two can play this game*. I sent him to the other side of the truck with his pick and shovel and told him to start working on his own.

After a few minutes, when I didn't hear anything from the other side of the truck, I went over and found him leaning on the shovel with a blank look on his face.

I told him, "I am not going to fill this truck by myself. I don't give a shit who you are, but you either do your share or you won't be here."

I must've hit a soft spot because he grabbed the pick and started swinging it like an old woman. It was pitiful to watch.

Relenting, I showed him how to swing the pick and let its weight break the ground. He caught on pretty quickly, so I went back to my side and started loading the truck.

When I heard a bit of gravel landing in the box from his side, I took a peek. He was actually shovelling, but again it was pitiful to watch. I left him alone to struggle awhile. That first load, I probably filled over three-quarters of the truck, but I figured that was okay because he was actually trying.

On the second load, I showed him how to stop relying so much on his arms and to put the shovel against his leg and use the leg to push the shovel into the gravel. Again, he caught on pretty quickly.

Over the next couple of weeks, Gordon told me his sad story. He was from Seattle, but due to a series of unbelievable circumstances was staying with his uncle, who was the big boss of the power plant.

He told me that a few days earlier he had been at home in south Seattle, walking past the Boeing aircraft factory and airfield, when he had spotted a little two-seater Taylorcraft plane just sitting there, idling away, without anybody near it. He had crawled under the fence, walked up to it and got in. He'd never been in a plane in his life, but from avid reading recognized most of the controls. He sat there for a while, imagining all the motions of flying the plane. In the midst of his reverie, one of the mechanics spotted him and came running across the field, waving and yelling at him. Gordon saw him coming and panicked, or so he told me. He released the brake and revved up the engine, and the plane slowly started to move, then went faster and faster down the runway away from the wrench-waving mechanic. The next thing Gordon knew, he was flying. He took the plane up to two thousand feet and flew over his home in Seattle.

Then the sudden, impetuous lark turned into a serious crime. *What do I do?* thought Gordon. *Land and face the music? No. Why not fly to Canada, and they can't touch me. My uncle lives in Princeton, and they have an airport. The fuel gauge says Full. Canada here I come!*

He headed north out of Seattle on the old Highway 99, turned east and followed Highway No. 2 over the Coast Mountains via Stevens Pass to Wenatchee, then north on Highway 97 to Oroville, and then north through the border to Osoyoos, up the No. 3 to Keremeos, Hedley and, following the road, to the Princeton airport. That's over four hundred air miles. Amazing!

I thought I had done some crazy things, but this took the cake. How he had found his way, or why he hadn't run out of gas, was a mystery to me.

There was a reception committee waiting for Gordon when he managed to land the plane without smashing it up: the Airport Authority, the Provincial Police, Canada Customs and his uncle. Gordon was charged and taken into custody, and then released to his uncle to wait for a court hearing. But then, incredible as it might seem, the plane's owner refused to lay charges. He had gotten his plane back in good order and believed that any kid who could pull off what Gordon had done didn't deserve to go to jail. Unfortunately, Canada Customs wasn't as generous, and Gordon was sentenced to one year's probation under the supervision of his uncle.

Gordon and I worked together for the remainder of the summer, and he ended up completing high school in Princeton. He joined the Canadian Air Cadets and then the Canadian Air Force, where he worked his way up through the ranks and joined the air demonstration squadron, precursor to the Snowbirds.

The last I heard of Gordon was in 1959. He was doing a power dive at an aerial show in Nova Scotia and crashed right in front of his family and the grandstand. A friend of mine, Cliff, phoned to let me know. Gordon had died doing what he loved.

Off to a Bad Start

When I returned to Vancouver in September to start Grade Twelve, I found that Van Tech was a working-class school with many boys, like me, attending from out of town and serious about learning a trade. The school had a list of families eager to board students, and I ended up staying with Lillian and Tommy Brown and their two small children for forty dollars a month. My roommate, Bob Ostrom, was from a fishing family who lived up the coast. He was in his fourth year at Van Tech. We hit it off just great and became lifelong friends.

Van Tech was very different from Kitsilano High. While Kits had been focused on academics, it also had a relaxed, casual atmosphere. Focusing on the trades, Van Tech was much more conservative and disciplined. Unaware of this difference, I inadvertently got off to a bad start.

On the first day of school, my homeroom teacher, Mr. Cowan, a tall, distinguished-looking man, walked into the room and greeted us with "Good morning, boys." Everyone in the room except me knew the drill: they jumped to attention and, in unison, shouted, "Good morning, sir." Mr. Cowan spotted me slowly getting to my feet in confusion, and he muttered, "Humph, new boy. At ease. You may be seated." From then on I didn't need to be told to stand up when a teacher entered the room, but my poor reputation with Mr. Cowan had been sealed.

My clothes also gave a bad impression. Before the school year started, I had decided to splurge and buy a new pair of pants for school. Strides were all the rage, and I had gone to a Chinese tailor and ordered a pair of these baggy, high-waisted pants with forty-two-inch knees and sixteen-inch cuffs in bright blue corduroy. Strides were worn with an open-necked sweater and no shirt underneath. At Kitsilano High, this outfit would have been the "in" thing. But on the first day at serious Van Tech they immediately branded me as flashy and lightweight.

I also breached the rigid social rules almost right away. In his Welcome Back speech in the main hall on the first day of school, the principal announced that there would now be two hundred girls attending Van Tech to learn secretarial skills and hairdressing. There had never been a girl in the school before, the principal said, and he hadn't wanted to admit them now, but he had acquiesced with the understanding there would be no fraternization between the sexes.

Alan wearing his blue corduroy strides,
Granville Street, 1947.

He threatened dire consequences if any boy was caught talking to a girl. I couldn't believe what I'd just heard from a principal.

When I looked at the bulletin boards advertising the various extracurricular sports and activities available, I noticed that one of the activities was Scottish dancing. Being of Scottish ancestry, I was intrigued and signed up. At the first session I discovered I was the only boy in the club. I was having a great time until the principal stopped in, looked daggers at me and left. I had just broken one of his new rules.

Fortunately, the No Fraternization rule didn't last long. Many of the girls were from the same families as the boys, and there was no way they weren't going to fraternize with their brothers.

In spite of these problems with the conservative style of the school, it didn't take me long to realize that all the teachers I had at Van Tech were excellent and highly committed. Some even had advanced degrees and could have taught at a university, but had chosen Vancouver Tech.

In mid-October, as I was settling in, I managed to get into trouble again. Vancouver's streetcar drivers and bus drivers went on strike, and the school was closed for the duration, so I decided to head home and get a job to make some money. I asked a secretary at the school to phone me in Princeton when the strike was over. Bob Ostrom came along, and we hitchhiked the three hundred miles together.

Back home, we both got work pouring concrete for a new bridge. Two weeks later, we heard on the radio that the strike had ended. School had started up two days earlier, although no one had phoned to let us know. In a panic, Bob and I immediately quit and headed back on my motorcycle.

We took the Fraser Canyon highway and were coming into Boston Bar when the connecting rod on my bike broke. It took a day to arrange for the bike to be shipped to our place in Vancouver. Then we tried hitchhiking in what was now pouring rain, but nobody would pick us up. We finally caught the cattle train instead, and arrived in Vancouver wet, hungry, tired and smelly—as the saying goes, "The smell would have knocked a duck off a gut-wagon." I vowed to never, ever again ride a train with pigs and cattle.

We reported for school the next day, but the principal had already labelled us truant and would not accept any excuses or reasons we gave for our absence. It seemed I just couldn't get a break.

Meeting a Celebrity

There were a few bright spots in this period of my life. Dad would take me to the occasional hockey or basketball game and wrestling matches. And each month when he gave me the money for my room and board, he invited me to their apartment for supper.

Dad and Eleanor lived across the street from the elegant Vancouver Hotel. One night as I was on my way to catch the streetcar that would take me home after supper, I stopped to look in the hotel's small display windows. One featured a beautiful crystal vase cut in a pinwheel design. I had been intrigued by cut glass ever since I saw my grandmother's extensive collection, and I was admiring this piece when I caught sight of a movement to my right, farther down the dark deserted street.

Walking toward me was an apparition—a tall, broad-shouldered, older woman, dressed all in black, with a flowing skirt flapping around her ankles, a large ankle-length cape and a big floppy black hat. Following thirty feet behind her was a younger man, also tall and also in black. He looked like he was stalking her, but she appeared unconcerned.

After keeping an eye on her for a few steps, I turned back to the cut glass, but then the woman came right up behind me, peered over my shoulder into the display case and casually said, "I see you like cut glass."

Turning to answer, I was startled to recognize her. It was Eleanor Roosevelt, widow of U.S. president Franklin Roosevelt.

By this time, the man following her was right beside us. I commented that he must be her guard, and she glumly said that she couldn't go anywhere without one. We walked together to the hotel lobby entrance, and as she went in, I bid her good night. The next day there was a piece in the paper about her visit to Vancouver.

I didn't tell anyone about this for a long time, feeling that no one would believe me. But many years later a French-Canadian logger taught me the trick of telling a hard-to-believe but true story. He was a master storyteller and would lead in with a comment like "Something very unusual happened to me, but you wouldn't believe it if I told you." He would pause expectantly or turn away and wait until you asked for details, and then he knew you were hooked.

Slave Labour

To become certified as an automotive mechanic, which was my plan, I had to work as an apprentice in the industry for two years (this was a good deal, as anyone who didn't graduate from Vancouver Technical

School had to apprentice for four years). As our year at Van Tech came to an end, our teachers took us around to visit businesses that were looking for apprentices, hoping we would find employers. We were all excited to see the prospects for our future.

On the first visit we went to Vivian Diesel Works, where they made large diesel motors. As we were being escorted around the shop, we spotted one of Van Tech's top recent mechanical graduates sweeping the floor! Talking to him, we learned he had been doing nothing but cleanup for the past year at the low rate of thirty-two cents per hour. He was not a happy camper.

We then visited a large automotive supply business. Upstairs, where the mechanical apprentices were repairing generators, carburetors and fuel pumps, the working conditions were no better than the worst sweatshops, crowded and stuffy with poor lighting. And the wages were just twenty-five cents an hour.

After these tours, I became disillusioned. I knew I couldn't live in Vancouver for two years as an indentured apprentice at twenty-five cents an hour without financial help, and Dad wasn't prepared to give me any more support—he had his own money problems. This was a huge disappointment, as I had invested my whole last year in preparing for a career in mechanics and had dreams of becoming a certified tradesman. In retrospect, I probably could have figured some way to complete an apprenticeship somewhere, but I had been drawing a man's wages for the previous four years doing unskilled labour, so with the short-term thinking of a teenager, I decided to chuck it all. Reflecting back over the years now, I can see that I kept the dream alive: I still love cars and have rebuilt more than ten of them.

Manual Labour

My school life had ended, and with it my room and board at the Browns. I was at an impasse, so I decided to get a temporary job until I could figure out what to focus on as my future occupation. I went to the Labour Exchange and ended up digging ditches by hand in downtown Vancouver, where they were laying transmission cables. The ditch was being dug along Seymour Street in twenty-foot lengths. It was three feet wide and eight feet deep, with no shoring to prevent the sides from collapsing on you. When you finished digging one section, you leapfrogged ahead to another section. It was boring work.

The men I was working with were right off skid row or immigrants who hadn't learned the language yet.

One fellow, Paddy, was an Irishman who always worked with his shirt off, showing a thick mat of black chest hair. One day at lunch, he solemnly announced to all and sundry, "I'm now going to do something you've never seen before, and I want your full attention because I can only do it once every year." With that, he struck a match and drew it slowly across his belly at the belt line. The hair on his stomach and chest burned like a grass fire, right up to his neck. We were all horrified. He put out the embers with his hands and laughed.

After two weeks of nearly solid rain, I quit, figuring I could find a better job with some possibility of a future. When you're eight feet down, shovelling sloppy mud, and half of it slides back down on top of you, and the sides of the trench start collapsing inward, it's time to move on.

Moving Furniture for a Living

At the time I quit digging ditches, I was going out with Nancy, the daughter of a wealthy family, who encouraged me to go to work for her dad's furniture-moving company. Taking that job was a big mistake and I regretted it for the rest of my life.

The tightly knit group of men at the company had worked together for years. The last thing they wanted in their circle was someone with connections and the ear of the man at the top. I tried my damnedest to win them over. They were nice to my face, but their tone of voice was never sincere, and I frequently overheard them hatching various plots to get rid of me.

One Saturday morning, after I had been working there about three

Ron and Alan after work, Vancouver, 1949.

months, the dispatcher told us that a piano needed to be moved into a West End apartment building. Doug, the designated truck driver, picked me as his swamper. I had never been on a piano move before, and I should have known something was up when I saw all the other guys looking at each other with smirks on their faces.

We got to the apartment building and discovered the piano wouldn't fit in the elevator. Doug said we had to carry it up to the fifth floor. The piano was one of the lighter, wooden types, weighing around 450 pounds. Doug lifted the front end and I, as the low-ranking helper, had to lift the back end. Because of the steep slope going upstairs, this meant that the vast majority of the weight was on my end. With five floors at sixteen steps per floor, this meant I lifted almost 350 pounds over eighty times. Doug refused to spell me off on the bottom end. After all, he was a truck driver; he didn't have to do that heavy bull work. It wasn't until later—much later and too late—that I learned Workmen's Compensation Board regulations required three men on a piano move.

The next stunt they pulled was even worse. A family was moving by rail from Vancouver to Toronto, and for some reason I was given the job of checker, which meant I stood at the door of the boxcar with a check sheet and marked off each piece of furniture as it was moved into the car. When I had to go for a pee, Don, one of the other crew members, quickly volunteered to take my place. When I came back, I saw that the stove, fridge and washer had been checked off. I was surprised they'd been loaded so quickly, but Don and the rest of the crew assured me they had been put in the car.

After we finished loading the car, I signed the check sheet and gave it to the foreman. Three weeks later the big boss, the foreman and an insurance agent came into the warehouse to see me. The three appliances were missing, and my signature was on the sheet. The bosses searched everywhere but couldn't find anything. I knew I would be digging my own grave if I explained what had happened; it was my word against the crew. So I had to take the blame. This was duly marked on my record, and I was never allowed to be checker again.

Another time, Doug the truck driver took me as his helper on a furniture move from one side of an exclusive neighbourhood to the other. He also took Ralph, who had just been hired that day. I later learned that Ralph had recently done time in jail for stealing—I guess he had lied to get his bonding papers, and the company hadn't checked his background yet. On that day, we were doing what was called a "company contract move," which meant we made it possible for the owners to walk out of their old house in the morning and walk into their new house at night, with everything already in its place.

When we arrived at the first house, the two packers had been at work for a full day, boxing up all the clothes and dishes, and were still going at it. When we went to move a dresser in the master bedroom, a huge pile of unpacked jewellery was still on top of it. Someone on the crew collected the jewellery into a box and put the box in one of the dresser drawers.

It was an easy, straightforward move. We put everything in its place in the new house and went home at quitting time. But at one o'clock in the morning, two plainclothes detectives woke me at my apartment and asked what I had done with the $2,000 diamond necklace that should have been in the box in the dresser. Fortunately, before things got too serious, another policeman showed up and said they had found the necklace at Ralph's place.

The next day we heard the story Ralph told the detectives. He said he thought it was costume jewellery, and he believed there was so much of it that the owners would never miss it. Besides, he had just got out of prison and times had been tough, so he thought he would cheer his wife up with a little present. That $2,000 necklace, in today's money, would be worth at least $20,000. Ralph went back to jail for another two years.

The only bright spot in the moving company job was Jerry, one of my new co-workers. He was a fun-loving guy who had hired on at the same time as me. Unlike me, he was perfectly happy to move furniture for the rest of his life. He lived in the old Martin Hotel at the south end of Granville Street, just before the bridge. It was a seedy area, and the hotel attracted all kinds of characters. Jerry lived on the top floor in the low-ceilinged attic of the building, along with Freddy, who worked as a desk clerk for the hotel.

Freddy was a heavy-set, middle-aged man with a great sense of humour. One Sunday afternoon, Jerry and I were sitting in the lobby, kibitzing with Freddy, when a straitlaced young fellow, neatly dressed in a suit and tie, asked for a room.

Freddy said, "Certainly, sir. Would you like that furnished or unfurnished?"

Confused, the man looked at Freddy and asked, "What do you mean?"

With a straight face, Freddy replied, "Blonde, brunette or redhead?"

The poor fellow was very embarrassed, but Freddy told him not to worry, he'd put him on one of the higher floors, where it was quiet and he wouldn't be bothered. Freddy did a marvellous job of reading people and placed them on different floors according to his assessment. The second floor was for drunken parties and patrons wanting call girls; the higher you went, the less commotion there was. The hotel generally catered to miners, loggers and fishermen, and Freddy supplied their every need.

On another day, Freddy sent Sue, a call girl, up to a room directly above the lobby. Soon we began to hear thumps and loud voices.

Freddy said, "It's only a drunken logger. Sue can handle him; she's a practical nurse and knows ju-jitsu."

Then we heard breaking glass, and a body bounced on the awning over the hotel entrance, flew by the window and landed in the street. I rushed out and stopped traffic while Freddy phoned the cops and the ambulance.

By the time the police arrived, Sue had cleaned up and was cool as a cucumber. She said that the logger had been drunk, turned ugly and was beating her. She grabbed him by the shoulders, dropped to the floor with her feet on his gut and flipped him over the low window-sill and out, where he slid off the awning and down onto the street. We found out later that, surprisingly, he wasn't hurt very badly and no charges were laid.

Taking Dad to Alcoholics Anonymous

Around this time, Dad and Eleanor split up due to his drinking, and Dad came to live with me in my apartment in the West End. He had had a good job as an electrician on the oil tanker *Imperial Edmonton*, running from Vancouver to Venezuela, but thanks to the drinking he had got into a fight with the chief engineer while they were in port at Long Beach, California, and had been fired. This all sounded so familiar.

We were getting along pretty well, but every two or three weeks he would start to get antsy and pick an argument with me. That would give him the excuse he needed to go out and get stinking drunk. He would be gone for two or three days, and then I would get a phone call, sometimes very late at night, sometimes early in the morning, and the stranger on the line would ask, "Is your dad Joe McGowan?" The caller would then tell me that my father was passed out on the floor, and if I didn't come and pick him up, they would call the police to take him to the drunk tank. I would get the address, usually in Hogan's Alley or some other bootlegging joint, phone a cab, pick him up, pour him into the taxi, take him home and put him to bed. The next day I would say something to the effect of "Dad, you were in one sorry state last night, and I'm getting fed up of packing you home." His response: he didn't want to talk about it. Then I'd warn him that I wouldn't always be available to pick him up and that he'd end up in the drunk tank.

One time I happened to be walking down Robson Street on a sunny Sunday afternoon, and as I rounded a corner, who did I see staggering down a side street toward me—and I mean staggering—but dear old Dad. I turned to avoid him, I was that ashamed. He eventually came home under his own steam a couple of days later. I felt really bad about it, but at the time I was near the end of my rope.

Finally I woke up one Sunday and there he was, sitting on the end of my bed. He had been away on a drunk for several days, but the first thing he said to me was "Alan, I want to quit drinking. Will you help me?"

Dad was a proud man, and it took a big effort for him to say this. I told him that I'd help him, but I didn't know how. He told me about a new organization called Alcoholics Anonymous that he thought might be able to help.

I got up, dressed and made breakfast for both of us. Over coffee, I looked at him and said, "Are you really serious about wanting to stop drinking? Because I don't want to waste my time."

He said, "Yes, I am, and I've been thinking about it for a long time."

We phoned AA and were told to come right down, so we caught a streetcar and went up the long flight of stairs to the organization's office on Granville Street. The first step was for Dad to stop drinking.

We filled out some forms and were sent to a drying-out place, which was a big old boarding house down by the railway tracks. It had many bedrooms and a large central meeting area. To a nineteen-year-old, this house and its inhabitants were one sorry sight.

At the house we met with a large, no-nonsense manager, and Dad was given a room. He was going to undergo what they called "Cold Turkey Drying Out," in which alcoholics went off the booze completely and immediately. They either toughed it out or were shown the door.

I went home to pack up Dad's toiletries and a few clothes, and took them down to him. Every few days I dropped in to see him. He seemed to be coming along okay, and after three weeks he was let go and moved back in with me. He talked enthusiastically about the experience and the supportive meetings. He was required to go to two AA meetings each week, and I went with him to support him on the twelve-step program to sobriety.

As a young person at these meetings, I learned a lot about the older adults I had previously looked up to. AA members were doctors, lawyers, secretaries and prominent businessmen. All who attended these meetings were required to admit their weakness for alcohol.

In addition to these meetings, and to have something to do at night, Dad joined a bridge club, which met near where we lived in the West End. The club was composed largely of older women. Dad, a reformed gambler, had been a very proficient poker player and enjoyed the sessions, but the women did not. He won consistently, and they accused him of cheating and eventually barred him from attending.

He remained sober for over three months, but one day we were on a streetcar heading to the Highland Games at Brockton Point, which Dad enjoyed, when a fellow got on and sat down behind us. He had been drinking beer, and the smell on his breath was very strong. When I wasn't looking, Dad slipped away from me and off the streetcar. The smell of the beer had triggered his craving.

A couple of days later I got the usual phone call and had to go pick him up and bring him home again. I was really disappointed, but Dad

Joe McGowan, 1955.

never drank to the same excess as before, and he slowly drank less and less. In the end, he and Eleanor got back together, and he moved out of my place.

Mr. P.

This was the year of the big snow in Vancouver—1948 to 1949. We had three feet of snow that stayed on the ground for nearly three months, and the city had to hire over two thousand men with shovels to keep the tracks clear for the streetcars. I even went ice-skating on Lost Lagoon several times.

Every morning at seven o'clock, I would trudge through the snow to the corner of Davie and Denman, just off the beach at English Bay, and freeze my butt waiting for the bus to work. And every morning while I was waiting there, a very distinguished-looking, middle-aged gentleman—I'll call him Mr. P.—came out of his fish and chip shop on the opposite corner. Dressed in a bathrobe and slippers, with a towel thrown over his right shoulder, he shuffled across the street to the beach and walked through the sand and snow to the water's edge. He stood there, calmly looking around, possibly admiring the scenery, before taking off his slippers with his feet. Then he stooped down, knocked the sand off the slippers and put them neatly together beside him.

He slowly took off his dressing gown and folded it up into a small bundle, which he placed precisely on top of his slippers. Then he carefully folded the towel and placed it on top of the dressing gown.

At this point, naked other than his bathing suit, he flexed his arms a few times and slowly walked into the water until it was well over his hips. Then he slowly sank down and did the breaststroke out into deep water. He swam back and forth parallel to the beach a couple of times, then slowly waded ashore, walked to his clothes, picked up the towel and unhurriedly dried himself off before slinging the towel around his neck and putting on his dressing gown and slippers. After taking another moment to stop and look around, he walked back to his shop.

I never saw this performance all at one time, but I'd watch segments of it each day until a bus came along and interrupted the sequence. Mr. P. took his swim every day, winter or summer, whatever the weather.

A Life-Changing So-Called Accident

In the early spring we had to move another piano, and Carl, one of the company's truck drivers, picked me to help him. He said this was an easy move, as we only had to lift the piano a few steps up to a front porch. However, the piano had one of those horrible cast-iron frames that weighed over seven hundred pounds and, as usual, when we started lifting the piano, I was on the bottom end.

Carl had backed the truck up sideways to the stairs so we could slide the piano off the tailgate, over to the fourth step and up, saving effort. We were nearly to the top step when Carl looked down at me over the top of the piano and then let go of his end.

The piano started coming down the stairs on top of me, and I realized if I stayed in position, it would pin me by the neck against the side of the truck and take my head off. I squeezed up against the wall, and the piano hit me along my left side, tearing all my muscles. Carl called the office, and another crew came out to move the piano. I went home badly beaten.

I was in bed for a week, in horrible shape. Dad made me an appointment with a chiropractor, and I crawled the two blocks to the bus stop. When I stepped off the bus downtown, I felt a sharp pain shoot up my back, and then I couldn't move. The bus driver had to ease the bus a few feet forward to let the other passengers off. After three or four minutes, when I was frozen like the Statue of Liberty, my back relaxed enough for me to crawl up the stairs to the chiropractor's office where I got temporary relief.

Dad had some experience with these things, and he talked me into making a Workmen's Compensation Board claim, something I knew nothing about. When I got the WCB report form, I wrote down exactly what had happened and then gave the report to the company owner, who read it and got upset. Ashamed, he admitted that WCB regulations required three men on a piano move. His company would be heavily fined if I reported what had really happened. He asked me to change what I had written and say that a box had fallen and hit me on the back in the warehouse.

I felt sorry for him, as he had been nice to me, even though I was no longer going out with his daughter. So I did as he asked. That was a big mistake.

I reported to the WCB for assessment and discovered that all the back muscles on my left side were torn, and the vertebrae in my back were badly out of alignment. I was prescribed eight weeks of daily heat and massage treatment at the WCB clinic.

A big, blonde, middle-aged woman administered this treatment, the same routine every day, complete with an embarrassing addition. She would start by massaging my back, working her way down to my buttocks. Just as she finished, she would touch a spot above my tailbone and up would come Oscar. She then rolled me over, hitting him gently with her hand, and down he would go. She would place a towel over him, as if it was a normal occurrence, and went on with the rest of the massage. I dreaded going for my treatments due to the embarrassment, but I kept it up because I wanted to get better.

After the eight weeks was up, I was paraded in front of five WCB doctors to assess my progress. It was obvious to me that there was not much improvement.

One of the doctors asked if I could bend over and touch my toes. When I said I couldn't even touch my knees, he said, "Give it a try anyway." So I tried, and with excruciating pain got my hands to just above my knees.

The doctor then said, "You're doing fine. Would you like to go back to work? They have a checkers job for you where you won't have to do any heavy lifting."

Totally overwhelmed by the five doctors, I said that I would very much like to go back to work but was worried that I couldn't stand for any length of time without a great deal of pain.

One of the doctors said, "Well, give it a try and see how it goes. But to get started you'll need to sign this form stating that you are willing to go back to work."

Intimidated, I signed the form in front of all five doctors and went back to work the next day. I only lasted until noon; the pain was so bad I had to go home.

I reported back to the WCB officer the next day and told him what happened.

He said, "Sorry, that form you signed released WCB from any further responsibility. You're on your own now."

I said, "But I can't work. What should I do?"

His response: "Sorry, fella, you shouldn't have signed that release."

With no alternative, I left Vancouver for Princeton, where I knew my family would take care of me. I had constant pain from that injury for the next thirty years—and lost thousands of dollars on chiropractor fees and missed work. What a rotten system to take advantage of a nineteen-year-old youth.

Learning the Painting Trade

I returned home to Princeton, bent and bowed, but not broken. Things had changed in the last year. Mum and Pat were living in a tiny cabin in town, and Mum had borrowed money to buy a coffee shop, the Snack Bar, and was very happy with life. She let me sleep on a couch in the kitchen. Just being home among friends and relatives did me a world of good.

Construction of the Hope–Princeton Highway was in full swing, and there were jobs everywhere, but I had to find something that was easy on my back. The right opportunity came from Louis, a painter who was working on a scaffold on the main street, painting the Princeton Hotel. As I walked by, he yelled out, "Do you want a job painting?" I thought, *Well, painting doesn't require too much lifting and can lead to a trade.* So I agreed to meet him at Mum's coffee shop to talk about it.

Louis was a big, strong, family man with a laidback, country attitude. He agreed to take me on as a registered apprentice, at half wages, for the first year. If everything worked out, he'd give me full wages for the rest of the three-year apprenticeship. We got along great, and I found the trade interesting. In those days, painters bought the basic ingredients and made their own colours, which was a real art. The jobs were varied and challenging, and we had many adventures together.

One time we were painting a shake roof, taking turns hauling the bright red paint up in five-gallon pails. It was Louis's turn to bring the pail up to the top of the ladder at the roof level. He carried it up, and I reached down and took hold of the pail. But then I slipped and over went the pail, dumping five gallons of red paint right onto Louis's head and face and down his back. Luckily he shut his eyes. When he finally opened them, all I could see were two light blue eyes peering up at me out of a totally red face. Stupidly, I blurted out, "Gee, Louis, I didn't know you had baby blue eyes!" This did not go over well, but later on we laughed about it.

Louis bought a spray-painting system, complete with spray gun and compressor, even though neither of us had a clue about how to use it.

He decided to try it out on our next job, painting the inside of the government liquor store. We started in the back storage room, filling the tank with paint and plugging in the compressor, which made a loud racket so we couldn't hear each other. Louis was up on the scaffold, painting the walls and ceiling so fast that I could hardly keep up, moving the scaffolding along for him.

We were just finishing the storage room when we heard the store manager shouting from the front of the shop, over the noise of the compressor, "Stop, for God's sake, stop!"

We stopped and for the first time looked around. The whole place was full of off-white paint mist, which was settling on the thousands of exposed bottles on the shelves. Fortunately it was casein paint, which can be wiped off glass when it dries. Even though it took two days, we were able to clean off all the bottles.

Needless to say, Louis became gun-shy after that. Because I was younger, with no hang-ups, I researched the whole thing and discovered that we had set the pressure too high and used a paint that was too thin, which generated the mist. I became the "expert" with the spray gun.

Painting the Local Whorehouse

One day Louis announced, with a mischievous smile, "I have just closed negotiations on a contract, and you'll never guess what it is!"

I couldn't begin to guess, so he explained, "We are going to wallpaper and paint the local whorehouse, and tradition says that you get double pay when painting a house of prostitution." Apparently this was due to the supposed stigma attached to being seen coming and going from a brothel.

That night, thinking I would shock her, I told Mum, and others in the kitchen of her café, "As of Monday, we're going to paint the local whorehouse."

Mum stopped stirring the soup she was making, put one hand on her hip and pointed the large wooden spoon in her other hand square at my face, saying, "Alan, wipe that silly grin off your face. Those ladies are no different than anybody else. I expect you to treat them with respect. You don't know the circumstances that turned them into prostitutes."

She then told me that around 1910, when she was growing up in Princeton, there were twelve houses of ill repute servicing the two thousand single men working in the local gold, copper and coal mines. The local doctor inspected all the ladies regularly, and every Wednesday morning they were allowed to come downtown and do their shopping. Needless to say, all the so-called respectable ladies stayed home that morning, so they wouldn't be seen with the scarlet women or—heaven forbid!—be mistaken for one.

On Monday morning we started work, and the madam, a black woman named Micki, greeted us as any other house owner would. Louis did the paper hanging, and I glued the wallpaper and painted. Throughout the morning, the "girls" slowly appeared and sat around having breakfast in the kitchen. Seeing I was young, and nervous, they kidded me a bit, but then left me alone.

As I worked, I eavesdropped on the girls' conversations, and this was certainly interesting. Some of their customers would surely have had red ears if they heard the comments made about them.

During the afternoons, a few customers usually came by, and the girls greeted them like old friends.

Within a week, the place looked really nice, and we bid the girls goodbye.

Rang-a-tang Times Down on the Farm

Hughie, my older brother, was batching it down on the farm. He had bought it from Mum when she needed money to pay the mortgage on her coffee shop. She'd had the farm appraised, and it was valued at $14,000, but she sold it to Hughie for $2,000, which was all she needed to pay for the café.

Unfortunately, the story didn't end there. After they both signed off on the sale, Hughie decided not to pay Mum the $2,000. He had developed the idea that, as the oldest son, he should inherit the property and not have to pay for it. Mum tried to be patient, but two years later she had to take him to court. She won the case, and Hughie was forced to pay, but as a result he never spoke to her again, and he did not allow her contact with the children he eventually had. It was a devastating fracture, with repercussions that are still felt today. And people wonder why I won't borrow money from, or lend money to, relatives!

At any rate, Hughie was living on the farm and working as a first-class steam engineer at the mine in Copper Mountain. When he heard that a man called Frank McGowan was in the local hospital, having lost his leg in a mine accident, Hughie decided he should go up to the hospital to see Frank. He shared our name, and Hugh thought we might be related somehow. Hughie and Frank hit it off, even though they didn't discover any blood connection, and when he was convalescing, Frank came to live on the farm. He was from an Alberta coal-mining town, and before long, Frank's brother Ted and three friends, Buster, Hubert, and Clarence—who I soon began calling "the three clowns"—also came to visit. They all ended up staying on the farm and getting jobs on highway construction.

With these new residents, the farm was now the site of some of the wildest parties in the area. What a contrast for a place that had never seen a bottle of booze or a cigarette in fifty years.

Around this time, Hughie sold me his old 1928 Model T Ford for forty dollars and helped me learn how to drive it. The Model T had no roof and needed a lot of work, so I rented the funeral parlour garage and had fun completely rebuilding it. I even built a roof for it. It was the greatest car to take into the backcountry for hunting, and I drove it everywhere—though it wasn't much good for picking up women in the winter.

One day I drove out to the farm. As I approached, I heard the blast of shotguns. When I pulled into the yard, I saw Hughie, Frank and Ted McGowan and the three clowns out on the side lawn, skeet shooting. The skeet looked awful big, and as I got closer, I could see they were shooting at Granddad's gramophone records. These were the old

Alan in 1928 Model T Ford, 1949.

quarter-inch-thick by twelve-inch-diameter records, and they included recordings of speeches by David Lloyd George, announcing the end of the First World War in the House of Commons in London, as well as opera featuring Enrico Caruso, Paul Robeson and many others. Pearls before swine. I was so disgusted I turned around and left.

Another time, Hughie and I had made arrangements to go fishing on Sunday, and I went to the farm the night before so we could leave early in the morning. When I arrived, there were ten cars, or more, parked all over the place. Oh-oh! Another party was going on.

I could hear Grandmother's piano and a guitar banging out the rhythm of a conga, and when I opened the kitchen door I was nearly bowled over by a long conga line, led by a beautiful, stark naked brunette woman, followed by twelve men, also stark naked. Even Frank was dancing naked in the line with his one leg and crutch. Needless to say, they were all very drunk.

I found Hughie in the kitchen, making sandwiches. He was sober and promised to have breakfast ready for us at six in the morning. I went back to my car and spread out my sleeping bag.

The next morning the house was a mess, but Hughie was up, and breakfast was ready. We went fishing, and he explained what had happened.

The party was supposed to have been a more sedate affair, and it had started well, with all the men bringing their girlfriends and everyone dressed up in nice clothes. But later in the evening, the beautiful brunette I had seen leading the conga line had arrived, uninvited. Dubbed "The Snake Charmer," she had moved to Princeton a few months earlier and had instantly established a reputation for wild living. When one of the girls at the party snottily declared that she and her friends would not stay at a party where "that thing" was present, the Snake Charmer threw down the gauntlet and said, "Never mind, little lady, you and your friends can go home. I'll take care of the men." With that, all the girls and two of the men who were engaged left, and the party was really on.

A spinoff of this party was that a number of the men got a dose of crabs—you'll never guess from whom. They all went to the drugstore for the blue ointment treatment that was then used to get rid of crabs. One of the men burned his scrotum with the ointment and ended up in hospital with an infection of the testicles. When Hughie and I visited and asked him how he was, he said, "See for yourself," and threw his blanket aside. What a pitiful sight. His testicles were swollen to the size of ostrich eggs. With the skin stretched shiny tight, they were resting on a thick layer of cotton batten that had been fastened with adhesive tape across his thighs. We laughed and left him to his misery.

Clarence and the Bull

Sometime after this party, Hughie phoned me and bluntly asked if I had any money. Apparently Clarence, one of the three clowns, had been arrested and charged with assaulting a police officer, a very serious offence. I only had seventy-five dollars, and it didn't sound like that would be enough to get him off the hook.

Clarence was five foot ten and 250 pounds of solid muscle, but not too smart. When he was drunk, all he wanted to do was beat people up. He would ask a guy to fight, square off with him, then grab the guy by the front of the shirt and knock him senseless with one punch. The grin never left his face from beginning to end.

Clarence and the boys had been in the old Tulameen Hotel beer parlour. When it closed, they moved the party upstairs to somebody's room. They were just sitting around talking, with the door open, when the manager asked them to keep the noise down; they paid him no mind and kept talking, so the manager phoned the police.

Officer Howard, a member of the Provincial Police, arrived, and in a very high-class English accent asked them to vacate the room. When Clarence made fun of Howard's English accent, the slim young policeman tried to arrest him. Clarence just grabbed the officer, swung him around, laid him on his stomach on the bed and sat on him. The men then continued to talk for another hour. When Clarence finally let Howard up, the policeman cuffed him and took him to jail.

Hughie and Clarence's pals and I took my seventy-five dollars to the courthouse for the trial. After the judge called the court to order, Officer Howard, very embarrassed, explained what had transpired.

When he was finished, the judge said, "You are a trained police officer. How could you let this man subdue you and then let him sit on you for one hour?"

Poor Howard was speechless. He gestured at great, hulking Clarence, sitting at the front of the court with his sleeves rolled up and muscles bulging all over, and said, "But, your Honour, just look at him!"

The judge laughed, and everybody joined in. Clarence was fined $150 and received no jail time, and we all chipped in to pay the fine.

The Nearly Great Train Disaster

One afternoon I dropped in to the local General Motors garage, where the foreman, Floyd, pulled me aside and said, "I don't know how to put this, but those three guys from Alberta, the ones staying on the farm with your brother, were in here to get an oil change, and when they left, a ten-gallon can of grease went missing. Do you think you could get it back for me quietly? If you do, nothing more will be said about it."

I told Floyd I would mention it to Hughie, as I was going out to the farm that night for a corn roast.

I forgot to bring it up with Hugh, and a few hours later, at 10 p.m., as we were all sitting around the campfire, we heard a horrendous screeching of train brakes. Then the train whistle started blaring, and the noise went on and on.

Hughie and I jumped in the car to go and see if there had been a train wreck. The three Alberta clowns didn't want to come, which seemed rather strange.

At ten every night we would usually hear the freight train from Vancouver chugging its way up the steep incline behind the farm on its way to Penticton. At 2 a.m. we would hear a passenger train going down the same hill to Princeton. The hill was the second-steepest grade in Canada, and it was tough for the train to slow down and make the sharp turn at the bottom before heading across the Tulameen River to Princeton.

When Hughie and I got to the train crossing, there were people everywhere, and a passenger train was stopped at the bottom of the hill, around the corner, in the middle of the Iron Bridge that went across the river. It seemed that the passenger train had been early that night and came down the hill at 10 p.m. The CPR people and the BC Provincial Police said the tracks had been heavily greased from two hundred yards above the crossing to one hundred yards below. All the braking the engineer had done to slow the train so it wouldn't miss the corner and end up in the river had flattened every wheel on the train.

By the time we got back to the farm, I had a pretty good idea what had happened to the train—and to that ten-gallon pail of grease from the garage. I pulled the number one clown, Hubert, aside and said, "You stole that grease, and you greased those tracks, didn't you?"

He looked at me with a smirk on his face and said, "You'll never find out."

I replied, "For Christ's sake, the foreman at the garage knows you stole that grease. All anybody has got to do is put two and two together, and you're all heading for the crowbar hotel."

Panicked, Hubert confessed, "We thought it would be fun, stopping the train from getting up the hill. How were we supposed to know that they were going to change the schedule, and the passenger train would be coming down the hill instead of the freight train going up?"

Two days later, the three clowns left town, though they didn't tell Hughie why they were going.

The next week when I went down to the farm, Hughie told me he had found the empty ten-gallon bucket in the back of the woodshed, and Floyd had phoned him about the missing grease. Hughie had put the missing grease and near train disaster together and realized the three clowns added up to big trouble. He paid Floyd for the missing grease, and nothing more was said.

There was never a dull moment when the Alberta boys were around, but it was a big relief when they left.

Bears, Fish and People Don't Mix

Hugh had heard about a great new fishing spot in the middle of nowhere and talked me into going up there with him. Rumour had it that twenty years earlier, somebody had stocked Murray Lake with rainbow trout, and you could now catch five-pound trout on a fly, a fly fisherman's dream.

We took the 4 a.m. CPR train to Brookmere and then hiked in to this pristine lake, where we set up camp in a Forestry tent that was already there. This tent was in the rough style; it had no floor, but a roof and walls were suspended from a large ridgepole hung from two trees.

We discovered there were indeed lots of fish in the lake. Hughie caught the first big trout, as usual with much whooping and yelling. We had fresh fish for breakfast, lunch and supper, plus three large ones to take home. We hung these three trophy fish in the corner of the tent, away from the sun and the flies.

Tired by the long day, we were sleeping in the tent by nine o'clock, dead to the world. A few hours later I woke up, panic stricken. I was lying on my back, but I couldn't see, and I couldn't breathe—something was pressing heavily down on my face, trying to suffocate me. I couldn't even cry out.

Desperate for air, I pushed up frantically with my hands and grasped a heavy, furry object. Next thing I knew, someone or something hit my chest hard, knocking the wind out of me. There was the sound of ripping canvas. Then the pressure let up and I could finally breathe.

Hughie woke up yelling, "What in the hell is going on?"

It was pitch black, so we turned on our flashlights and saw that the tent wall directly behind my sleeping bag was ripped from the ground to the ridgepole, half of one fish was missing and there was coarse black hair under my fingernails.

Piecing it together, we figured that a bear had smelled the fish and come into the tent. Stupidly, in my tired state, I had put my sleeping bag directly under the hanging fish. In order to get at them, the bear had stood over me, with one foot on each side of my head, and then had sat back, right on my face, while eating. When I pushed him, he had torn through the tent wall to get away, but not before one of his back feet stomped on my gut. I was lucky that when he launched himself to get away, he didn't claw my face off. I must have been protected by my sleeping bag.

We hung the remaining fish in a tree outside, hoping the bear couldn't smell them there and wouldn't come back. The next day we caught another large trout and spent the rest of the day nude swimming and sunbathing before it was time to catch the train for home.

There are not many people who can say they woke up with a wild bear sitting on their face—and survived.

Hughie and Marriage

With construction of the Hope–Princeton road finished, and things settling down around town, Hughie was now living alone on the farm.

He was also going around with the prettiest girl in town, and things were getting serious.

He phoned me one day and, in his usual style, without any preamble, said, "How would you like to be my best man?"

Knowing Hughie as a real ladies man, I had to take a poke at him, so after a ten-second pause I said, "I hope it's Ruby."

Pretending to be offended that I might imagine there had been any others, he came back with "Certainly it's Ruby. Who else could it be?"

I left that alone.

They had a lovely wedding with a reception at the in-laws, and they took off in my newly acquired 1941 Pontiac for their honeymoon. I can just imagine the job poor Ruby had when they came home, straightening out the mess at the farmhouse.

Shellac Mystery

Around the time Hughie was married, Louis got the contract to paint the new Highways Department camp halfway between Princeton and Hope. We had five painters to paint the inside and outside of the forty-eight-room Highways camp, including the large garage. I was put in charge of the paint shop and supplies.

Government regulations required that all plaster surfaces had to be first sealed with shellac. With forty-eight rooms to coat, this required at least forty-eight gallons of shellac, which I carefully monitored. But halfway through the job I noticed that shellac seemed to be disappearing at a higher rate than the rooms were being sealed, and that it was vanishing overnight. I decided to investigate.

The next morning I got up at 1 a.m. and saw a light under the door of the paint shop. I opened the door to find Martin Gill and Fred Brown, two old more experienced painters from our crew, sitting there drinking alcohol. They shamefacedly explained what they had been doing.

Shellac is made up of one-third shellac bugs, which produce the shellac resin, and two-thirds methyl hydrate, which is industrial-strength alcohol. Martin and Fred, who were old drunks, had been siphoning off small amounts of alcohol and hiding it in a glass jug. Over a period of time, the bugs and resin settled to the bottom of the jug, leaving clear methyl hydrate on top. Martin and Fred would then pour the clear alcohol off the top into a hollowed-out loaf of bread to filter any remaining shellac from the liquid and, voilà, out the bottom of the loaf came the pure alcohol they were happily drinking.

Louis gave them a firm talking-to and let them continue working, but they took no more shellac. I learned later that too much of that stuff can make you go blind.

Master Storytellers

We had very basic facilities at the construction camp: just one large room with lousy lighting and double bunks. We had nothing to do in the evenings, so all of us would all sit on our bunks and tell stories and jokes.

After three snowbound months telling stories to fifty grown men every night, we all recognized some champions. One was Louis, my boss, and the other was Paddy, a big, red-haired Irishman. Both Louis and Paddy would tell three or more stories and jokes each night, and in the three months neither had ever repeated themselves. They had it down to an art: the attention-getting cadence, the dramatic pauses, the variance of volume and the imitation of accents.

Other men contributed to round out the evening, and Martin Gill, a tall scarecrow of a man (our shellaced painter), was one of them. One night I was the straight man for Martin and asked him how he got the two scars on the front of his neck and another two at the back.

He explained, "Well, I'll tell you. A long time ago, I got to know a married lady who lived in a floathouse. I visited her when her husband was on night shift in the pulp mill. One night he came home early and caught us. I snuck out the window and headed straight up the floating gangway to safety. I heard a rifle shot behind me and felt a bullet go into the back of my neck and come out the front. I was so scared, I put on a burst of speed, and that was when I caught up to that bullet.

It went back in the front of my neck and then came out the back. And that's the truth, so help me God, how I got the four holes in my neck."

I Don't Owe You Squat

Louis's two major painting contracts were coming to an end, and he decided to lay off all of his crew but me, as I was still working through my apprenticeship. He asked me to take half of my wages up front and promised that when he got paid for the contracts, he would give me the rest.

Six months later the large contracts were finished and he laid me off. But he didn't pay me the final half of my wages. He owed me $2,150, which in those days was a lot of money—equivalent to well over $20,000 today.

Hughie felt we should pay him a visit and try to work this out, so with a lot of trepidation on my part, we took my time books and payment records and went to his house. After Hughie explained the situation, Louis looked me square in the face and said, "I don't owe you one red cent. Now get off my property." All of this was a big shock to me, as I thought that Louis was a good friend, and I had trusted him.

I hired a lawyer out of Penticton and took Louis to court. However, it turned out that my lawyer, Louis, his lawyer and the judge were all Masons. Before the trial started, and in front of everyone, my lawyer, Louis and the judge talked together like brothers about a meeting they had been at the previous night. We went through the whole court charade. By tone of voice and insinuation, I was made out to be the bad guy, and Louis the good. The final result: I was awarded a lousy token $250, and it took me two years and another, non-Masonic, lawyer before I could collect even that money, most of which went to cover my $200 in lawyer fees and lost wages.

I learned two things out of this experience: when money enters a friendship, friendship goes out of the window; and when a boss owes you money, he pays as you do the work.

Later, I also learned that Louis had not registered me as an apprentice, so my time working for him had not contributed to my obtaining tradesman papers. Fortunately, many years later, through the painters union, I wrote a test and was "grandfathered" in as a journeyman painter.

Confessions of a Milkman

With no painting work, I took a job for the winter delivering milk for the main distributor in Princeton. The work was hard, with long hours and low pay, but full of interesting challenges.

I had one particular sadistic female customer. I'd put her order on her porch, pick up the empty bottle and head to the gate when, *ouch*, her small collie dog would appear from nowhere and nip me on my right ankle.

After two bites I grew suspicious, wondering where the dog came from and why it bit me at exactly the same place every day. The next time, I spun around just before I got back to the gate. There she was, opening the door, letting the dog out. Caught in the act, she slammed the door shut.

I reported this to the manager, who phoned and told her if she didn't keep her dog inside, we would have to suspend delivery. Everything went fine for a week, and then, *wham*! I was nipped again. That got me thinking—two can play this game.

The next day I switched hands and, just as the dog was ready to nip me, I brought the empty milk bottle down full force on his head, knocking him out cold.

I turned around and there was my customer, looking out from behind the living room drapes. I smiled and waved at her. No more trouble from her or her dog.

I also had one seductive female customer, a long-limbed, middle-aged blonde who was married to a local businessman. At least twice each week she would "forget" to put out her empty bottle, and I would have to knock on the door. Within seconds she would open the door, standing there in a sheer negligee and a carelessly open dressing gown. A blind man could spot the invitation, but . . . a married woman in a small town? No way, Jose. After a month of these shenanigans she gave up. From then on, the empty bottle was always outside when I came to the door.

After a few months delivering milk, I applied for a good steady job working in the Copper Mountain mine as a sample punk. A sample punk goes underground to all the working sites in the mine to collect samples of ore, which he brings back to the assay office for analysis. The sample punk then plots the results of the analysis on a chart. Thanks to my education, I got the job and was due to start in two weeks.

When I gave notice to Johnny, the manager of the milk delivery company, he asked me to train a replacement. I agreed, and two days later I started training the new man he had hired.

At the end of the two weeks, I went to see Johnny to collect my wages. His response: "What do you mean, two weeks' wages? I'm not paying two men to do one man's job."

Big mistake! Johnny was taller and much heavier than me, but I hit him so hard he slumped to the floor.

I waited for him to get up and said, "Do you want more, or are you going to give me my wages?"

He sat down and, shaking a bit, wrote me my cheque. Six months later, Johnny was caught embezzling the company's money and sentenced to two years in jail.

Jail for the Winter

Billy Scales, a local logger, loved life and fast living. He'd work between binges, and he partied all spring, summer and fall, but when winter came he'd be broke, with not enough employment stamps to get benefits. Somewhere in his addled brain, a strategy emerged—find a crime he could commit that would be just serious enough to send him to jail for the winter. Then he would have a warm bed and three meals every day until spring.

On December 1, at ten in the morning, Billy got drunk with the last of his money, picked up a large brick, went to the middle of the main street and threw the brick through the big window of Black's jewellery store, one of the largest windows in town. Billy then stood in the street, pretending to be drunker than he was, as a crowd gathered.

Mr. Black, a thin, nervous man who was considerate of everyone, lived with his family in the back of the building, behind the jewellery store. He heard the crash and phoned the local member of the Provincial Police. Billy was soon handcuffed, arrested, jailed, sentenced to three months and shipped off to Oakalla, the provincial jail. Everything worked as planned, and Billy spent the cold months of winter in the crowbar hotel, nice and warm with free meals.

He came out in the spring, was hired back for one of his many logging jobs, and the cycle started all over again: payday, partying and broke in the fall. So the next year, on December 1 at 10 a.m., he smashed Black's window and went off to jail for the winter once more.

By now, Mr. Black's insurance had gone up, and he had noticed the date pattern, so the next fall, when he met a sober Billy on the street, Mr. Black asked him, "You're not going to throw another brick through my window on December 1 this year, are you?"

Billy said, "Why, no, of course not," with a smile on his face. But a few local citizens overheard the conversation, and word spread quickly that Billy was going to do it again.

As December 1 approached, all the busybodies in town were chatting Billy up, anxious to be the first to find out if he really was planning to break the window again. Their attention made Billy believe, in his befuddled mind, that he had become a celebrity, since people who, in earlier years, had avoided him like the plague were now talking to him.

Mr. Black grew more nervous and worried about all the extra expense, and he unintentionally stirred things up further by going to the local lawyer for advice. He found out that the police couldn't charge Billy until he actually smashed the window. Mr. Black then asked the one local police officer, Joe Blair, if he could be on hand on December 1 at 10 a.m. to prevent Billy from smashing his window. Joe agreed to be on hand but said he couldn't do anything until Billy actually threw the brick.

All of this got the rumour mill grinding harder and faster. "Nobody within the law can stop Billy from smashing Black's window," some of the busybodies tut-tutted, while others exclaimed, "Then what the hell is the law or lawyers for?"

Finally the great day arrived, and a crowd started gathering in the street before nine in the morning. By ten, the atmosphere was reminiscent of an old-fashioned hanging, where everybody is having fun but the hangee—in this case, poor Mr. Black. Billy was in the Tulameen Hotel beer parlour with a group of hell raisers who were treating him like a hero, egging him on to smash the window again.

Just before ten they spilled out of the beer parlour and headed two blocks up the street to the jewellery store, all of them swaggering, with fists clenched. Some of the local citizens backed away; they didn't want any part of this. Mr. Black was standing in front of his store. Constable Joe Blair was now on site, standing off to one side.

Billy, puffed up by his notoriety, had a brick in his hand. Without any preliminaries, he pitched it through the glass—even though Mr. Black was standing nearly in front of the window.

The constable walked over, cuffed Billy, told the crowd to disperse and took Billy to jail. When it came to trial, the judge, due to the danger and the proximity of Black to the window, nailed Billy with two years in the federal penitentiary for endangerment of human life. Black's problem was solved.

* * *

Unfortunately, those last five paragraphs are totally fictitious. I had left town by December 1 and never did find out what "the final solution" was. But I think it's a nice ending.

Life in a Mining Camp

Working in the mine as a sample punk was a great job. I was on a steady day shift and only spent about four hours underground; the rest of the time I worked in the assay office. Even the time underground was good, especially in the winter. When the outside temperature is thirty-five below, it's a nice constant sixty-five degrees underground, with no wind, rain or snow. And the characters I met in the mine were second to none.

Silent Scotty

On my first day in camp, Bill Richmond, the Head Bull Cook and Company Cop, said, "You're in Bunkhouse Number Three, room 208, and your roommate is Silent Scotty. Scotty can talk, but he just doesn't want to. You'll get along fine."

Silent Scotty was a short, portly middle-aged man. I explained that I was his new roommate, and he gestured to my bed and locker. I put my things away, and he pulled out a bottle of Scotch whiskey and two small glasses. He silently filled both, handed me one and signalled a toast. Whenever I spoke to him, he would respond with a movement of his head indicating yea, nay or okay.

After asking Scotty's permission, I set up my portable electric record player for seven-inch 45 RPM records. These players were all the rage, but Scotty looked as if he had never seen one before, and he stood watching, fascinated. Two weeks later, he came back from town with two records featuring bagpipes and Scottish folk songs. I helped him put them on the record player, and from then on he used it more than I did.

Scotty had one other weird, unsettling habit. He would sit staring at the far wall for the longest time, then tip his chair back really far on two legs, start grinning, then slowly open his arms wide and throw back his head. Then he would slowly fold his arms back over his gut, return his chair to its four legs and resume staring at the wall until he started the whole process again. The first time this happened I was alarmed, but after a while I got used to it and figured I had the perfect quiet roommate.

Ivan's Drift

Most of my sampling was done in a slushier drift, a 250-foot-long tunnel located directly under an ore body and above the ore trains. Ore

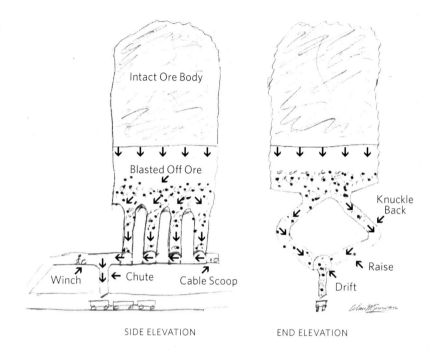

Intact Ore Body

Blasted Off Ore

↓ ↓ ↓ ↓ ↓

Winch ← Chute Cable Scoop

SIDE ELEVATION

Knuckle Back

↖ Raise

Drift

END ELEVATION

The operation of a mine slushier drift.

was blasted off the bottom of the ore body (stope) and fell down into the slushier drift in chunks, which were pulled to a grizzly chute and then down into ore cars below.

The slushier drift operator has a lonely, dangerous job. He works in the dark, with no lights other than his headlight. His job is to break up the large rocks that are too big to go down through the grizzly chute to the train. To break the rocks, he peels the wax paper off one, two or three sticks of dynamite, then shapes the explosive into what is called a pancake. He places the pancake on the rock where he thinks the grain is just right to split the rock, inserts a cap and fuse, lights it and goes behind a timber wall to await the explosion. At this point, he is also supposed to sound a whistle to warn anybody nearby that there is going to be an explosion.

My job was to go down the drift and randomly pick up small chunks of ore for analysis. All of the slushier drift operators I collected samples from were a bit odd. The strangest of all was Ivan, an operator from Russia, who would never use a whistle when blasting, wouldn't answer if you yelled you were coming through the drift, and wouldn't tell you he had lit up any charges. Only after the blast would he yell out in a deep voice, "Coompts the Reevolution!" which would echo up and down the tunnels. I don't know if his elevator went to the top floor.

To get to Ivan's drift from another drift, I crawled through a "coyote hole," a four foot by four foot shortcut that opened into the back end of his drift. One day I came through the coyote hole and yelled that I was there, but, as usual, Ivan didn't answer. I was halfway down the drift to the grizzly chute when I saw smoke coming from a large rock: a big lighted pancake!

I immediately turned around and ran back down the drift, passing two more smoking rocks that I hadn't noticed the first time. I leaped up into the coyote hole just as the closest one let go.

Ivan thought it was a huge joke, and when I told the shift foreman that Ivan hadn't blown the whistle, he blamed me for going through the shortcut. So much for safety.

Greasy Mike

After I had been working a week, I went into the mess hall for a late Sunday breakfast. A middle-aged man was sitting alone at a table, and I decided to join him. He didn't acknowledge me when I sat down but just stared at his meal, a large bowl filled with every form of breakfast food—oatmeal, bacon, eggs and corn flakes—all mixed together. It was disgusting.

He proceeded to eat the whole mess with his mouth open, shovelling food in with great gusto and washing it down with great gobs of coffee. He made such a mess that the table all around us was soon covered with bits of food.

I finished my own breakfast quickly. As I was leaving, the flunky grinned at me and said, "Congratulations, you are the first person in a year to sit down for a meal with Greasy Mike."

Prisoners of War

The company had hired twelve former prisoners of war, highly educated members of a German submarine crew, to work in the mine. This was the fall of 1951. Apparently this group had fallen through the cracks and hadn't been released until now. They had only been over from Europe for a few weeks, and none of them could speak much English. They stuck together and showed a certain joie de vivre as well as a great sense of humour.

One night we had a talent show in the community hall, and one of the Germans volunteered to play a classical piece on the piano. He played like a professional and got an enthusiastic round of applause. The Germans then began to pressure Fritz, another of their group, to perform. In spite of his protests, they carried him up onto the stage, chanting, "Sing, Sing, Sing." We all joined in. Relenting, Fritz turned serious and surprised everybody by singing a stunning German aria. The community had never heard a classical singer like this before, and he brought down the house.

Fritz was always pulling stunts, and one day he went too far. On a Sunday morning, when the mess hall was full, he stomped in and stopped in the doorway wearing the full dress uniform of a German submarine captain, complete with purple-lined cape, medals, and high leather boots. He then clicked his heels together and gave the German salute. "Sieg Heil!"

All talk stopped. There were over fifty war veterans in the room, and after a long, deadly silence they rose up as one with a roar, all heading for poor Fritz. He turned and ran out the door and down the road out of camp, his fancy cape and high boots flying in all directions.

They didn't catch him, and when he crept back into camp later, he was warned to keep his so-called jokes to himself.

The Chinese Flunky

After I had been in camp for a few months, I was awakened at 5 a.m.

by a violent banging on the wall right beside my bed. I was alone in the room as Silent Scotty was working the graveyard shift. The wall was actually shaking, so I pounded back with my fist and yelled, "Shut up in there."

The banging slowly stopped, and I went back to sleep.

My next-door neighbour was a tall, quiet Chinese man who worked as one of the cook's flunkies. He had a room to himself and kept to himself, so the noise was highly unusual.

When I got up to go to work, I looked at my neighbour's door. It was still intact, but I was shocked to see the flunky's twisted, bloated face staring at me through the glass of the transom window, above the door. He had some binder twine around his neck, fastened to the window latch, and he had obviously committed suicide.

The Head Bull Cook later told me that he had played poker with the man a day or two earlier, and he had been very depressed because the doctor had told him he had stomach cancer.

I felt kind of weird. There was this poor guy strangling to death, kicking and banging against the wall, and I was on the other side, pounding and yelling at him, telling him to shut up.

Another Camp Bully

We had a bully in camp, a tall, rangy miner named Arnie, who enjoyed beating the living daylights out of people, especially smaller guys. One day, as the sample punks and surveyors were all going down into the mine in the cage, somebody said, "Something should be done about Arnie beating up all these little guys."

Our cage tender, Tony the Greek, had been a professional wrestler and said that if we could give him fifty dollars, he could arrange to have Arnie worked over by a group of professional wrestlers that were coming up to the community hall the next week.

We easily collected the fifty dollars, and Tony told us to make sure we brought Arnie to the match. He said that we needed to encourage him to get into the ring for a round with a wrestler called the Avenger.

We all went to the match, including Arnie and his entourage. The preliminary wrestling match got everybody primed, and then the manager stepped into the ring and asked for volunteers. He said they would give one hundred dollars to any man who managed to stay three minutes in the ring with the Avenger.

We all started chanting "Arnie, Arnie, Arnie," and quickly the whole crowd picked it up. You could see Arnie was a little doubtful, but he put on a good front, took off his jacket and flexed his muscles.

The Avenger leaned over the top rope to give Arnie a hand into the ring, then yanked him clear over the top rope to land smack on his back in the middle of the ring, knocking the wind out of him.

The manager went through his usual introductions, and the fight was on. Arnie was flipped, flopped and twisted all over the ring for one minute. Then the Avenger pinned him to the mat and it was over.

Arnie was not at work the next day; I guess he was a very sore miner. Word eventually got back to him describing how he had been suckered, and after that he was a reasonably good boy.

Caught Cheating

Late one night my friend Eddie showed up at my door, carrying his suitcase and his .22 rifle. He told me that the "Bank of China" had caught him cheating at cards and had taken all his money.

The Bank of China was an old Chinese man who worked as a cook in the mess hall. He was also a ruthless "ten percent" loan shark and ran the poker games in the back of the pool hall with an iron hand. His men harshly punished anyone who didn't pay up or who cheated at cards, so Eddie had a big problem. He had managed to escape through the toilet window before they could beat him up for cheating. Now he needed money to get out of camp fast.

I could only give Eddie twenty bucks, as it was two days before payday, but he said that was enough. He gave me the .22 rifle and asked if I could keep the suitcase until he was able to send for it. I reluctantly agreed, and Eddie slipped out of camp on foot in the dark.

I dragged that suitcase all over for the next twenty years—back to Princeton, over to Penticton, then to Castlegar and finally way up to Kitimat. Still no word from Eddie. I put it in my attic, and years later, when I moved to Terrace, where I still live, I finally threw it out.

Where are you, Eddie? Your suitcase and everything in it are now long gone.

One-Gun Blackie

One evening my friend Pete came to visit, accompanied by Blackie, a short, dark little fellow I had never met before. They wanted to borrow my shotgun for a skeet shoot.

I opened my clothes closet and took out the shotgun from my collection, which also included two rifles and a .32 Belgian automatic pistol. When I turned around with the shotgun, Blackie's eyes were bugged out, staring at my guns. I didn't give it too much thought, because a lot of people I knew had guns.

The next night at 2 a.m., Bill Richmond, the Company Cop, knocked on my door. Bill was an ex-Mountie and one of the fairest men you could ever meet. He settled camp problems discreetly and efficiently without involving the Provincial Police. On this occasion, he came into my room and thrust my pistol at me, advising me to get a lock for my closet. When I asked him where he had found the pistol, he said it was a long story and sat down on my bed.

Apparently Blackie, who it turned out was an ex-con, had gotten drunk, found a key to my room, taken my pistol, along with its holster and shells, and went down into the mine. Shouting and waving the pistol, he staggered through the lunchroom, car maintenance shop and electrical shop, scaring the bejesus out of everyone. Fortunately, even though Blackie had my box of shells in his pocket, he didn't or couldn't load the pistol, so no one got hurt.

Management fired Blackie over the incident, but two months later he was rehired. The miner he had worked with wanted him back—apparently he was very good at his job as a nipper.

Some Mighty Weird Hitchhikers

While I was working at the Copper Mountain mine and staying in the camp, I spent many weekends driving the eighty-eight miles to Penticton to see various girlfriends. On the way, I usually picked up hitchhikers. Having been a hitchhiker myself, I had a soft spot for fellows with their thumbs out. Besides, they made the trip more interesting. But two hitchhiker incidents were more than interesting.

The first was a slim, red-haired young man, neatly dressed in a suit and tie. After I picked him up, we went along for a few miles, but he didn't say a word. To me, this was against the Hitchhikers Creed. Drivers who pick up hitchhikers are lonely or want somebody to talk to in order to keep them awake. A good hitchhiker will entertain the driver. Chatting it up as a hitchhiker, I have received many kindnesses from grateful drivers, including free meals, accommodation and even an offer to be adopted by an older couple who owned a shipyard in Seattle.

To break the silence, I asked him where he was going. He said, "Penticton" before clamming up again.

I thought to myself, *Either you talk or I stop, and out you go.* So I asked him why he wanted to go to Penticton.

He replied, "I don't want to talk about it."

Now I had my dander up and told him, "Either you talk or you walk. Now suit yourself."

After a couple of tense minutes he blurted out, "I have a girlfriend there, and she's been cheating on me." He started crying, and the whole story came out.

For two years, for reasons he didn't disclose, he had been locked up in Essondale, the insane asylum in Vancouver. When he heard about his girlfriend, he broke out so he could go and see her. I commiserated with him and asked how he was going to handle the situation when he saw his girlfriend.

He said, excitedly, "I'm going to kill her."

Not surprisingly, our chitchat for the next few miles was strained. I was trying to figure out what to do next. My passenger told me he

Alan with 1941 Pontiac Silver Streak, 1951.

didn't have any money, that he hadn't eaten for over a day and that he'd been sleeping in the bush, so I offered to treat him to lunch when we stopped in Keremeos. When we got to the restaurant, he didn't want to get out of the car. I guess he was scared of being seen or caught, but I definitely wasn't letting him stay in my car alone, and I told him so. He reluctantly crawled out and walked up the street with me, looking wildly in all directions.

In the restaurant he settled down a bit, and when our lunch came he tore into it like he was starved. I ended up giving him half of mine and then excused myself to go to the can. I snuck out, jumped in my car and took off for the local police station. Luckily the one policeman in town was on duty and had been on the lookout for the escapee. I told him where to find him and then left for Penticton and a weekend of uninterrupted frivolity.

Another time, I came down from camp and stopped at the nearest gas station. Two men approached me while I was fuelling up and asked if I was heading south to Penticton. They were both dressed in rumpled black suits and looked like they had slept in their clothes. No packsacks or suitcases.

A bit intimidated, I said yes.

One got in the front with me and the other got in the back seat, and away we went. They told me they were from Chicago and had driven up to Vancouver to look around. One said their car had broken down; the other said they ran out of money. When I asked what had happened to their suitcases, the man in front said they had lost them, but at the same time the fellow in the back seat said that they forgot them.

I asked where they were ultimately going, and there was confusion again as they both started to say different things. Something definitely wasn't kosher here.

They finally both agreed that they desperately wanted to get back to the United States. I told them I could let them off at Keremeos, as the U.S. border and the Nighthawk customs office was just a few miles east of there.

The man in front then dropped the bombshell. "We can't go through customs." When I asked why not, the guy in the back seat said, "Because when we ran out of money we tried to rob a bank."

I was now getting into deep water. Having worked in logging, construction and mining camps, I was used to being around ex-cons. But I realized that these men might also be carrying weapons. Pressing for details, I asked, "What do you mean, you 'tried' to rob a bank?"

They both started stammering and, slowly, out came the whole stupid story. Apparently when they ran out of money, they spotted this bank in Vancouver and impulsively pulled up right in front of it. They got out of their car, walked in without looking around and demanded money from a teller. It was only then that they noticed two policemen doing their banking on the other side of the room. Panicked, they ran out of the bank and down the street—leaving their car and belongings behind. No one came after them, so they sneaked back hours later, but their car had been towed away. Where, they were scared to ask.

I now realized these two were pretty stupid and that I could probably find a way to get rid of them before they got any bright ideas about taking my car or my money. They didn't want to stop in any towns for fear they would be recognized, so I pulled over beside a farmhouse, got out my map and showed them a route where I convinced them they could walk across the border at night without being bothered. After a few minutes of suspicion, they agreed to this plan.

I drove them to a spot half a mile from the border and let them out, advising them to stay in the bush until nightfall, when the little customs office was closed, and only then walk into the United States through the bush. After that, I turned the car around with a big sigh of relief, feeling very lucky to be rid of them.

Looking back now, I realize I wasn't too smart either. We were in the middle of nowhere, and they could easily have killed me and taken my car—but obviously that thought didn't occur to them at the time.

How to Bamboozle the Public

We had a long weekend coming up, and I wanted to see my old girl-friend Nancy, the daughter of my boss at the furniture-moving company in Vancouver, 175 miles away. For some reason, even with all the women available locally, my thoughts kept returning to Nancy. Our parting had been my fault. She was away on a two-month holiday when I graduated from Vancouver Technical School, and I needed a date for the graduation festivities. So I invited one of the girls who was graduating to be my date. To make a long story short, when Nancy got back, somehow she found out about this and wouldn't forgive me. However, three years had passed now, so I tracked her down and we agreed to meet at her parents' house in West Vancouver.

When I knew I was going to Vancouver, I put a notice on the bulletin board by the mess hall in the mining camp, asking if there were any fellows wanting to go to the Lower Mainland who would share the cost. Two middle-aged miners, Bill and Fred, asked to come along. They were the guys earning the big money on contract in the mine, so I was happy to split the bills with them.

Bill and Fred didn't talk much on the long drive, but I did learn that they were both bachelors. When we got to Vancouver, I dropped them off with their luggage at a three-storey house downtown. Fred asked me in for a drink, and I locked the car and followed them inside.

A woman Fred introduced as Chanel brought us drinks. Next thing I knew, there were five more women in the room, greeting Bill and Fred like long-lost friends. Well, what do you know—we were in a house of ill repute! And Bill and Fred were going to stay there for the weekend.

I was introduced to everyone, and if you didn't know any better, you would think it was a family reunion. Fred was talking to one woman about her kids, and Bill was off in the corner in serious conversation with another woman.

I was making small talk with Chanel until the phone rang. When she came back from answering it, she was dead serious. She told the women to go to their rooms and politely asked us to take our drinks and go sit out in my car for about thirty minutes. It seemed the house was going to be raided and the police were kind enough to let her know in advance.

In the car, I turned on the radio, and we nursed our drinks. I asked Fred, "How come the police let her know they were going to raid her?"

Fred explained, "Chanel pays to be notified."

After about ten minutes, six scruffy old rubby-dub guys came wandering down the street and, to my surprise, went up to Chanel's house. She greeted these bums at the door, and through the living room windows I could see her pouring large drinks for them and handing them each some money.

After a few minutes we heard sirens. Then police cars surrounded the house, and a bun wagon pulled up to the curb. Six policemen went right past my car, up the steps and into the house. A *Vancouver Sun* newspaper van also pulled up, and a reporter jumped out with a flash camera.

After a few more minutes, down the steps came the six bums, now handcuffed. They happily stopped on the steps, and as they were loaded into the bun wagon, to have their pictures taken by the reporter. Then they were driven off to the local jail.

Chanel watched out the window until all the looky-loos on the sidewalk had left and then came out and signalled us to come back in. I was now running late and needed to get to my friend Doug's place, where I was spending the weekend, so I gave my glass to Fred, asked him to thank Chanel for the drink and took off.

The next morning at Doug's place, the whole family was sitting around the large breakfast table, catching up, when Doug's grandfather brought in the morning Sun newspaper. On the front page was a big picture of the six bums climbing into the bun wagon, with the caption "Patrons of Brothel Arrested."

Doug's mother said, "Well, it's about time they arrested some of these awful men. Chief Mulligan is doing such a wonderful job." I kept my mouth shut about the truth behind the *Sun* photo because Doug's family wouldn't have believed me anyway. But Walter Mulligan, the chief of police, was run out of town for corruption a few years later.

I spent the day with Nancy over at her parents' place. She had matured and so had I, and we agreed to write to each other. Sadly, nothing ever came of it, and over the years I regretted losing touch with her.

On Sunday afternoon I picked up Bill and Fred from Chanel's for the trip home. They told me that the bums each got twenty dollars from Chanel for their "work." They had a warm night in jail and a good meal, and were released the next day. They also didn't get fined, as even the police realized you can't get blood from a stone.

Back in Princeton, I dropped in at the Snack Bar to see Mum and Pat. Mum told me that Pat had become engaged to a good-looking young fellow, Curt Vesper, who had moved to nearby Hedley. His family was mainly in the trucking business. A few months later they had a big wedding in town, with everyone from both families attending. Even Mum and Hughie got along. I borrowed a friend's new yellow convertible and drove the bride and groom around. After the honeymoon, they went to live with Curt's family—and later I got to know the Vespers quite well as I continued to search for my place in the world.

PART FIVE

Finding My Future

Buried Alive

In my job as a sample punk, I took samples of ore once a week from every site that was producing ore in the copper mine. Some ore bodies are very rich in copper, and some are very low. The samples I collected helped the mine managers balance the overall concentration of copper coming out of the mine at a constant two percent. If the overall ore concentration was too high, copper overflowed into the tailings pond and was lost; if it was too low, the company lost money.

If you ever get the chance to go deep underground, at least a thousand feet, do so, as it is an impressive experience. Once I had to do some sampling in a very remote area that was two thousand feet below ground. Just for the experience, I sat down on the side of the drift, leaned against the wall and turned off my headlamp. I sat there for over half an hour. The first impression was the absolute darkness. I couldn't have seen a piece of white paper in front of my eyes. I couldn't see my hand moving in front of my face. I could not see any form of movement. It was absolutely black.

At first, it was also utterly silent. But soon I started to hear the earth moving—a tiny tick here or a crick there. The earth is not solid; it is composed of large sections that are constantly moving, ever so slightly. If you walk down a drift and look for fault lines or fractures between these sections, you'll find one every few hundred feet. If you touch the fault, your finger will come away with finely powdered rock, ground down by thousands of years of pressure and tiny movement.

One day, the boss told me to take my partner, Hank, and sample a raise being drilled from six level up to a drift on five level. (A raise is a forty-five-degree shaft that is blasted out from a lower level upward, to gain access to the upper level.) The boss mentioned that the miners had nearly broken through to the drift above, so we should be careful as it might be unstable.

To get near the rock face, we needed to go along six level drift, then up the four-hundred-foot raise being blasted out. Near the bottom end of this raise was a long, gradual curve up to the left, which meant we couldn't see where the miners were working up on the face until we were well around the curve and committed to climbing the raise. We yelled as we went up, but everything was deadly quiet. Usually you could hear the miners drilling. We cautiously climbed around the curve and still there was nothing—no noise, no signs of life; there weren't even air hoses going up to the rock face for the drills. This was all very strange, but we decided that the miners must have left for the day, so we proceeded to climb up the ropes dangling from the sides of the raise.

We got about two hundred feet up when we suddenly heard rocks rattling down toward us. We both dived for a foxhole—a two-foot by eight-foot depression in the side of a raise that has a twelve-inch plank as a protective fence. Foxholes are put in the side of a raise every hundred feet to store the heavy drilling equipment between blasts. Hank dove in behind the plank first. I landed on top of him, partially hanging out of the foxhole.

The rocks, some the size of footballs, came ricocheting down from several hundred feet above us, hitting all four sides of the raise and crashing down past us at a tremendous speed. Whenever there was a lull, we prepared to head down out of the raise, but then another avalanche of rock would come barrelling by. I was hit on the shoulder by a small rock, but luckily it didn't break anything.

This was a very unusual situation and had us baffled. Normally if a miner is cleaning up rock that wasn't broken by a blast by pushing it down the raise, he will be on a platform where he can see down the raise, or where we would be able to see him. We screamed and shone our lights up the raise, but there was no response and no one in sight. We couldn't figure out what was going on or what we could do about it.

Hank was a big, strapping, happy-go-lucky man who lived life to the full, drinking and fighting, but after an hour or so of this he started to cry and panic. Getting desperate myself, I started to pray, and a wonderful thing happened. I felt a gentle hand on my shoulder, and a soothing voice said clearly, "Don't panic, Alan; you will get through this." It had a great comforting effect on me, and I was able, in turn, to calm Hank down.

We continued to shout and flash our lights up the raise at regular intervals. After we had been trapped for almost two hours, I saw a flickering light far up above us. I turned on my light and shone it back up the raise. After a terrifying minute, the other light shone directly at us. Saved! Thank God.

The rocks stopped falling and we climbed out of the foxhole and up the 250 feet to the top of the raise. There we found the miner, Emerald Ortwine, and his helper looking at us through a small three-foot opening, which we climbed through onto the five level drift.

Emerald said, "When I looked down that raise and saw your light, I couldn't believe anybody could have survived all that rock we dumped."

Emerald was part of the crew that our boss had warned us about. He had been working on the face of the raise, and the night before had actually blasted a small hole through to the upper drift. When he returned in the morning, he found a lot of loose rock had fallen forward into the five level drift around the hole and left a real mess. He and his helper had cleaned up the bottom of the raise, then climbed to the top and crawled through the breakthrough hole. They were working in the upper drift, picking up the loose rock and throwing it through the hole and down onto us. They hadn't heard us screaming because a large, noisy ventilation fan was running in the drift right next to where they were working. Just before they spotted my light, they had been setting up dynamite around the breakthrough hole to blast a bigger opening. If Emerald hadn't seen our light, we would have been chewed to hamburger when they let off their charges.

By the time Hank and I got back up to the surface and went to the locker room, everyone had heard about our near disaster, and a bunch of men were standing around asking questions. I started getting out of my mining clothes and boots, but then I stopped, thought about it for a minute and put them on again. I knew if I didn't go back down into the mine right away, I would never be able to go underground again. The boss wanted to see me to ask about the accident, but he would have to wait.

I went down in the cage to the main six level drift in the mine. The main drift was very big and had lots of lights and ventilation, so it felt good, not claustrophobic; it was nearly like walking on a downtown city street at night. I walked around for an hour and then came up in the cage for supper.

For the next two weeks I had nightmares, and so did Hank. He was also worried that I would say something about him crying, but I reassured him that I would never do that.

My Education in Mining

I was eventually promoted to the position of surveyor's helper for the mining company, which turned out to be very interesting and challenging work re-calculating the surveyors' configurations. I was fascinated by a surveyor's ability to plot a 450-foot raise through twists and turns in solid rock and come out smack bang on target. As part of this job I went on many field trips, helping surveyors, staking claims and gathering all forms of mineral samples as well as doing exploration work.

The biggest trip I went on was to northern B.C. and Alaska to evaluate and stake a large deposit of copper ore. When word of the find came in from the prospector, we had no time to waste, as there was a risk of losing the claim to wildcatters. So the next day we jumped into my car and drove to Vancouver, where we had chartered a plane to Prince Rupert, the nearest city to the find. On the trip were Jack, the engineer and boss; George, the geologist; and me, the grunt who would do the grid sampling, mapping and claim staking.

When we arrived in Prince Rupert, we checked into the hotel where we were to meet Carl, the promoter. According to Jack, Carl was a millionaire who owned several mines and a helicopter fleet.

Carl wasn't in his room. None of us knew what he looked like, but I was sent out on the street to look for him. There was no one around the front of the hotel except an old bum in rough clothes and a battered felt hat. He was sitting on the curb, placidly smoking a pipe.

I asked him, "Have you seen a tall, well-dressed, middle-aged man come out of the hotel in the last few minutes?"

Without looking around he grunted, "Nope."

I ran around the block and back to the entrance. No sign of Carl. The old bum was still there and asked me if I had found the man I was looking for. I said, "No."

He slowly turned around, looked up at me and asked, "Why are you looking for this well-dressed man?"

I explained that we were going to go up north with him to look at a mining site. As I talked, I noticed that while the "bum" wore a soiled felt hat and old clothes with the pants cut off, his boots were first-class.

Carl stood up, stuck out his hand and said, "You thought I was an old bum, didn't you? Don't always judge people by their clothes, son. I'm dressed ready to go into the bush." Boy did I feel stupid.

We took off the next day in a Beaver floatplane and landed in Stewart, B.C., right smack on the Alaska border. There we met Tommy, the prospector grubstaked by Carl, who had discovered a mountain of low-grade copper ore thirty miles away, high up in the mountains.

Tommy was a quiet, middle-aged man with a sly sense of humour who had spent his life in the woods, prospecting. He and I seemed to be kindred spirits, and we got along well. The morning after we arrived, he said, "I'm going to take all of you to Concrete Mike's Café for breakfast. You'll find it interesting."

According to Tommy, Concrete Mike started the café to make a little money after he burned out on mining. "He doesn't talk, and he doesn't have a menu," Tommy said. "You just tell him what you want to eat."

The café was in a long, narrow building, sitting all by itself out in an open field. The five of us sat down at the long counter, and Concrete Mike came out of the kitchen. He was a serious-looking man, in his mid-fifties, with a powerful build. I was the closest to the kitchen, so he stopped right in front of me and just stared at me. After a long silence, Tommy said, "Alan, give him your order." ·

So I mumbled, "I'll have bacon and eggs and a cup of coffee."

Mike gave a slight nod and then stared at Carl, George, Jack and Tommy in turn. They all said they'd have the same. Without a word, Mike went back into the kitchen. I looked down the counter at Tommy, who had a twinkle in his eye and a slight grin on his face. He was enjoying his little prank.

Twenty minutes later, Mike came out with five twenty-ounce T-bone steak dinners. Tommy said, "Eat up, or you'll make Mike mad, and you don't want to do that." Even though it was just eight in the morning, we tucked into these huge dinners.

We finally finished all we could eat and got up to pay. At that moment Mike came out of the kitchen carrying five large slabs of homemade apple pie with a large slab of cheese on top. He gave us a dirty look, as if to say, *Aren't you going to eat my pie*? Like little kids being scolded, we swiftly got back on our stools and forced ourselves to eat the pie. Tommy later told us, laughing, that Concrete Mike served nothing but steak dinner and apple pie, day or night. That's all he knew how to cook.

After "breakfast" we went up to Crawford's, the only store in town. We ordered two sets of groceries—one set for our base camp and one set to be dumped by air at our "dry" camp out on the claim site. We took the one set of groceries and hired a taxi to take us to the base camp, which was at a long-abandoned mine site with a few habitable cabins ten miles out of town.

From here, we weren't going to be hiking through devil's club, or over glaciers and mountains, with one-hundred-pound packsacks. No, we were going to use one of Carl's newfangled machines, called a helicopter, to go the thirty miles to the claim site. The only problem was that the helicopter couldn't fly when the weather was bad, which was most of the time up there in the north country autumn, because Fred, the pilot, was worried the rotors of the helicopter would freeze on the way to the claim site, which was at a much higher elevation. So we were stuck for a week at the base camp, wasting time, waiting for the weather to clear. The booze ran out the first day, and the tobacco ran out the next. It was like being trapped in a cage with four bored and angry old lions, so I found an old single shot .22 rifle and some ammunition in the cabin and took off hunting every day after I'd finished my assigned chores, staying well out of their way and keeping everyone stuffed with ptarmigan.

Fred knew his job. He had been a fighter pilot for England throughout the Battle of Britain and told many harrowing tales of survival. He decided to do a short test run and casually asked if I wanted to go along, I jumped at the chance.

Fred started the engine and let it idle for quite a long time. Then we took off, nearly straight up above the camp.

We got to about two thousand feet when Fred said, "Well, here goes," and casually reached over and turned off the ignition. We dropped like a stone. But the wind generated by our fall started the blades rotating, faster and faster, and we were able to land without turning the motor on.

I was half scared and half mad, and asked Fred, "Why didn't you warn me before we took off?"

He asked, "Would you have gone with me then?" No argument.

Later, Fred told us that his little Bell helicopter was the first one ever to land in the area. He had flown it up to Stewart new from the factory in Texas and landed it on the school grounds to get gas before coming to our camp. The whole town had turned out to see it, and some kid had even managed to carve his initials in the Plexiglas cab, much to Fred's dismay.

* * *

While we were grounded, a tall, old, English gentleman prospector and his young Japanese wife came into camp and politely asked to meet with us. This was common whenever we got to a new area. Word would get around that there were mining experts in town from a large mining company, and every two-bit promoter or wannabe prospector would be knocking on our hotel room door, showing us samples of their great claim and asking us to come out and take a look. Most of these were "heartbreak showings," with no potential; others were promising but didn't have the tonnage required to establish the large mining operation needed to make it profitable.

The old gentleman explained that he had developed a very small mine nearby, and over the last twenty years he had been drilling a drift deeper into the side of the mountain, following a vein of ore, hoping to hit the mother lode. He then, with a flourish, dumped twenty-five pounds of ore on the table in front of George, the geologist.

George's eyes bugged out when he saw it. "Electrum!" he exclaimed. "The only time I've ever seen this was a small sample at university."

Electrum, he explained, is fifty percent gold and fifty percent silver. The old gentleman had been high-grading enough of the Electrum out each year to keep financing his operation, and his winters in Victoria.

We took a rainy day and went up to the little mine, and George spent an hour studying the flow of the mountain, the grain and the slope of the rock. Unfortunately, his professional opinion was that this small high-grade vein was not going to lead to a large mother lode.

When he broke the news, the old gentleman thanked him but said that he was going to continue digging deeper as long as the seam held out and continued funding his tiny operation.

Being young and direct, I asked, "Aren't you getting too old for all this nonsense?"

He said, "Son, I love the life I've led, and my greatest desire is to die on the trail."

That really shut me up. Over the years I've often wondered what happened to that old man and his little mine.

* * *

The weather finally broke, and Fred ferried us all up to Tommy's mine site, which was in a spectacular location near the top of a mountain. A glacier filled the valley below. Fred left with orders to pick us up in four days.

A bush plane had gone up nearly two weeks earlier to drop a tent, an airtight stove and groceries for us. To me, this was luxury prospecting—no slogging through bush with heavy backpacks. But then we discovered that bears had gotten into the food, and the only thing left was half a bag of flour. The bears had even smashed our cans of milk against a tree and licked the bark. And what they couldn't eat they had peed and crapped on.

Surprisingly, Tommy wasn't overly concerned. He told me to go up on the tundra above camp and write "FOOD" in three-foot letters, using toilet paper held down by rocks. He said that bush pilots flying over always kept an eye out for any party in the bush if they were in the area. Sure enough, that afternoon a plane came by and wagged its wings, and the next morning it dropped more groceries for us.

George developed a sampling grid across the site, and Tommy and I went out to collect trench samples. We put them in canvas bags and labelled them according to the grid. From our samples, we eventually determined that one-third of the side of the mountain was low-grade copper ore with gold showings, a big find.

At noon on that first day, I had returned to camp to make lunch when, looking back, I saw Tommy five hundred yards away, bent over facing the hillside, breaking rocks with his prospector's pick. Coming straight up behind him was a medium-sized black bear. I had my rifle handy, but the bear was too close to Tommy for a clear shot.

The bear, without hesitation, walked right up to Tommy and started sniffing his rear. Tommy was still oblivious, so I fired a shot into the air. Tommy looked up, turned around and saw the bear. He half-heartedly swung the pick at him, the bear backed up a few feet, and Tommy turned around and returned to breaking rocks.

The bear stood there looking confused, then slowly walked away. He probably had never seen a man before and was just curious. Tommy called them "Glacier Bears"; they lived around glaciers and ate the tubers that grew around the edges of the ice.

That night, Tommy and I went to bed in our large old tent, each of us in our sleeping bags about six feet apart. Some time later, in the pitch dark, I woke up to hear Tommy yelling at me to stop pushing him.

I replied, "Tommy, I'm away on the other side of the tent!"

I finally found my flashlight and turned it on just in time to see the rear end of a big fat black bear waddle out through the flap. I asked Tommy if I should go shoot him.

He replied, "Naw, you'll just scare those city types. Now shut up and go to sleep."

I guess that bear hadn't sniffed enough of Tommy during the day to figure out who and what he was, and had decided to come back for another try.

The next day we went out to stake our claims on the mountain of low-grade ore that Tommy had found. We were busily doing our staking when, lo and behold, we found a claim certificate in a can by a stake. The site had already been staked by somebody else. We opened up the can and took out the claim certificate. It was dated a few days earlier. I had my little Brownie camera in my packsack, so I asked Tommy to hold up the certificate so I could take a picture of the paper with the date and all the details. For some reason he was reluctant to do this, but he finally agreed and I got the picture. Tommy then folded the certificate up and put it back in the can. Too bad we were delayed nine days getting to the site by that so-called efficient new method of travel.

I had no idea how important this little episode was. When we went back to camp, Tommy took Carl aside, and he got very upset. Carl said he wished he had the helicopter there right then so he could fly out immediately and register the claims before the "wildcatter" got to the government office in Prince Rupert and registered his claims. (The first person to actually register the claims is awarded the find, not the one with the earliest date on the claim paper.)

In mining exploration, you never tell your business to anybody. This might seem paranoid, but a slip of the lip can mean big bucks. Tommy had discovered this valuable site all on his own and had told no one but Carl. All we could think was that maybe the Stewart phone operator had listened to the conversation when Tommy phoned Carl in Vancouver to tell him of his discovery. The phone operator could have told someone, who had then hiked in and wildcatted the mountain while we were stuck waiting for the helicopter to fly us in. There definitely had been a leak somewhere.

When Fred finally came back with the helicopter, we had gathered our samples and were ready to leave. Tommy suddenly asked to borrow my rifle and a box of shells, and then told Fred, "You're taking me for a little ride."

Carl overheard and protested that he needed the helicopter to get to Prince Rupert to register the claims, but Tommy said, "To hell with your precious claims. I've got something that has to be done."

He came back an hour later. When I found three shells missing from my box, I realized what he had done. Earlier, he had told me that the bears that had eaten our food would be very dangerous to lone prospectors because now they related the smell of man to food and wouldn't hesitate to kill if they were hungry. Now there were three bears that wouldn't kill a prospector or ransack his camp.

Fred then flew Carl out to Prince Rupert to register the claims. The next day Fred returned and took us back to Stewart. When we landed there, half of the close-knit little town knew something was going on.

After returning to civilization from this trip, there was an old prospector's ritual we observed: pick up a bottle (preferably rum), go to your room and take off the one set of dirty clothes you have worn for over a month. Fill the tub with hot water, get pleasantly drunk and soak for two hours to get off the grime. Then flop into a real bed and stay there for at least twelve hours.

The next morning at breakfast, Jack said, "Do you guys realize that we have been running around for over three weeks and we haven't tipped anyone yet?"

The exploration company's policy was for employees to tip five dollars a day to anybody catering to them on an exploration trip. The idea was that it would pave the way for another member of the company later on. So as we were leaving the restaurant, each of us each slipped a twenty-dollar bill under our plates.

We were just to the door when we heard crashing dishes. We turned to see our waitress with a shocked look on her face. The eighty dollars we had left would be equivalent to over $1,200 today.

That night, Carl got back from registering the claims in Prince Rupert, but he wouldn't say whether he got there before the wildcatter. After supper he took me aside and said, "If the results of our sampling work out, along with Jack's engineering feasibility study, I'm going to set up a new mining company with the shares opening at roughly twenty-seven cents. By spring, they should be up around twelve dollars. I can let you in for two thousand dollars. What do you say?"

I had seen so many shysters in the mining game by then that I immediately turned him down. I thanked him and told him that I had been saving my money for a trip to Mexico. In my innocence I didn't stop to think why I had been singled out for this generous offer. As you will see, it took a couple of years before the reason for this life-changing proposal dawned on me.

* * *

When we got back from the prospecting trip, sailing into Vancouver in the middle of the night on the old *Camosun*, we landed at Pier C and did something you would never do today: we walked the four blocks up Granville Street in downtown Vancouver with packsacks on our back, and me with a rifle over my shoulder. We walked into the Georgia Hotel, took off the packsacks, and I leaned the gun against the counter and registered. The clerk didn't bat an eye.

I drove the men back to Copper Mountain, and the next day we checked in at the mining company's head office. I walked into the office of Howard, my boss, to discuss the trip with him. Halfway through my account, Howard interrupted and asked me to show him the pictures I had taken of the claim site. Somehow he knew about the pictures, and when we came to the photo of Tommy with the claim paper, he started asking all kinds of questions. Then he asked if he could have the negatives and the photos so he could make copies for his boss. I thought nothing of it at the time and gave them to him. Two days later he handed me an envelope with my pictures and negatives in it. Without looking at them, I put the envelope away and never opened it for four long years.

Howard then sent me, post-haste, out to the middle of nowhere to do mine assessment work for three months. I worked with a ten-man team of samplers, core drillers, handymen and cooks, assessing two old abandoned mines—the Silver Cup and True Fissure—in the Kootenay Lardeau district.

Mum had gotten married while I was away in the north. The groom was Frank Mitchell or "Mitch," a tall thin taxi driver with a dry sense of humour. He was a regular customer in Mum's Snack Bar Café. I thought they were a perfect match, and over their forty-seven years together they successfully ran several small businesses. I brought Mum back a set of earrings and necklace of Alaska black diamonds as a wedding present.

Ghosts of the Silver Cup Mine

The Silver Cup mine, which had been closed since 1932, was located five thousand feet up a mountain near the tiny ghost town of Ferguson. Apparently the bunkhouse and machinery were still in good shape, as the syndicate from Boston that owned the mine had paid a local man to look after them for all these years.

On our way to Ferguson, we stopped at Beaton, a little town of two hundred people, where the only place to eat was a small hotel restaurant. When we told the hotel owner we were going up to Ferguson to check out the Silver Cup mine, he said very seriously, "That mine is haunted. You don't want to go near that place."

We laughed it off, paid our bill and carried on up the narrow, winding, twenty-mile road to Ferguson. In its prime, Ferguson had a population of over two thousand people, but now only three families still lived there, and it was just about a ghost town, with abandoned stores, hotels and bars.

The mine site was the eeriest I had ever encountered. It was five thousand feet up the side of a mountain overlooking the valley far below. The forty-man bunkhouse featured a calendar for October 1932;

there was kindling neatly stacked in a wood box beside the stove, along with newspapers from 1932. The long mess table was set for three people, and all the beds were fully made up with beautiful Hudson's Bay wool blankets. There wasn't a speck of dust anywhere. I went to check out the forge shop, and all the blacksmith tools were still lying on the forge, as if the smithy had just left; they weren't even rusty. It felt like the miners had walked out the day before, not twenty years earlier.

Everybody picked a room on the bottom floor, and Jesse, the cook, rustled around and got our supper together.

That night, sleeping in one of the beds that had been made up for twenty years, I was roused from sleep to a feeling that something was chewing my hair. Still half asleep, and lying on my back, I put a hand to my head and felt something move over my arm and down my chest.

My eyes were wide open now, and I could see a large rat sitting on my chest, staring at me, not ten inches from my face. There was a full moon, and the light pouring through the window made his little eyes glitter.

I knocked him off my chest and got up, took a flashlight and wandered around downstairs, upstairs and into the attic. The place was crawling with bloody rats!

I rang the dinner bell and told the newly awakened crew to go out to the forge shop and wait until I gave the all-clear. Then I fired up my carbide lamp and put it on my miner's helmet, loaded my .22 Remington pump-action rifle and went pit-lamping rats. When I shone the light in their beady little eyeballs, they glowed, which made for easy shooting. In the attic, where they had most of their nests, I got about ten. Then I went through each room and got another eight.

It turned out that Jesse the cook, a big six-footer, weighing 250 pounds, was scared out of his tree about rats, and from then on he treated me like the great white hunter.

The next morning we set out to enter the abandoned mine. Two locals working with us, Wolf and Charlie, had cleaned out the mine portal and braced it up so we could go in and do our Moyle sampling.

Dead rats from the bunkhouse, Silver Cup Mine, 1952.

Now they started babbling about the ghosts and said that they would do anything outside, but they wouldn't go into the mine.

I said to Glenn, my novice helper, who had never been in a mine, "Well, let's go say hello to all those ghosts!"

According to the maps, there was a main drift, five feet wide and seven feet high, which zigzagged over two thousand feet back into the mountain. Along the way there were three empty ore stopes, or caverns, the size of a five-storey building, that had been blasted out.

We lit our carbide lamps and slowly walked in. There was only about three inches of water on the ground, and the timbering in the main drift was still sound. I felt a faint draft, and the carbide lamps were flickering a little bit. This was good news. It meant there was an air vent somewhere, so there was no dead air that would eat up our oxygen. At 1,400 feet in, we encountered the first stope; it was so big it had an echo. Then we went around a corner and got to the second stope, 1,800 feet in.

As we stood there looking at the large stope, some small pebbles rolled down the slope and landed with a splash near our feet. Glen flashed his light up the slope to the far wall.

We saw two large ghostly white shapes slowly floating high up across the wall.

Glen let out an ear-splitting scream and took off, splashing up the drift, with me not too far behind him. As I ran, something big and solid pushed me from behind. I slammed into Glen, and we both fell, face forward, into the mud and water. Both our lamps were doused in the water, leaving us in total darkness.

As we tried to get up, another something ran right over top of us, pushing us back down into the mud. Totally soaked, we picked ourselves up and tried to light our carbide lamps, but the sparking mechanisms had been submerged in water. It took a while to wipe them off.

When we finally got the lamps lit, we splashed out to the portal, completely soaked and terrified. There we found Wolf and Charlie, leaning on their shovels and laughing. They asked us if we had seen the ghosts. When we confessed what had happened, they told us that two white mountain goats had come flying out of the portal just ahead of us. With that, a great twenty-year legend bit the dust. I still don't know how the goats could see in the nearly total darkness.

Axel the Foreman

Axel, foreman of the contract core-drilling team, was a grouchy old Swede who was fanatical about his coffee. He demanded the cook keep a large two-quart pot on the stove for him at all times, with instructions that a half cup of fresh grounds be added each day without disposing of the old grounds. How Axel could drink that crap was beyond me. When the pot was completely full of grounds, it was emptied and the process began again.

Over the next few weeks, I noticed Axel spending an inordinate amount of time looking at the core-drilling results. When I asked why he was doing this, he reacted as if he'd been caught with his hand in the cookie jar. Many core-drilling foremen took retainers or bonuses from big mining stock promoters in return for passing on tips about discoveries in the field. First news of a new mining strike was worth a fortune to these speculators. Axel said he would make it worth my while if I helped him out. We never did find anything decent, so fortunately it wasn't a temptation.

Living for Revenge

Over the next week I often overheard Wolf and Charlie, the locals, talking conspiratorially in whispers. I caught some pieces of the conversation—"I'll get that son of a bitch" or "You wait, I'll knock his block off." Wolf was a quiet, intense fellow, very strong and tall with wide shoulders and slim hips. Charlie was shorter, chubby, easy-going and not too smart, a natural-born follower. When I asked them what the problem was, they clammed up and said it was personal.

They asked me if I could drive them to town on Saturday night to go to the beer parlour. I had my doubts about going along with them but agreed, even though I don't drink beer, and got permission from the foreman. For the whole twenty-mile drive down the mountain and into Beaton, neither one of them said a word. They seemed all tensed up, and when we arrived they didn't wait for me but hot-footed it into the beer parlour while I was parking the jeep.

The beer parlour was a long narrow room with no tables, benches or chairs down the middle. About fifteen men sat on wooden benches with their backs against the wall and tables in front of them. Nobody faced the wall.

This was not a good sign. It meant they were preparing to fight or to dodge beer bottles thrown in a fight. I was surprised to see two middle-aged women sitting at a table at the far end of the room. In B.C. at this time, a beer parlour was supposed to have two rooms—one for men only, and one for ladies and escorts—so having a single room was unusual. Apparently the town was so small that the good, the bad and the ugly all sat together.

The atmosphere was so thick with tension that it felt like a blanket around me. People would walk in, stop in the doorway, warily look around and then quickly sit down at their special spot. There was hardly any talk or laughter, just serious drinking and looking around.

I tried to get a conversation going with Wolf, but he was spending his time glaring at a fellow against the opposite wall. Charlie was glaring at another man, but he outstared Charlie, and Charlie ended up looking down at the floor.

A small, heavyset, middle-aged French-Canadian logger wearing a red shirt with wide blue suspenders, cut-off jeans and logging boots was sitting across from us. He was the only person who seemed to be having a good time. As usual, his name was Frenchy. According to Wolf, the two husky middle-aged women sitting at the far table, wearing long dresses, were hand loggers.

Pretty soon the room was full. Everybody had had enough to drink, so now they started talking and got a little careless. One of the lady loggers stood up to go to the ladies room. As she walked by Frenchy's table, he sprang to his feet, bent down, and with both hands pulled her dress up over her shoulders. He couldn't pull it any higher because she was taller than him, so he jumped on the bench and pulled the dress over her head. He then jumped up on the table, and with one hand holding her helpless with her arms above her head inside the dress, he did a little tap dance on the table.

At this point, all hell broke loose. You'd think a boxing-ring gong had gone off. Wolf leaped up, jumped on the bench, then over the table and launched himself clear across the room, square at the man he'd been staring at. Somebody else came across at Charlie, who was sitting beside me. A man got up from the table to our left, and somebody across the room made a flying tackle at him. They both smashed into the entrance door and ended up outside, with the door and frame under them. I took cover under the table and missed the rest of the action.

The smacks and thuds went on for another two or three minutes. Then the lights went out and it was totally dark. The thuds, bangs and moans slowly faded away as nobody could see to fight.

246

Then Cliff, the bartender, said, "All right, you guys. Are you ready to stop?"

Moans and groans.

"I won't turn the lights on until you guys say you won't fight anymore."

More muted swearing and muttering, and then, "Yeah, okay, all right."

Cliff said, "What about you, Doug? Tom? Wolf?"

They mumbled, "Oh, okay."

Cliff turned the lights back on, and I got out from under the table. What a bloody shambles.

But, strangely, everyone got up off the floor and started straightening the tables and benches. Cliff ordered the guys who had knocked the door down to fix it, and two guys who, five minutes earlier, were pounding each other, went outside together and rehung the door with breakout wedges—no screws or nails—so the door and frame would come out easily next time. Pretty smart.

Two other men got up and helped Cliff serve the beer. The broken glasses and spilled beer were left and forgotten.

Then the quiet talks started up. Wolf whispering to Charlie, "Did you see me hit that big son of a bitch? I sure got him good, didn't I?"

Charlie replying, "Yeah, I just saw the first punch before Frank was on top of me."

Everyone was laughing about what Frenchy did to Nancy, and she was laughing too. And so it went for the next half hour, whispers and threats about what would happen the next Saturday night—but you could count me out.

An Unusual Mine

George the geologist and I finally took a day off from our seven-days-per-week, twelve-hour workdays, and went down the mountain to the foreman's office in Ferguson. As we were having coffee with Fred, the foreman there, an old prospector came in. Mike was a seasoned veteran at the prospecting/mining game, and he had heard that George was a geologist. He was hoping George would give his claim a free assessment.

Mike's story was incredible. He had found samples of high-grade lead zinc and silver across the scree at the foot of a glacier and had staked his claim right on top of the glacier. Staking a claim is not a casual thing. Each claim staked cost $135 per year as a maintenance fee, and a lot of prospectors had little income.

Eager to see Mike's unusual claim, we headed up there. All on his own, he had started working at the foot of the glacier and hand-chopped a raise in the ice over one hundred feet up, following the trail of little pieces of silver ore until he found a small vein of silver in the solid rock. The glacier was alive and was moving downhill at the rate of twelve inches per day. That meant every spring, when Mike wanted to develop the drift in the rock, he had to cut through another hundred feet of ice to get to the rock drift portal. Every day after that, he had to cut away another foot of ice to make sure it didn't close off his portal underneath the glacier, either while he was inside the drift or from the outside. The rock drift he had blasted out went over eighty feet into the mountain. He had been taking the high-grade ore from the small seam for the past few years and selling it to keep the claim going.

Going into the elaborate ice tunnel Mike had cut was eerie. It didn't help that the glacier was moaning and groaning around us all the time. I couldn't get out of there quick enough. How Mike had worked it all alone, I can't imagine, but prospectors are driven by the dream of a big payday.

George's rough assessment gave Mike some good news. George thought there was a better than fifty-fifty chance that deeper in the mountain there was a small ore body.

Over the next few years I occasionally wondered how Mike was doing. Did he ever get caught in his tunnel and have to dig himself out? And what would happen to the glacier when he let off the explosions that were necessary to access the main ore body? Normally a blast shakes the surrounding rock. Would it bring the glacier down on his ice tunnel? A scary thought.

True Fissure Mine

When we finished assessing the Silver Cup mine, we moved over to another old abandoned mine, the True Fissure, for more exploration work. It was located higher up, at the opposite end of the valley.

Over many years, miners working the True Fissure had dumped thousands of tons of rock down the steep slope of the mountain. This tailings dump had created a smooth surface, 250 feet wide and over 1,500 feet long, on a forty-five-degree slope, perfect conditions for an avalanche in winter. To make matters worse, the road up to the mine traversed this tailings dump twice. If we ever slid off that road, we would roll 1,500 feet down to the trees below and our camp.

In our first month at the mine, we had over fifteen feet of snow, and an average temperature of forty below zero. And every day when I was taking the crew to work, I had extra trouble in the middle of the dump traverse. A spring of water was flowing out onto the road there and freezing, tilting the road at a dangerous outward angle.

One particular morning, we awoke to two feet of fresh snow, so I sent Bob up ahead with the bulldozer to clear the new snow and the ice from the spring off the road. When I got out of the jeep at the edge of the slide area to watch him working, I could feel the ice under my feet vibrating from the heavy steel pads of the bulldozer. It occurred to me that this could create an avalanche, so I backed up about a hundred feet!

As Bob was clearing above the switchback, the snow on the slope below the Cat started to move. The next second there was a great roar, and the entire snowpack rushed down the slope, just missing us. It thundered down and then up into the trees on the far slope, just missing the camp. The wind the avalanche generated knocked over ten-inch-diameter trees on the far slope as if they were matchsticks.

We waited for Bob to come down and clean the road again. Then we went up to work. At lunchtime I came down to check out the slide; I could walk on the snow, as it was packed like concrete. About a thousand feet down, I spotted our one and only crowbar sticking up out of the snow, but two shovels that had been left at the spring were nowhere in sight. I had an awful time pulling the heavy crowbar out of the snow. It was bent like the letter C.

Conditions in this camp were pretty crude, and there were no washing facilities. In our two crowded eight-man shacks, the only way to bathe was to put a bucket of water on the heater and two basins on the floor for your feet. When the water was heated, a buddy would pour water from the bucket over the bather's head, while the peanut gallery made comments.

After a month of twelve-hour workdays and cramped quarters, the men started to get bunkhouse happy, and the comments got uglier and uglier, often leading to fistfights.

To dispel the tension, I decided to hook up my little mantel radio. We climbed two trees to string an aerial, and at first it was a wonderful break from the monotony. But over time the radio created even more arguments and fistfights as men quarrelled over which of the two stations to listen to and when to turn it on or off.

One night I walked into our bunkhouse to find Blackie holding court around the airtight heater, trying to stir up trouble. Blackie was a mean little man who had been in and out of prison all his life, and he blamed everything and everybody for his lot in life.

Blackie was telling the guys that Jimmy, our old Scottish cook, had been putting saltpeter in the food and the salt shakers. Saltpeter allegedly stops men from having an erection and supposedly makes them less rambunctious.

Blackie was what's called a "Bunkhouse Lawyer," a fellow who has twenty-five percent of the facts and pretends to know the remaining seventy-five percent. Blackie had stolen a salt shaker out of the mess cabin and was going to run a test on it. He said, "You get the top of the stove hot, sprinkle the so-called salt on it, and the salt will turn brown and burn, but the saltpeter will melt before it burns."

Sure enough, some of the salt melted and some of it burned.

With this supposed "evidence," Blackie accused Jimmy the cook the next morning, but Jimmy just snorted and replied, "And why would I do that?" and calmly walked back into the kitchen.

I never did find out if Blackie's accusation was true—and to tell the truth, at this point I didn't care. I'd had enough of all the bitching and fighting in our bunkhouse, so I found a small shed in the camp, six feet by six feet, and covered the inside with cardboard for insulation, then moved in. I strung some electrical wire and hooked up a three-hundred-watt lamp. This made my little home warm and cozy, and I could read without interruptions. I left my radio with all the crazies.

* * *

Thirteen-year-old Benny, who worked as the cook's flunky, was small for his age. He was Bob the Cat driver's adopted son. Bob was a bachelor and a drunk, so little Benny had been raised real tough.

Blackie, who was small himself, couldn't pick on any of the crew because they were all bigger than him, so he started picking on Benny. One morning he went too far and yelled out, "Hey, you little bastard, bring me some more coffee."

In camps, the coffee is in heavy, two-quart earthenware pots. Little Benny struggled and picked up the coffeepot, came up behind Blackie, grabbed his shirt at the neck and poured the scalding coffee down his back.

Hearing Blackie's howls, Jimmy came out of the kitchen and without hesitation stripped Blackie's clothes off, grabbed a pound of butter and slathered it on Blackie's backside.

Bob later explained to us that Benny was legally a bastard, and Bob had only taken him in when some women had left him behind in Ferguson. Understandably, Benny was touchy about being called a bastard.

Fred, the boss, listened to both sides of this conflict and delivered a backwoods judgment: Benny wouldn't be fired. Blackie was off work for two days, and from then on treated Benny with respect. You could say that Blackie was now also, colloquially speaking, "a tough little bastard" for surviving the burn without complaint.

* * *

One morning, we were all getting dressed when we heard Fred coming up on his weekly trip with the camp supplies and mail.

It was forty below zero, but Doug, one of the miners, didn't want to miss him and rushed out into the snow wearing only his underwear and no socks. Doug was a tough man who hardly ever said a word, but his wife in Princeton was pregnant with her third child and was having serious trouble. Doug was worried sick, not knowing what was happening.

Doug ran up to Fred and asked for his mail.

Fred said, "Oh hell! I must have forgotten it."

Doug just stood there in the snow, stock still, in his bare feet, not talking, moving or shivering, but staring blankly. Nobody knew what was going on or what to do, so I went to Jimmy, our seasoned old camp cook, and explained what had happened.

Jimmy quickly produced a bottle of Scotch and told me to force it down Doug's throat. I took it to Doug and, with a little trouble, stuck the neck of the bottle in his mouth, then slowly poured.

After twenty minutes of steady administration of Scotch, Doug started to relax. We slowly walked him back to his shack and got him dressed. Then Fred put him in the truck and took him down to base camp. When Fred came back the next week, we anxiously asked about Doug, but he wouldn't say anything. We never did find out what happened to Doug or his wife.

The Fired Geologist

Along about this time we got a new geologist, Joe Emerson, a small, quiet, thirty-five-year-old man. As the head sampler, I had to work with Joe. I didn't enjoy it, as he was as miserable as a dog with a sore tooth. Something was really bothering him, so I made sure I was extra nice, with a sympathetic ear, and finally the story came out.

Joe had been the geologist of a thriving medium-sized East Kootenay mine for five years. One morning, when he was underground, two miners came to him because they had found something special in the drift they were drilling. Joe checked it out and discovered they had accidentally blasted into an unbelievably large, high-grade ore body that nobody knew existed. The drift face was solid lead zinc and silver with gold tracings, a big discovery.

Excited, Joe went back up to the surface to tell the mine superintendent. The super immediately ordered Joe to go back down and tell the timber men to clean up the ore and seal off the drift. Joe thought this was odd, but the boss was the boss.

After the drift had been sealed, Joe was told he was fired, along with the two miners who had discovered the ore body and the two timber men who had sealed it off. Joe had a wife and two kids to support, and now that I knew his story, I didn't blame him for being so miserable.

And, of course, now that we'd got to know each other, Joe became a little more friendly with me. This was a good thing because he, like all geologists, was a source of fascinating stories. One night when we had nothing else to do, he came over to my small cabin and told me about one of his mother lode theories. (Every geologist has one.) He unfolded a large map of the West Kootenay and Okanagan areas. On it he had painstakingly marked in all the known ore bodies by size and direction of shape and flow.

Joe said, "My theory is this: all these smaller ore bodies create a shape and direction to where the large ore body should be." He then pointed to the Peachland area. "That's where it is going to be found." I couldn't dispute it as all the many tiny arrows pointed there.

(Nearly ten years later, when I was long gone from the mining exploration business, a big discovery was made in Peachland. Joe was bang on.)

A few days before they were going to close the camp for Christmas and January, Joe finally decided what to do about the company that had fired him.

"Obviously they want to keep the big strike secret until they can come up with a glowing prospectus and make a fortune selling shares on a rising market," he told me. He explained that he was going to take a mortgage out on his house and put together every cent he could scrounge. Then he was going to buy shares in the company before they made the announcement and the shares went through the ceiling. He advised me to do the same.

I didn't have the heart to tell him that I had seen so many crooked things in the mining exploration game that I was leery of putting any money in it. I said I was heading to California and Mexico with a friend for the break. We parted company, wishing each other a Merry Christmas and promising we'd all be back in a month.

I headed straight for the Copper Mountain mine office to pick up my paycheque. I was looking forward to seeing my boss, Howard, and the rest of the office gang. To my surprise, they all treated me like I had brought a skunk with me. Howard called me into his office and abruptly gave me my cheque. I left feeling rather strange but was looking forward to my five-week holiday.

Two Country Boys in California and Mexico

My friend Jerry and I had been planning this trip for months. Jerry worked underground in the mine, on the timber crew, and we had become friends because we both had girlfriends in Penticton. Jerry's parents had a house there, and it was somewhere for us to stay each weekend. Jerry was a good, upstanding person who counteracted my irresponsible ways, and we got along great. He had only one flaw: he was horny as hell and would crawl ten miles over broken glass for a piece of tail or even the promise of one, which gave us some trouble when we travelled south.

I had made that motorcycle trip to California in 1946, and we had been hearing good things about how warm and inexpensive Mexico was, so we decided to go there during the winter break. Earlier, in the summer, I had traded in my old Pontiac for a 1949 Chevrolet Del Ray with a teardrop backend. I decked it out with running lights and lights on the mud flaps; to me, it looked great. I even modified the seats so they folded down into a bed—very nice for camping or to accommodate the ladies.

We first hit Portland, San Francisco and Los Angeles, and then we took the coast highway down to San Diego, saving some money by camping out at Balboa Animal Park. This was a very large park where, from a distance, it looked like the animals were roaming free; when you got closer, you saw the park management had dug deep moats that the animals couldn't cross.

The only local entertainment was the Sea-Dog Inn, a dive for visiting sailors. They had a band, and there was a good crowd, but the women looked pretty rough.

We had just sat down at the bar to check the place out when one of the women perched on a stool beside Jerry, who lit up like a lantern and bought her a drink. The bar was so dark I could hardly see her, and when I tried to talk to her over the loud dance music, I had to bend close to her ear. And, uh-oh, there was the shadow of a dark beard. I settled back in my seat to await the fun, as Jerry was a country boy and a little naïve about sexual variations.

Jerry started nuzzling her. Soon she had her hand on him, and he had his hand up her skirt. This was getting interesting!

Then he jumped up, backed away with a horrified look on his face and yelled, "You're a man!"

The "woman" casually got up and moved down the bar with her drink. It didn't help matters that I was laughing so hard. It took Jerry an hour and two drinks before he got over it and latched on to another woman, Betty.

I danced a couple of dances with a little gal from Louisiana with the cutest accent. But then I cooled it—a lot of these lonely women were the wives of sailors as this was the home port of the Fifth Fleet, a dangerous combination. Meanwhile, Jerry was doing great with Betty, and he came up to me, gave me a wink and said he wanted to borrow the keys to show Betty our car.

An hour later he hadn't come back. At midnight I went outside to check on him, and the car was gone!

When the bar closed at 2 a.m., there was still no Jerry. No car, no hotel, no way to contact him, and I was thoroughly pissed off. What could I do? The San Diego waterfront is about as tough as you can get, so I stuck close to the bar, walking around the four street corners.

About an hour later, two men came walking toward me along the dark, deserted sidewalk. Just as they got abreast of me, they split up, as if they were going to pass me, one on each side. Before I could move, one had my arm behind my back, and the other had my head in a hammerlock.

They started frisking me. One pulled out my wallet, opened it and took out my driver's licence. He said, "Oh, you're a Canadian are you?"

I managed to squeak out "Yes."

They released me, and one of them asked, "What are you doing walking the streets at 3 a.m.? We're San Diego detectives, and someone has reported that you are behaving suspiciously."

I explained my dilemma, and they said, "You better get off the street before somebody robs you."

I said I'd give Jerry until 4 a.m. to show up, and then I'd go to a local hotel for the rest of the night.

As I continued doing my rounds of the four corners, another two detectives came along. This time I was able to spot them by their clothes and heavy black shoes, so as they approached and started to split up, I yelled, "Hold it!" I held my hands up and backed against the wall. Then we went through the same interrogation.

After that, I decided to call it a night. I went to the closest fleabag and checked in. I had a hell of a time locking the door and finally got two dinner knives from the night clerk and jammed them in the doorframe.

I woke after a restless sleep, had breakfast and resumed my post outside the bar. About 11 a.m., who pulls up beside me with Betty in my car but Jerry, with a big grin on his face.

I yanked open the door, pulled Betty out onto the sidewalk, jumped in myself and said, "Let's go."

Jerry said, "But what about Betty?"

I said, "If you want her, get out and find your own way home."

I don't think I have ever been so impotently mad in my life, but it didn't seem to bother Jerry in the least. We fought over it for two hours, and I finally told him that from then on I would never trust him when it came to women. With that, we set off for Mexico and Ensenada, 130 miles beyond the border on a dead-end gravel road.

We stayed at a beachside motel for a couple of weeks, met some nice Mexican people and relaxed in the sun.

On the way back, we decided to stay overnight near the border in Tijuana and got a hotel room and a kid to watch the car for one dollar a night. After supper, for our last night in Mexico, we decided to kick up our heels at a popular local tavern with good music and tequila.

We were having a great time dancing with the bar girls when I noticed the locals were slowly disappearing and only American sailors and tourists were left. The bartender, Sanchez, out of the blue announced he was giving everybody a free round. Good old Sanchez— if we had only known that he was setting us up. We all drank to his health, but I saw that the bar girls were no longer laughing or smiling. It was as if it was the end of their shift.

Suddenly the front door flew open, and the Federales, the Mexican police, came charging in. The sergeant announced that we were all under arrest for "being in a bar after closing time." All sixteen of us males, but not the bar girls, were hustled into a bun wagon, taken to jail and jammed into one small cell.

After a while an older sailor in our group said, "Don't worry, this is a local rip-off. We will be released and over the border before morning."

Soon the sergeant came in and announced that charges had been laid against all of us. We would be brought up before the judge the next morning for sentencing. We all started babbling about how unfair this was.

A while later the sergeant came back with a wizened old Mexican who kept saying, "Go your bail, fifty dolla. Go your bail, fifty dolla," with his hand held out.

Nobody had issued charges to us or even taken our names, so I wondered how he could go our bail. But then one of the sailors stepped forward and handed him fifty dollars. The Mexican took the money with a "Gracias" and stuck it in his coat pocket. No receipt, no nothing. Fifty dollars was a lot of money in those days. Nevertheless, we all ended up forking over the money.

At four o'clock in the morning the sergeant told us to be back at the courthouse at 10 a.m. for sentencing. Then he ceremoniously flung open the cell door and stood to one side as we walked out.

Jerry and I were groggy and still a bit confused about what had just happened, but as we walked up the street to our hotel, the U.S. border looked mighty sweet and very close. We picked up our bags, paid the boy watching our car and in ten minutes flat were across the border. Good riddance to Mexico!

Laid-Off and Footloose

Back home, I reported for work at the mine and, surprise, was told that I had been laid off! The excuse was there had been a cutback in exploration work, but I couldn't understand why I was laid off when I had two years' seniority over others in our group. It wasn't fair, and being out of work in the late winter was not a good situation, especially after I had spent nearly all my money on the trip.

Hugh and his wife, Ruby, were still living in Copper Mountain, where he was in charge of the steam plant. I went to his house and complained about what had happened. He got upset, and at the next union meeting he accused the president of favouritism and not adhering to the union seniority rules. It didn't do any good, but we both felt better.

A few years later, in 1956, when a delegation of businessmen came to inspect the new aluminum plant up the coast where I was now working, I happened to be at the entrance to the plant when the buses came in and all the business types got off. Was I surprised to see all my old bosses from the mine, including Carl, but not Tommy. I went over to greet them like long-lost friends and got the cold shoulder. It hurt and it bothered me. Why was I still a pariah after all this time? What had I done wrong?

The full story behind this situation did not come out until a few months later, when I was reading an article in the *Vancouver Sun* newspaper. It all had to do with that claim we staked near Stewart in 1952. Turned out that the wildcatter who had staked the site before us worked for a large mining company, which was now fighting my old employer for the claim, that was said to be worth $30 million.

I thought back to the photos I had taken of Tommy holding up the claim papers we had found. I hadn't looked at them since that trip, but now I realized they were evidence, dated days before we got to the site. Now where were they?

I went up into the attic and dug up Eddie's old trunk, which I had dragged all over the country, hoping he would someday claim it. I had stored the envelope with my pictures in the trunk, but when I went through the photos, the shot of Tommy holding the claim paper was missing. I went to the negatives, and that particular negative had been cut off the strip. So that's what had happened when Howard borrowed my pictures. Now I knew why Carl had offered me shares: they were trying to buy my loyalty. When I had refused the offer, they sent me off to the Kootenays so I couldn't say the wrong thing to the wrong person, and as soon as they could, they laid me off. The whole state of affairs made me very sad about the greed of my fellow man. (And in case you are wondering how I could remember all that was said and done to me sixty years ago, if some people mistrusted you for no reason and temporarily wrecked your life when, in your view, you hadn't done anything wrong, I'm sure you too would remember the details.)

In the end, Carl and his company won the court case. And over the next fifteen years they pulled out more than $130 million worth of copper and gold.

Downward Spiral

From this point on, things started to spiral downward for me. I went in to the Penticton employment office, but there was no work for painters. However, a new outfit called the O.K. Food Plan had started up and was looking for salesmen. I had tried selling insulation in Vancouver and cars in Copper Mountain, via a dealership in Penticton, so having nothing else to do, I decided I would give it a whirl.

My new employer gave me a one-week training course in salesmanship that was very informative. Then I was sent out on the road to sell the latest appliance that was all the rage: deep freezers. Buy one of our deep freezers, we told potential customers, and you can buy all our frozen food at a large discount. During my first week of selling, I learned that the other three salesmen were all ex-con men who had been in and out of jail. I concluded that something was wrong with the whole scheme and quit.

My sister, Pat, and her husband, Curt Vesper, were moving to Castlegar with Curt's family and talked me into going along with them. Columbia Cellulose had bought the timber licence in Castlegar and was going to build a big pulp and sawmill complex. With all that construction, the Vespers thought there would be a good chance for them to sell lumber and for me to get a steady job. They sold their farm and garage in Hedley and packed all the furniture onto their trucks, and we moved to Castlegar with high hopes.

Once we got there, Harvey, Curt's father, a real smooth horse-trader type, talked me into going into partnership with him on a used car lot, selling cars to the construction workers.

We found a spare lot that was right next to a B/A garage and gas station, which was ideal. Harvey arranged the rental of the lot and also arranged for dealers in the Okanagan to lease us vehicles to sell.

I soon discovered that while Harvey was a great organizer, he was also allergic to physical work. I ended up as lot attendant, mechanic and salesman. And the cars that he had arranged for us to sell turned out to be oddball ones that the previous dealers hadn't been able to unload, like Kaisers, Edsels, Studebakers and even an old Diamond T truck. We managed to sell and trade a few of them, but I found myself living on the little money I still had left in the bank.

The used car lot lasted three months and then died, and all the hoopla about the pulp and sawmill quieted down when the entire project was delayed for five years. I went back to my old trade and worked for a local painter until that job ran out too.

Sexually Frustrated Housewives

Just a month after I arrived in Castlegar, Donald, a new friend, told me about a dance that was being held at the Kinnaird Community Hall. I got all cleaned up, even scrubbed the grease out from under my fingernails, and with my nearly new 1951 Pontiac Silver Chief car, I picked up Donald for a night of dancing and fun.

We drove the couple of miles up the road to Kinnaird, found the hall and parked the car on the large unlit parking lot. We could hear the dance music through the open windows and doors of the hall; it sounded pretty good.

It was a warm spring night, so before going in we opened the car windows and sat there having a couple of drinks. We then paid our dollar entrance fee, went in and ran into the usual situation. The women were on one side of the hall beside the orchestra, and the men were against the opposite wall. I recognized a couple of tire kickers from the car lot and went over to talk to them for a few minutes so I could get the lay of the land.

Donald turned out to be shy and wouldn't dance, but spent his time socializing with some friends. A nice waltz had just started, and I spotted a woman across the hall who looked interesting. She was standing in a group of five women. I went over and asked her to dance. She said yes without any hesitation.

We swung out onto the dance floor, and right away I was pulled in close. Well, who am I to resist? We were snuggled up until the waltz ended. Holding my hand, she turned toward me, looked me square in the eye and said, "I'm getting awful warm. Would you like to go out and get some fresh air?"

I thought this was rather sudden and very trusting of her, as I had barely spoken to her during the dance. I didn't even know her name. Taking a good look, I could see she was a few years older than me, and she had a wedding ring on. I spotted her friends looking our way, and Donald was standing there looking at us with a silly smirk on his face. Behind Donald, a group of young men were also looking our way.

Something didn't feel right, so I asked her if she was married. Without a moment's hesitation she replied, "Yes, but once a month, I'm let out." What a strange comment.

Well, I thought, *in for a dime, in for a dollar*, and out we went. She put her arm tightly around me and we walked a few paces in the dark. Then she had a strange request: she asked to see my car. I found it in the half-light, now tightly packed in among all the others. I showed it to her and then she swung me around and pushed me up against the driver's front door, crawling all over me, even zipping down my fly.

This was way too much and I tried to push her away. I suggested we slow down a bit and get in the car and out of sight.

She replied, "My husband won't allow me to get in a car because then he can't protect me."

Can't protect you, I thought. *What is she talking about? Where is this husband?*

At this point I concluded she was a nut job. I pulled her hand out of my pants and asked what she meant. Before she could answer, I noticed a man standing in the dark to the right beside my front fender, five feet away, blocking the way between the two cars. Could this be the husband? What in hell was going on?

I tried to gently push her away, and in doing so I glanced to my left. There, between the two cars at the rear bumper, was another man who was also just standing, looking at us, blocking the way out. Alarm bells went off in my head—get me outta here!

She said, "Don't get excited. It's only my husband and his friend. They're here to protect me."

Again I tried to push her away, but in that narrow space, and with her clinging to me, there was no room.

I said to her and the two men, "I'm sorry, but I'm outta here. If you don't let me go, I'll be the one yelling rape or help."

She backed off, and I had just enough room to slip by the supposed husband. I said again that I was sorry, but I couldn't go through with whatever they had planned. I crossed the parking lot without looking back and entered the hall to find Donald and his friends standing there with knowing looks and smirks on their faces.

He said, "My, you're back early. What happened? Didn't you like what she offered?"

I was obviously upset and asked him what the hell was going on.

He just laughed and explained that in the local smelter, where these men worked, there was a division that smelted lead. Each month the company took blood samples to monitor the lead build-up in their bodies; when they got over a certain limit, they were moved to another division. Unfortunately, by the time the men became "leaded," they also became impotent and lost interest in sex. Some of the men also got the lead in their joints, causing pain and inflammation. On the positive side, after six months out of the lead division, most of them fully recovered.

Working in the smelter was the best-paying, steadiest job in the area, and these men did not want to quit. But some of them had realized how frustrating it was for their women to do without sex for up to a year, and they had come up with various compromises. Donald explained that the woman I danced with was one of a group of five with leaded husbands who were at the dance to get laid.

"With you," Donald said, "it was going to be strictly 'Wham, bam, thank you, man,' you big stud horse you! But with your vanity, you didn't want to be the screw-ee, you wanted to be the screw-er and screwed everything all up." With that he nearly fell over, he was laughing so hard.

At this point I was wondering if I had fallen through a hole in the ground and come out in Alice's Wonderland. I decided to go home.

A Turning Point

I wasn't making any money during this period, due to the used car lot fiasco with Harvey, but I was still sending five dollars each month to the "friendly" finance company that covered the loan on my own car. The Pontiac was now over ninety percent paid for, and the law at the time was if it was over sixty-six percent paid for, and you were still making some kind of payment, the finance company couldn't seize it.

But one dark night after supper, I heard a heavy vehicle on the road adjacent to my basement suite. Looking out, I saw a tow truck backed up to my car. I ran outside to find Ralph, an old friend of mine from Penticton, who worked for the finance company, directing Bill, the local tow truck operator, to hook onto my car. Bill hadn't known it was my car. When he saw me, he backed off.

I told them that I was in good standing with my loan and they would be stealing the car if they took it. But Ralph had come all the way from Penticton, over two hundred miles of gravel road, and he wasn't planning on going home empty-handed. He convinced Bill that he should go ahead.

When Bill moved to get under the car to hook it up, I told him there would be violence if he touched my car. Bill looked at me, knew I meant it, and refused to follow Ralph's orders, saying that he had to live in this town.

Ralph said he'd get another tow truck. I replied that then he would be the one lying on the road with broken teeth. I knew I was right and I wasn't going to be bluffed and bullied into giving up my car.

Ralph mumbled a few threats, but that's the last I heard from him. Just for good measure, though, for the next two weeks I parked my car at a friend's house, out of sight.

This incident was probably the lowest point in my adult life, and it made me vow to do something to get myself off this insecure bottom level of society.

Around the same time, I added to my feeling of hitting bottom when I got a copy of the *Vancouver Sun* and checked the mining shares. Carl had been pretty accurate when he offered me shares in his new mine. The stocks had started at twenty-seven cents and had quickly shot up to over twelve dollars. If I had taken his advice and used my savings to buy into the mine, instead of going to Mexico, I would have made a bundle that would have set me up for life. I don't think I would have been laid off from my job at the mine either.

Joe Emerson's old mine had also come out with a glowing report on the new ore body, and the stock price had tripled. I'm sure Joe made a killing—and he deserved it. But obviously I was going to have to live and learn the hard way and dig myself out of the pit I had found myself in.

Back to Painting

I went back to work as a painter, teaming up with an older man, Orton Pelton, who knew all the ropes along with all the right people in the painters union, and he got me into the union. We hired on with City Decorators in Trail, and our first job was painting the big old Rossland post office.

The basement had to be spray-painted with whitewash, which is made from slaked lime, but Kelly, the boss, had mistakenly bought unslaked, or raw, lime. The next day we started spraying the white-wash. Before we got very far, the fire alarm went off. I had forgotten to turn off the basement furnace fan, and it had sucked all the strong dust fumes from the unslaked lime through the whole building. Everyone had vacated, and there were thirty people standing outside on the street, coughing, with tears in their eyes. We eventually got the job done, but was I ever embarrassed!

One of our most gruesome jobs was repainting the inside of a house where the tenant had put a shotgun in his mouth and blown his brains all over the ceiling and walls.

Another time, Kelly got us a job painting a house in Trail. The groom had just brought his new bride back from Italy, and they wanted the interior of their house painted. Orton and I were just finishing the bathroom when Kelly came by and asked us to put some white enamel on the toilet seat. He thought it looked grungy. I obliged and moved on to work on the living room ceiling.

The groom came home at lunchtime, and we could hear a loud

discussion in Italian going on in the kitchen but paid it no mind. Then he came out of the kitchen, chuckling, and said to us, "My new bride sat on the newly painted toilet seat. Will you repaint it? She wanted to tell you, but she doesn't speak any English and was too embarrassed to try!"

A couple of weeks later we were taking down our scaffolding on a house, finishing up for the week, when Kelly came by and told us, "I know it's payday, but the cheques haven't come in. I should be able to pay you in two weeks."

Orton said, "Well, if we got to wait, I guess we've got to wait."

We finished putting everything away and jumped in Orton's car to head back to Castlegar.

I said to Orton, "Drop by the office in Trail. I want to see Kelly."

Orton knew about my wages hang-up and protested that I was only going to make Kelly mad. But I said, "Orton, if I've got money coming, I'm going to get it."

Afraid to be associated with me, Orton parked his car two blocks away down the street.

When I walked into the office, I didn't say anything, but Kelly knew why I was there. Standing behind his desk, he immediately started mouthing off and threatened to fire me if I didn't leave.

I told him if he didn't sit down and write me a cheque right now, he'd be going through the wall. He wrote the cheque. I said thank you and left, fired.

When I got in the car, Orton said sarcastically, "Well, did you get your money?"

I said yes, but he wouldn't believe me until I showed him the cheque. I quickly cashed it and we drove home in silence. (It took Orton over two months to get his back pay.)

Painting High Steel

Orton and I hired on with Bedard of Vancouver, which had the contract to paint the new Waneta Dam project a few miles below Trail, where the Pend d'Oreille River flows into the Columbia River. It was to be a very high dam, with the steel structure over 165 feet high.

The dam was only half finished, with ninety percent of the concrete poured. Over one hundred feet above the concrete deck was a half-mile-long aerial tramway that spanned the entire gorge. The tramway was used to bring up large buckets of concrete and to lift the large steel floodgates into the slots, as well as to put the structural steel in place.

I'd never worked on a big-time construction project, painting high steel, so I had a lot to learn. The foreman was Bert Martin, a feisty little middle-aged Scot from Vancouver, who ruled with an iron hand. Some of the sixteen painters had worked for Bedard for years, and they really knew their jobs, be it high-steel bosun's chair work, swing stage or heavy-duty spray painting.

Orton, being older and a top-notch brush painter, was given a nice inside job painting offices and workplaces. I was younger and stronger so was given the rough heavy work, mostly hanging from a bosun's chair, painting the exterior high steel.

My first job was working with another young fellow, Wally, brush-painting the inside and outside of the steel walkway at the top of the sluice gate structures. This meant we had to climb over the railing 165 feet up, hook one arm over the railing and paint all the exposed steel. One mistake and down you'd go.

I talked to Wally and suggested we should have safety belts. He agreed and we headed down to the paint shop at the outside base of the dam. Wally was walking ahead of me. Bert stood on the front step of the shop and watched us wend our way down.

When we got close to the paint shop, Bert said, "You boys need something?"

Wally said, "Yeah, we came down to get some safety belts to do this job because it's unsafe without them."

Burt looked only at Wally and said, "You're fired. Collect your things and leave the property."

He deliberately did not look at me, and I turned around and went back to work. No safety belt.

* * *

The next day I had a new partner, George, a young Russian Doukhobor man. He was very nervous, and when we got up to the walkway he said he had never painted high steel before, but he needed the money.

I let him start by painting some of the inside steel to get used to the height, the wind and all the moving distractions around us.

After lunch, I suggested he try painting the outside of the walkway. He tentatively climbed through the railings and got his arm hooked around the lower rail. I passed him his paint and brush and went back to work.

Soon after, I heard a squeal and looked over. George had both arms hooked around the railing, but his feet were dangling in mid-air.

I rushed over and pulled his feet up to the horizontal I-beam. When I looked more closely at his situation, it appeared he had painted the I-beam that he had been standing on, then stepped on the slippery wet paint and lost his footing. His pot of paint and brush had gone flying.

Even though his feet were on the beam again, he was still clinging to the handrail for dear life. I talked to him quietly, but he wouldn't look at me or respond; he just stared straight ahead, clinging to the railing. I couldn't figure out what was the matter with him.

Joe, one of the old-time Bedard men, was below us on a bosun's chair. He pulled himself up, hand-over-hand, and went over to look at George clinging to the rail. Joe's diagnosis: "He's frozen, and you won't be able to pry his hands loose. We have to slowly work him out of there."

When I asked how we would do that, Joe said that we had to make him feel safe. We had to get a scaffold plank and put it under his feet so he couldn't look straight down, and then we had to tie him to the railing and keep talking to him. Eventually he would relax and we could get him to let go. Joe said all this as if it had happened many times before.

I stayed with George, saying anything that came to mind, while Joe went scrounging for a rope and a plank. We got the plank in place, tied it down tight, and slowly convinced George to step on it. We then tied his body up tight so he could try to relax his death grip on the railing.

Over time, his eyes started to move around again, but he still wasn't talking. Then, after a while, he started trying to say words, but they were just babble. Eventually I got one or two words out of him.

At this point we gradually loosened his ropes, and he crawled through the railings onto the walkway. Boy, was he ever glad to be on terra firma. We escorted him off the walkway and down to the paint shop. Bert made him a hot cup of coffee. Joe and I went back to work, and that was the last we saw of George.

The winter winds came, and some days we were working in thirty degrees below zero. I was given the nearly impossible job of painting the exposed steel edges of the large sluice gate guide channels that were reinforced with six-by-six angle iron embedded in the concrete. These channels were partially covered by a thin layer of concrete that was also often coated with rain, ice or snow.

Each morning I would collect my red lead paint primer, brush and acetylene torch, and climb into the bosun's chair. To paint the steel, I heated a three-foot section with the torch, wire-brushed it and then slapped on a coat of paint. When it was finished, I would drop down, repeating this in three-foot sections until all fifty feet had been painted. Then I would pull myself, my equipment and the bosun's chair back up the fifty feet, pull up my 250 feet of rope, drag everything over to the next channel guide and start all over again for each of the eighty channels.

One day when I was working close to the far side of the dam, hanging down below the sluice gates, I saw a crew of three men adjacent to me, hanging on the cliff face, prying or "barring" off the loose rock with crowbars. None of them had safety belts.

I heard a scream and looked over just in time to see one of the men fall into the large whirlpool at the base of the dam. He never came back up.

When you're barring rock off a steep slope with a crowbar, you put the crowbar in the crack and pull back on it. Apparently this man hadn't been instructed on how to do this properly. He had been pushing on the bar, not pulling back on it, and when it slipped, over he went.

On heavy construction projects, the attitude of the day was "You can kill one man for every million dollars spent." This project had a value of three million dollars, so they were allowed to kill three men. If I remember correctly, they managed to reach their target.

* * *

At lunch in the paint shop, the big topic of conversation was that men from the Kahnawake Reserve near Montreal were coming to put up the top sixty feet of high steel on the dam. These Natives had no fear of heights. They were also "highballers," paid by the ton on contract, so the quicker they worked the more pay they made.

Ten of them arrived at the camp, along with seven Texans, and they were treated like royalty. The second day they were there, one of them didn't like the soup in the mess hall, took it back to the kitchen and poured it over the cook's head. Crazily, he didn't get fired, but the cook did.

They took over the tramway crane to lift the steel from inside the base of the dam up to the top deck. With nothing to hang on to, they would stand on an eighteen-foot by twelve-inch beam as the crane lifted it two hundred feet into the air. Once the beam was swung into position, they would casually walk along the narrow beam to the other end and, with a spud wrench, fasten it in place. Then, just as casually, they would walk back to the other end. To get off the high steel, they slid sixty feet down on a vertical I-beam, their boots on the inside and their hands, in leather gloves, on the outside. When they got close to the bottom, they would put pressure on their boots, slow down and nonchalantly step onto the deck, as if getting off an elevator.

I was doing my usual boring bosun's chair painting job, so had a grandstand seat to watch them work above and below me. One day it was about twenty below zero, with a twenty-mile-an-hour wind, and one of the Natives started walking across that eighteen-foot beam in mid-air, hanging on to nothing. He got halfway across, slipped on some ice and went down, with his right arm hooked around the beam and his body and legs swinging below the beam. Almost before I realized what had happened, he swung his legs up, then stood up and continued his stroll to the other end—nerves of steel, and the reactions of a cat.

In three weeks, those men from Kahnawake had all the high steel in place and nobody got killed. You can have your show-off rope walkers with their long poles to help them balance, but give me a Kahnawake doing his high-steel work; that's far more thrilling.

* * *

During heavy rain and snowstorms, when it was impossible to paint outside, I was given a spray gun and joined the gang of guys inside, painting the seventy-foot-high ceiling and structural steel of the powerhouse.

Sixty feet below us were construction crews hand-fitting the thousands of components of the generators. The ceiling painters would cover two squares of the roof's structural steel with planks to stand on. Underneath each square we suspended a large canvas drop sheet to prevent paint dripping or tools dropping on the men and generators below. Naturally, there were no hardhats or safety belts on this site.

Ed, our gang leader, was a tall, thin, serious, middle-aged man who knew every trick in the book for high-steel painting, but he had one of the damnedest scariest habits. He would come on-site, look up at the ceiling we were painting, then walk backward to check if we had missed any spots. Sometimes he would back up on a plank that overhung an empty square by a few feet. He would be talking to us, and the other end of the plank would slowly lift up off the girders. Then he would walk back up the plank, still talking. Boy, did he have our undivided attention.

He could get away with this because he was wearing the right shoes. When I first started my painting apprenticeship, Louis looked at my thick-soled leather work boots and said, "Have you got an old pair of dress or dance shoes?" He explained that, in the painting trade, I'd be spending over half my time standing on a twelve-inch scaffold plank. With thin-soled dress or dancing shoes I could feel the edge of the plank with my feet, which would make me much safer. That's why Ed could confidently walk backward, feeling the plank as he went.

One day Ed brought us a five-gallon pail of light green enamel and placed it right in the middle of two planks. He then pulled off his usual heart-stopping stunt, walking backward. But this time the plank that rose up was underneath half of the pail of paint. Up went the plank, and the pail rolled over and fell through the gap, landing on the canvas four feet below. The impact snapped one of the thin ropes holding a corner of the canvas. The pail rolled to the lower point and—miracle of miracles—turned sideways, with one end teetering on the edge of the canvas.

Sixty feet below us, ten men were busily bolting together generator plates, unaware of the danger. If the pail fell, the damage alone would be in the tens of thousands, even if no one were killed.

Quick as a cat, Ed slipped down between the planks, and with two guys holding his legs, he managed to retrieve the can of paint. Nothing was said and we all went back to work.

* * *

One lunchtime we were heading to the paint shop when we passed one of the inspectors. The whole front of his body, head to toe, including his face, was covered in dark yellow one-inch squares. He was glaring at us, as if trying to figure out which one of us had done this to him.

After we got by him and into the lunchroom, someone asked, "Well, all right. Who spray-painted the inspector?"

We looked around. Joe Goss and I were spraying light green; others were spraying red lead. The two guys who were spraying yellow were the only ones who had taken off their coveralls, but all of us painters knew to look at their shoes, which were splattered with yellow. Guilty!

It turned out these two guys had been down in a cramped concrete tunnel, painting the large turbine pipes of the generators. This inspector had gotten on their case and was lying on the catwalk grating above their heads, spying on them. The guys were dressed for the dirty job in coveralls and gloves, with rags wrapped around their heads and mouths to keep the paint out. One of them looked up, recognized the inspector and in a rash moment blasted him through the grill work with eighty pounds per square inch of yellow paint.

We all had a good laugh. The inspector never did find out who painted him, but he kept his distance from then on.

* * *

One morning I came to work in a heavy rain. I leaned over the edge and started pulling the bosun's chair and the 250 feet of rope up so I could get into the chair. It was an unusually tough job because the rope was soaked with water and weighed a lot more than usual, probably close to one hundred pounds.

I was bent way over, straining into empty space, pulling up with all my might, when some clown violently goosed me from behind. Your instinctive reaction when goosed is to step forward, but this would have meant stepping into empty space and falling 150 feet straight down. Luckily I had my wits about me and instead let go of the chair and rope, swung sideways and grabbed the upper steel sluice gate guide.

By the time I had recovered from the shock, the clown who goosed me was long gone. If ever I felt the urge to kill, it was then.

At one point the company decided to build a large cofferdam, a temporary watertight enclosure, below where I was hanging to paint the sluice gate guides. This meant that about three times a day they lowered a big five-yard bucket with twenty thousand pounds of concrete directly over and past me, then down to the twelve-man cement crew working inside the cofferdam far below.

One day I heard a frantic tooting of the crane whistle and looked over to see that the cable hooked to the bucket was breaking. Each time one of the segments snapped, the bucket dropped another foot lower, and the broken ends of cable curled up into a ball. Two snaps, three snaps and then the remainder broke.

The five-yard bucket with twenty thousand pounds of concrete was now falling a hundred feet directly onto the crew below.

Fortunately, the crew had heard the whistle in time. Those twelve men climbed the twelve-foot vertical walls of that cofferdam in record time to get out of the way.

The bucket hit like an explosion, splitting in half and splattering concrete in all directions. I'm sure that if those men hadn't moved so quickly, there would have been a lot more than one death per million dollars on this project.

During the coldest, most miserable part of the winter, I was still priming the steel guides, hanging from a bosun's chair. There was two feet of snow everywhere.

One day I overturned my pot of red lead paint. Down went the half gallon of paint, right onto the top of the concrete spillway. Because the paint was warm, it melted the snow and flowed down under the snow and onto the concrete spillway. Nobody noticed it at the time, and I wasn't about to tell anyone.

Months later, when they had all the brass and politicians there for the grand opening, the pictures in every newspaper showed the dam with my large red paint splatter front and centre.

When I went back a few years later, there was no sign of it. I guess the water had washed it off over the years.

Time to Settle Down

When I first arrived in Castlegar, I was going through an odd phase with regards to the female of the species. To put it bluntly, I had become totally disenchanted with the conniving ways of women trying to entrap me, or any man, into marriage and had decided to take it easy. This lasted a few months until a friend introduced me to Mary Wanjoff.

Mary was a Russian Doukhobor woman with a good education; she also ran her own grocery store on her family's farm. With her dark hair, brown eyes and olive complexion, she was very good looking. We enjoyed doing a lot of things together, including playing badminton, hiking and swimming. We also found we loved dancing together, and we went regularly to Playmore, a dance hall run by a couple who were former professional ballroom dancers. The highlight of every evening was at 10:30, when everybody would form a large circle. The lights were

Mary Wanjoff, 1950.

dimmed, a spotlight came on and the owners came out in formal dress and gave an exhibition of ballroom dancing.

A major feature of living in the Kootenay region of B.C. at that time was the presence of the hard-working, pacifist Russian Doukhobor community that Mary's family was part of, and I need to give a bit of background to that community to explain some of the difficulties that arose in our relationship. The Doukhobors had immigrated to Canada in 1898 to escape the persecution of the Tsar, Nicholas II. Canada offered them freedom to pursue their pacifist beliefs, promised they would never have to face conscription, and agreed not to interfere with the community's internal affairs. In many ways, the Doukhobors were

Mary and friend, 1950.

ahead of their time, promoting vegetarianism, cooperation and international unity as well as pacifism. Their credo is "Toil and Peaceful
Life" and their central pacifist belief is "The welfare of the whole world
is not worth the life of one child."

Mary's family were "Independent Doukhobors." They owned
their own farm, ran a small business and also worked for local non-
Doukhobor industries. Others, the "Orthodox or Community
Doukhobors," lived communally, operating some very successful
cooperative jam factories and businesses.

However, a third group, the Freedomites or Sons of Freedom,
caused huge confusion and pain for the more peaceable and hard-

working Doukhobors, particularly during the 1950s and '60s. The Sons of Freedom, under various charismatic leaders, took the Doukhobor philosophies to a radical and violent extreme. They believed that ownership of property or material wealth broke down communal values and led directly to wars, so they bombed and burned the houses and buildings of other Doukhobors, as well as government buildings and structures. No one was harmed, but a great deal of property was destroyed. They did not send their children to public schools, as they believed the governments that ran the schools promoted wars. And they did not believe in paying taxes, as this also supported war, and you really didn't own the land as long as you paid taxes.

The government of the day overreacted and kidnapped the children of the Sons of Freedom, incarcerating them in prison-schools and keeping them away from their families. The government also worked to break up some of the more successful communal farms and factories run by the Orthodox Doukhobors. To protest these actions and others, the Sons of Freedom staged highly publicized nude protests and marches. (They would strip off their clothes to show their renunciation of material possessions.)

At one point during this time, I was working with a group of Doukhobors, painting some Custom houses at the Paterson border crossing. Some of my fellow workers were Orthodox Doukhobors and some were Sons of Freedom. Most of the Sons of Freedom lived together in simple tarpaper shacks, while the Orthodox prided themselves on their well-built homes. One day Pete, a small, quiet, middle-aged painter who was a member of the Sons of Freedom, didn't come to work. When I asked one of the others why he wasn't there, the man told me quietly that Pete and his family had been burned out the previous night.

Pete came to work the next day and, working with him, I learned the gruesome details in dribs and drabs. Pete and his wife had bought some new living room furniture as well as an electric fridge and stove. Shortly after these new "luxury" items arrived, there was a knock on his door after the family had gone to sleep. Pete answered to find forty of

Alan and Mary, 1953.

his Sons of Freedom neighbours, men, women and children, surrounding the house. The leader told him to get his family out. Then the neighbours burned his house down. Everyone stood around until there was nothing left of the house, at which point the neighbours took the family into their own homes and looked after them. They had broken a rule: "You cannot have material possessions better than your neighbours."

Six months later, when Pete had saved enough money for concrete and wood, everybody in the Sons of Freedom community got together and built him another house. I won't go into any more details, but that is what they believed and practised at that time.

Because of all this turmoil, if Mary and I were driving to or from Playmore, we would be stopped by at least two roadblocks operated by the police. Everyone in the car would be asked their name. If they were all "English" names, like McGowan, we would be let go. If one of the names, like Mary's, happened to end in a Slavic-sounding "off," we would be ordered out of the car, and the police would search the entire vehicle for gas cans and explosives. It was a confusing and difficult time for everyone.

* * *

After six months going out with Mary, I started to think seriously about marriage. I broached the subject, but Mary had to think it over. Her mother and dad hated "the English," and to them I was "an Englishman."

During all this time, I had never come near her house or met her parents. She was scared about what her folks might do to me. Normally I would pick her up and drop her off at the home of an Anglo-Saxon neighbour down the street who was a friend of Mary's, but I was getting fed up with this strange arrangement. So I talked her into letting me pick her up at her family's front door the next day.

We were planning to go for a drive on that sunny Sunday afternoon, and as I pulled up to the house, there on the front porch sat Mary's mother, glaring at me. I have no idea how she knew I was coming.

As I approached the steps, I said, "Good afternoon, Mrs. Wanjoff. It's a nice day. Is Mary ready?"

She turned to the house and yelled for Mary to come out. I waited a minute, and as I stood there, I noticed Mrs. Wanjoff was cleaning tomatoes, picking them up from a box on her left side, inspecting and polishing them and putting them in a box on her right side.

Mary didn't come out immediately, and when I turned around to go back to the car, Splat! A rotten tomato landed with great force right in the middle of my back. I turned around and saw Mary's mum holding another tomato at the ready.

I applauded and yelled to her, "Good shot!" Laughing, I got to my car. My bright yellow shirt was now highlighted in red. I took it off and wiped most of the rotten tomato off with a rag.

Mary finally came out of the house and was very embarrassed. But I thought it was a great stunt; you could say I had at last met Mary's mother.

Mary had serious misgivings about getting married to me. Without her parents' approval of the match, she would have to give up everything she knew, including the store she ran on the family farm. To make matters worse, her parents had told her they would disown her if she married outside the Doukhobor community. I told her we'd better cool it until she could decide.

I mentioned all this to Orton, my older painting partner, and his wife, Kay. They told me they thought I was making a serious mistake, marrying someone from a totally different background. But I was in love and, true to form, didn't listen.

Two long months later, Mary finally phoned me and agreed to get married. We set the date for June 12, 1954. I checked with the local guys about where to get the best deal on a set of rings, and they sent me to Spokane, across the border, as it was the diamond centre for the entire Northwest and had a huge wholesale selection.

The wedding was going to be a strange affair, as none of Mary's family or the Doukhobor community would be involved or in attendance. Dad, Hughie and Ruby came over from Princeton a month ahead of time to meet Mary, but just Mitch and Mum were able to attend from my side. All the wedding arrangements were made by an older non-Doukhobor couple who were lifelong friends of Mary, and a week before the wedding she left her home of twenty-five years and stayed with them. We had a full white wedding in the United Church and a reception at a friend's house.

After the wedding, we headed to Vancouver for our honeymoon and to look for work. We had agreed that if we wanted to build a good life for ourselves, we would have to leave Castlegar and all the resentments that our marriage had created. We stayed with Mary's brother Pete in Vancouver. He and his common-law wife, Edna, an Anglo-Saxon,

Mary and Alan wedding, 1954.

Pete, Edna, Mary, 1953.

had no trouble with our relationship and were very supportive. Because Pete lived far from home, in Vancouver, his parents were not subjected to criticism from the Doukhobor elders for his conduct.

Fortunately, this story has a happy ending. A year later we had Joseph, our first baby, named after my father. Joe was born in the ramshackle beach hospital at Kitimat, B.C., where we had ended up moving. Mary wrote to her parents, but there was no response. I had two weeks' holiday coming, so a few months later we spent four days driving the 1,300 miles back to Castlegar—600 of those miles on gravel road. We got a room at a motel, and Mary phoned her mum and told her that this would be her one and only chance to see her grandchild. Mary had two older brothers, but neither had produced grandchildren yet. Her mother agreed; we could come and bring her only grandchild over to the house.

Mary Wanjoff, Sharon, Joe, Pete, 1957.

We got out of the car with great trepidation, and Mary walked ahead of me down the "rotten tomato" sidewalk with Joe in her arms.

It turned out that I didn't have to worry. When Mrs. Wanjoff saw her first grandchild, she came rushing out, grabbed him and wouldn't let him go until we finally had to leave. From then on, things were normal between Mary and her family. They were always a little reticent with me, but I could understand that.

Heading North

With the responsibility of marriage, I knew it was time to get out of construction work and settle down to a steady job. In 1954, everybody had heard of the largest construction job in the free world: the huge aluminum smelter Alcan was building in Kitimat, 450 miles up the coast north of Vancouver in the middle of nowhere.

I got an application form, but when I started filling it in, I stopped and stared at what I had listed for employment. I had an epiphany! Nobody in his right mind would hire me with all the jobs I'd had. Without realizing it, I had been following in my dad's footsteps, jumping from job to job all over the place. I focused my resume on three painting jobs and promised myself that I would become a responsible, solid citizen and do my best to stick to one job from then on, come hell or highwater.

With the new resume and my new resolutions, I went down to Alcan's hiring office on Howe Street to see if I could hire on as a painter. I was now a member of the International Painters Union Local 138, thanks to Orton, so I thought my chances would be pretty good, but Alcan's hiring agent said they were only hiring "Pot Men," whatever they were. Discouraged, I thought that was the end of it, but Alcan phoned me a few days later and told me to be at the Fraser River seaplane base the next morning to fly up north. I was hired as their first painter.

I said goodbye to my new bride, leaving her at Pete's place until we could secure family housing in Kitimat, which was presently a very closed company town. I boarded an old Beaver seaplane for a scary twelve-hour flight with a pilot who kept falling asleep.

There were 1,400 smelter workers coming to Kitimat at that time, so the place was chaotic when we arrived. I first stayed on a floating bunkhouse in the harbour. Then I was moved to the old *Delta King*, a beached paddle-wheeler. There, my bunk was right over the boiler room that supplied the entire smelter site with heat and light. It was so hot that I couldn't sleep inside, so I took my bedroll and slept out on the dyke that surrounded the boat.

The first morning I reported to work along with about fifty other men. We were herded like cattle into the plant's stores and outfitted with heavy wool clothes and boots. I didn't understand why, as a painter, I was being outfitted like this. We were then herded down to the smelter's potlines. This was where they would smelt the aluminum, and they were preparing the pots by doing something called "candle baking." You couldn't see thirty feet into the potline building, what with the smoke and heat.

Seeing these adverse conditions, I broke ranks, turned around and walked back to find the maintenance office, where I asked to see the superintendent. I informed him that I had been hired to paint, not work on the smelting pots. He told me that was all the work they had, and that's what I had to do for a few weeks. I told him that I was a journeyman painter and had hired on through Local 138 of the Painters Union, so Alcan would have to pay my way back to Vancouver if they didn't have work for me as a painter. After a long discussion, I was told to report to the temporary carpenter shop, where they would find some painting work for me.

The temporary carpenter shop turned out to be an old shack under the conveyor gallery down by the wharf. There I met Tommy, a journeyman carpenter, who became a lifelong friend. Tommy explained that Alcan was having lots of teething problems as it prepared to start up the smelter in the middle of the North Coast wilderness. They didn't know what to do with tradesmen like us, as Kitimat Contractors (KC), the construction company building the smelter and townsite, was in charge of everything related to the trades. So we were to cool it and get lost until KC completed the building phase and moved out in another month or so. At that point we would be able to take over the contractor's paint and carpenter shop and get to work in a big way.

In the meantime, to keep me busy, the foreman, Ben, took me up to paint one of the 125 small, temporary contractor houses that had been built at the smelter site. Basically, I was to occupy myself with this until they needed me. In other words, get lost until we want you.

The Prince Is Coming! The Prince Is Coming!

One afternoon a few days later, Ben came flying up in his old truck and rushed into the house I was painting. Ben was from South Africa and had a reputation for handling men as if they were slaves. He was middle-aged, excitable and could never stand still, so everything had to be done on the run.

With more than his usual panic, he danced around and announced that Prince Philip was coming in less than three weeks to officially open the smelter. Ben, a royalty fanatic, wanted to know if I could paint everything that Prince Philip and his entourage would see on their three-quarter-mile route from the dock to the smelter, and if I could get it done before the big day.

I was standing on the top of a stepladder, with a paintbrush in my hand. I pictured the route in my mind, and between the two points Ben had mentioned I realized there were 125 houses, a security office, a hospital, nurses' quarters, a bank, the cafeteria that sat over 1,000 men, five large bunkhouses for 2,500 men, a guest house, steam plant, the *Delta King* and God knows what else.

In shock, I sat down on the top step of the ladder in shock, staring at this madman.

Ben stamped the floor and demanded, "Well, can you do it?"

I thought for a few minutes: *Here I am in a brand new town and a new plant, where everything is organized confusion. But there's lots of enthusiasm and flexibility. I'm twenty-four years old and have never supervised a large group of men before, and any men we get to help will not be painters, but . . . what the heck. Let's go for it. It's not my money. What can I lose? And it might be fun.*

I told Ben that two and a half weeks was not much time, but with enough men, paint, brushes and equipment, and if the weather held, anything was possible.

Without waiting even ten seconds, he said, "Well, get me a list, and I'll see what I can arrange." With no more palavering, he tore out of the house and was gone.

I got down off the ladder, put away my equipment and apologized to the family for the delay in finishing their house. Then I grabbed a notebook and took a long slow walk over the royal route, putting together estimates.

That night at eleven, Ben woke me up where I was sleeping on the dyke, demanding to see my list. We sat on the dyke in the twilight, and I got out my notebook and told him that, due to the time frame, we could only paint the front of the buildings and fences along the route—like the false fronts of a movie set—because we didn't have time to paint the sides or backs. To even do this, we needed forty-eight able-bodied men and four hundred gallons of white and green paint. The *Delta King* painting would have to be subcontracted, because you need expert painters to do boat work safely. I thought maybe a contractor could do the land side that everybody would see. We would also need to take over the KC paint shop, with all its equipment, as the centre of operations, and we would have to start immediately.

Ben, surprisingly, delivered on every demand. How he did it, I don't really know. Kitimat at that time was a totally isolated community with no road out. We took over the KC paint shop. Ben begged, borrowed, bought and flew in all the paint and brushes that we needed. And he found the forty-eight men, who joined us ten at a time. I would line them up and ask them if they had ever done any painting. If someone said yes, he was automatically made a lead hand. For training the novices, I held a brush in one hand and a bucket of paint in the other, took the brush and demonstrated how to dip it in the paint and tap it on the inside of the pail to remove the excess paint so it wouldn't drip. Then I told them to paint the front of anything that didn't move, from the wharf to the smelter site gate. And away they went.

Not too long after we got started, the phone in the paint shop started to ring off the hook with complaints from people who lived and worked along the route: "Your stupid painter painted my doorknob." "My glass windows are painted over and I can't see out of them." "They splashed paint all over my roses." "One of your painters painted my dog's nose." "There's a painter peeking in the windows of the nurses' quarters." "Your men only painted the front of my house—why didn't they paint the sides and back?"

The many three-storey bunkhouses and the cafeteria were in pretty good shape, so, thankfully, we didn't have to paint up high and risk having inexperienced men fall off ladders. The land side of the *Delta King* was painted in time by a private contractor from Terrace and looked great. I'd hate to know what Alcan paid for that. Mercifully, the weather held, and at the end of the job, if you drove fast enough, the whole route looked pretty good. I personally thanked most of the crew, who then went back to the labour pool. But I kept six men for a few days, just in case.

The day before the big event, the general foreman of the casting department phoned out of the blue and wanted the monstrous-sized Number One straight-line casting machine painted with high-heat aluminum paint. This was going to be the centre of the whole affair. Prince Philip was supposed to stand at the end of the casting machine. He would press a button, and the machine would start up and drop hot ingots out of the moulds, *bang*, onto the steel table. Then the prince would declare the plant open. Photographers from around the world would take pictures for publicity and posterity.

Two of my novice painters worked overtime, spray-painting the whole machine, including the moulds, aluminum, and doing a fair job for novices. Casting then cast two complete sets of ingots and picked out the best ones. These were put back in the painted moulds and prepared for the button to be pushed. At that moment, the cold ingots would start moving and drop out onto the table. There is a famous picture of Prince Philip with his hand on the first ingot poured. Now you know why he didn't get his hand burned by what would normally be a 1,200-degree ingot dropping onto the steel table. One of those ingots ended up in the head office in Montreal.

The day before the big event, Ben was a nervous wreck and was driving me around the bend. Someone had told him that if the weather was sunny, the prince might come from the Alcan underground powerhouse in Kemano, fifty miles away, in a helicopter instead of a ship. Ben picked a site beside the soccer field, just below the smelter, and in the morning I had to find three large rocks, set them in a pattern and paint them red, as a landing site.

Ben had also inspected the guest house set aside for Prince Philip's private luncheon and had found that the toilet seat in the guest house was not up to his conception of the royal standard. He wanted me to paint it with white enamel.

Mary, Skye, Sharon, Alan, Joe, 1966.

"Enamel takes a long time to dry," I warned him, "and Prince Phillip might end up getting his bum painted."

He hesitated and then said, "Go ahead and paint it."

At that point I hoped the paint wouldn't dry, but I would never know if it did or didn't, would I?

The crowning frustration came that night at eleven, when I was roused out of my bedroll by Ben because he had spotted, believe it or not, a one-foot patch at the top of the flagpole in front of the guest house that had not been painted white. We went in Ben's company Jeep to the paint shop for white paint, a brush and an extension ladder. I climbed the pole and painted the bloody patch in the dark, and then took everything back to the paint shop and staggered into bed at 1 a.m.

Everything went off without a hitch the next day, and the press coverage went all over the world.

A few days after the big event, I was back painting the family's house, out of sight and mind again, when Ben arrived, looking dejected. He announced that he had just been fired and asked me to tell him what he had done wrong.

As far as I was concerned, he was the victim of a chaotic situation, where opinions may have clashed on how to handle the official opening. Or maybe it was his attitude toward men. Maybe he'd spent too much money on the opening. Or, who knows—maybe the paint on the toilet seat didn't dry!

The Long Haul

My time working for Alcan in Kitimat turned into thirty-six long years. If I had a dollar for every time I was going to quit, I could have bought a new car, but I stuck it out to retirement in 1990. I kept my promise not to be a "Boomer" like my dad, and my jobs at the plant over the years became more and more challenging and interesting. When I retired, I was working as an engineering technician. Mary and our three children never lacked for food or clothing, and the children graduated from higher education and are a tribute to society. I'm very proud of them.

ACKNOWLEDGEMENTS

I'd like to thank the many people who encouraged and supported me through the process of writing and publishing these memoirs. In particular, my daughter, Sharon, who worked with me at every stage, helping to pull it all together; my partner, Mary Jane, who read the early drafts and encouraged me to keep going, my sister, Pat, for finding some of the photos and reminiscing along with me; and my son Joe, who suggested I write these memoirs in the first place. And thanks to the creative professionals who gave so much of their expertise to this book: editor Mary Schendlinger who introduced me to renowned memoir editor, Barbara Pulling, for expert structural advice; skilled editor, Audrey McClellan; talented book designer, Frances Hunter; Peggy Thompson, Kristin Jackson, and Daniel Francis.